Farm and Factory

Midwestern History and Culture

GENERAL EDITORS
James H. Madison and Thomas J. Schlereth

Farm and Factory

*Workers
in the Midwest
1880 –1990*

DANIEL NELSON

INDIANA UNIVERSITY PRESS

Bloomington and Indianapolis

The paper used in this publication meets the minimum require-ments of American National Standard for Information Sci-ences—Permanence of Paper for Printed Library Materials, ANSI Z39.48-1984. ⊗ ™

Manufactured in the United States of America.

Library of Congress Cataloging-in-Publication Data

Nelson, Daniel, date
    Farm and factory : workers in the Midwest, 1880–1990 / Daniel Nelson.
        p.   cm. — (Midwestern history and culture)
    Includes bibliographical references and index.
    ISBN 0-253-32883-7
    1. Working class—Middle West—History—19th century. 2. Working class—Middle West—History—20th century. 3. Farmers—Middle West—History—19th century. 4. Farmers—Middle West—History—20th century. 5. Labor policy—Middle West—History—20th century. 6. Middle West—Economic conditions.   I. Title. II. Series.
    HD8083.M53N45   1995
    305.5′62′0975—dc20   94-45185
    1 2 3 4 5 00 99 98 97 96 95

Contents

Preface

This is a study of work, broadly conceived, and of the people who performed that work in the region of the United States generally known as the Midwest. I have arbitrarily defined the Midwest as the states of Ohio, Indiana, Illinois, Michigan, Wisconsin, Minnesota, and Iowa. Nearly everyone would agree that those states should be included, and for my purposes that consensus is sufficient. In the text I note many distinctions within the region, but my essential argument is that a commonality of experience overshadows geographic and other distinctions. The essential feature of the region's labor history that set it apart from other American regions was the sustained, simultaneous growth of agriculture and industry, a feature that produced notable patterns of individual mobility and that left a distinctive and inescapable heritage.

The rapid growth of agriculture and industry created two distinctive and separate paths to material prosperity and two largely separate labor forces. The classic transfer of labor from farm to factory, common to New England in the nineteenth century and the South in the twentieth, did not occur in the Midwest until the post–World War II years. As a result industrialists had to seek workers elsewhere. Midwestern factories, mines, and lumber camps became enclaves of European immigrants and their children and, in more recent decades, of migrants from the American South, as far from the surrounding countryside as Europe was from America.

This pattern emerged in the middle decades of the nineteenth century as substantial islands of industry began to appear in the Midwest. By 1900 the contrasting worlds of agriculture and industry were well defined. During the following decades, important changes in the midwestern economy reinforced the pattern. Agriculture continued to flourish, in part because farmers won government favors at the expense of urban groups. Industry, buoyed by technological and organizational innovation, also boomed. The depression of the 1930s, a devastating blow to both groups, paradoxically reaffirmed their importance, and World War II ensured that there would be no marked change in the immediate future. Only in the 1960s did serious problems emerge, and in the 1970s and early 1980s, like Oliver Wendell Holmes's "One Hoss Shay," midwestern agriculture and industry collapsed, provoking an unprecedented crisis and bringing to an end the pattern of work and employment that dated from the nineteenth century.

The title of this work, *Farm and Factory*, recognizes the two central employing institutions in midwestern history and, by implication, the relative absence of a third. A complete title might be *Farm, Factory, and Office*, but the omission is deliberate, suggesting another way in which the Midwest deviated from the national norm in the mid-to-late twentieth century. The organizational and technological innovations of the early twentieth century created not only opportunities for three or four generations of midwestern farmers and factory workers but also presumptions about the desirability of goods over service production. Both the economic reality and the assumptions that it fostered contributed to a relatively underdeveloped service sector and to agonizing problems of adjustment as agriculture and industry evolved in the late twentieth century.

Apart from this pattern, the midwestern experience was distinctive for the role of workers' "voice" in its labor history.[1] Organized labor, the most obvious manifestation of voice, became and remained a more formidable presence in midwestern industry than in the economic activity of other regions. It plays a major part in this account, though the emphasis here is on midwestern unions and union actions, not the labor movement in general. Farm organizations were also highly effective in articulating the interests and complaints of midwestern farmers. Other expressions of voice have appeared at various times, though they usually have not left a comparable record of institutional activity. In recent decades, as occupation has declined as a basis for organization and protest, the role of the Midwest in social-reform movements has receded. As agriculture and manufacturing have become less important, workplace institutions for expressing workers' voice have also become less prominent, at least for the moment.

How does one study work in a historical context? There are several essentials. The first is to consider the roles of demand and supply in shaping the midwestern labor force. They embrace on the one hand the operation of market forces, the technology of production, and the management of workers, and on the other, the processes by which workers acquired skills and experience, the predilections of particular workers and groups, and the efforts of workers to preserve their positions and opportunities. A second essential is to view midwesterners who were employees in an industrial relations context, that is, as participants in a structured relationship based on expectations about the individual's performance and reward. Third is the link between work and ethnicity. Most midwesterners chose to work with people who shared a similar cultural heritage, regardless of other characteristics. As a result employment and ethnicity have been highly correlated, though the meaning of this tie has changed over time. Fourth is the impact of work on politics. Midwestern farmers have been among the most successful and creative workers in enlisting government to assist them, while industrial employees have been only marginally more successful than workers in other regions. A historical account cannot provide a complete explanation for this phenomenon, but it can help place the respective achievements and failures of these groups in perspective.

Though my goal has been to consider each of these dimensions of work, I make no claim to comprehensiveness. Two limitations are especially noteworthy. I have made only passing references to the professions, which evolved in reaction to national and international more than regional influences, or the work of executives, merchants, and other wealthy and prominent individuals who have received disproportionate attention in biographical and other historical works. Even after excluding these groups the story remains uneven. The literature is remarkably skewed toward industrial work and union activity, and the modern historian is a victim (as well as a beneficiary) of the choices of those who have studied midwestern workers in the past. In many instances, I can do no more than point to the dark corners of midwestern labor history in the hope that others will illuminate what for now remains obscure.

I have incurred numerous debts in the course of this study. James Richardson, Judith Sealander, and George Knepper read earlier drafts of the manuscript and provided invaluable critiques. John Ball and the interlibrary-loan staff at the University of Akron were unfailingly helpful. Maryann Hamilton typed the statistical tables, and Winifred Dues freely shared her word processing expertise. Daniel Leab, Arthur DeMatteo, Stephen Amberg, David Harriss, Rene Perez Rosenbaum, Roger Horowitz, and Bernard Sternsher shared unpublished materials. My thanks to all of them. Most of all I am indebted to my wife, Lorraine, for her patience and cooperation.

Part I

The Midwestern Worker at the End of the Nineteenth Century

By the 1880s the seven states of the American Midwest were among the most attractive areas of North America. Except in a few remote counties, mostly in the far north, frontier living and working conditions were a memory. Abundant resources had attracted a burgeoning, vigorous population. Roads and railroads crisscrossed the region, facilitating the exchange of goods and ideas. A half dozen of the largest American cities punctuated the prosperous countryside. Social and cultural institutions mimicked the urban society of the Northeast.* Regional maturity was also reflected in the occupations of midwestern workers. Though most people engaged in agriculture, mining, forestry, and related activities dependent on natural resources, as they did in other areas of the United States, a growing minority had turned to commercial and industrial activities. By the 1880s it was possible to generalize about the region's potential. We start at that point.

Table I–1 summarizes the information on occupations that the U.S. census takers collected at the end of the nineteenth century. The data covers only workers who received a direct, material reward for their efforts and is therefore incomplete. But it does document the importance of agriculture and manufacturing and the growing significance of a third, highly diverse group of occupations that produced services rather than goods. The pattern is consistent with the evolution of the national economy in the nineteenth century and the northeastern economy in particular.

Chapters 1, 2, and 3 examine the major categories of jobs and workers at the end of the nineteenth century.

---

*See Jon C. Teaford, *Cities of the Heartland: The Rise and Fall of the Industrial Midwest* (Bloomington: Indiana University Press, 1993), chap. 1.

Table 1-1
Midwestern Workers, 1880–1900

	Rate of Growth 1880–1900 (Percentage)	Distribution 1880	1900
		(Percentage of all workers)	
Agriculture	19	46	32
Industry	103	20	24
Mining	265	<1	2
Construction*	66	5	5
Manufacturing	106	15	18
Trade and Transportation	187	10	17
Railroads	114	2	2
Personal and Professional			
Service	94	23	26
Domestics	50	5	5
Teachers	64	2	2

*masons, carpenters, painters, plumbers
Sources: U.S. Census, *Population*, 1880, table 34; 1900, table 93.

1.

Midwestern Farmers, 1880–1900

Were farmers workers? Certainly they toiled as long and as hard as the average factory worker or miner; their cash incomes were, on average, no greater; and they responded to economic opportunity and adversity in similar ways. Yet there were differences. Most farmers owned the land and tools they used in their work, performed their tasks without formal supervision, and labored within a family organization. Their income was only part of the return on their labor. As a result economists and statisticians often considered farmers a distinctive group, closer to professionals in outlook and behavior than industrial workers.

This inclination was even more pronounced among radical critics of the status quo. Most nineteenth-century socialists simply accepted Marx's dismissal of farmers and focused on urban, industrial workers. Nonsocialists influenced by Marxist theory, such as AFL president Samuel Gompers, adopted a similar perspective. Yet there were exceptions. They included the radical journalist Algie M. Simons, whose midwestern background had alerted him to the realities of farm work. In numerous addresses to socialist conventions and in a little-read treatise, *The American Farmer* (1902), Simons argued that farmers were part of an expanding American proletariat, subject to the same exploitative forces that affected factory workers and miners. Although Simons underestimated the farmers' ability to respond to adversity and to reshape their environment, he recognized that they were workers, not unlike urban artisans who used tools and machines to produce goods for the market. His insight is a first step toward understanding the history of midwestern workers.[1]

Natives and Immigrants

Though the midwestern farmer of Turnerian legend was a free-spirited individualist, hostile to institutional constraints, the real late-nineteenth-century farmer was much more tentative and circumspect. Perhaps because family fortunes depended so much on the effort of individual members, rural midwesterners sought to minimize the uncertainties of their environment by living and working in a setting they understood or, at a minimum, with people they thought they understood. Economic and social isolation were both undesirable and likely to be unprofitable. Communities based on ethnic and regional identities were thus prominent in rural areas. These identities were the critical variable in the dispersal of the farm labor force across the land. They proved to be remarkably durable in many rural areas and continue to be a hallmark of much of the rural Midwest.

The first extensive midwestern settlement, a century earlier, had been in the Virginia Military Reserve, a vast tract of southwestern Ohio that had been set aside to reward Virginia veterans of the Revolutionary War. The settlers who moved into the Reserve at the end of the eighteenth century re-created the life and work patterns of the Chesapeake region, except for chattel slavery. They brought the two-pen house, the traverse-bay barn, and an understanding of the beneficial interdependence of corn and hogs, thereby providing the initial stimulus to the rise of the Corn Belt. Most of all they provided a familiar setting for those who were less fortunate, less adventuresome, or simply younger. In the early decades of the nineteenth century, thousands of others followed, usually after a period of residence in Kentucky or, less often, Tennessee. The southern third of Ohio, Indiana, and Illinois, bounded at its northern extreme by the National Road, became an extension of Virginia and Kentucky.[2] This pattern became a model for the development of the region.

Thus the most notable feature of midwestern growth was the influence of initial settlement decisions. There is no evidence that Ohio or Illinois farmers remained in one place longer than farmers in other regions, yet large areas remained culturally homogeneous. The patterns have been plotted from the decennial census and, more sensitively, from architecture, language, and other expressions of folk culture.[3] These studies date from the 1940s and 1950s, suggesting the remarkable longevity of popular cultural forms and the persistence of people who shared a common heritage.

Indiana is illustrative. Scholars have identified three areas of the state, exclusive of a handful of counties, such as those of the northeastern border, where European-immigrant communities prevailed. The southern counties are representative of the South-Midland culture of the trans-Appalachian South. The extreme north, on the other hand, was an extension of the Yankee culture of Michigan. The center of the state was a mixed area of diverse cultural forms that reflected the subregion's commercial links with the Cincinnati hinterland of the early nineteenth century. The prevailing dialect was more southern than northern, but different from that of the southern counties. It suggests the influence of the dynamic and cosmopolitan Miami Valley of western Ohio.[4]

The pattern in other states is similar. The lines of settlement that divided Indiana into cultural subregions also extended east and west through Ohio and Illinois, though the influence of Cincinnati gradually overshadowed the

impact of early southern settlement in southwestern Ohio. The southern
third of Illinois, which was geologically distinct from central and northern
Illinois, remained an identifiable area, more closely associated with Kentucky
than the rest of the state. Other areas of Illinois and Iowa had separate
identities. For example, Allan Bogue describes the settlement of these regions
in the following terms:

> The sons of Kentucky, Tennessee, and Virginia settled in southern Illinois and
> southeastern Iowa particularly. . . . Especially important in central Illinois were the
> natives of Ohio and Pennsylvania, while the New Yorkers and New Englanders
> were most strongly entrenched in the northern section of the state. The southeast-
> ern two-fifths of Iowa especially attracted the Ohio-born. New Yorkers and
> Pennsylvanians settled all along the Iowa side of the Mississippi, but ultimately
> more of the latter lived in southern Iowa than did those born in New York.[5]

Such designations, based on census data, are only rough approximations of
the cohesive forces that operated in the frontier Midwest. Massachusetts
natives were not particularly interested in the company of Bay State natives;
they sought the company of family members, former neighbors, and friends.
The actual process can be observed only at the community level. The best
accounting to date is a study of the rural population of Claridon township in
Geauga County, Ohio, part of Ohio's Western Reserve, settled almost
exclusively by New Englanders. Judging from the census reports, Claridon
township was a tight-knit, homogeneous entity, not unlike its neighbors.
Most residents had roots in New England, usually in Connecticut. They lived
on moderate sized farms, engaged in dairy farming, manufactured butter,
cheese, and maple syrup, and introduced social, religious, and political
institutions common to Connecticut society. Yet a more detailed examination, based on diaries and material culture sources, suggests that the county-
level data obscures as much as it reveals. In fact the township population was
sharply divided into two separate and mildly antagonistic groups. One
consisted of families that had originated in two Connecticut towns; the other
was made up of families from Vermont and New York. The first group was
wealthier, Congregational, politically and socially dominant in the township,
and socially self-contained. The other group was poorer, Methodist, the
source of most of the township's artisans and shopkeepers, and similarly self-
contained. To characterize these groups as Yankees, Protestants, or dairy
farmers is to miss the details that were most important to them and that
explained their behavior as workers.[6]

Joining the natives was a rapidly growing population of immigrants. These
people constituted approximately one-quarter of the rural, agricultural population in the 1880s and a slightly smaller proportion in 1910, more than in any
other region of the United States. At the end of the nineteenth century, a half

million Germans, a quarter million Norwegians, nearly 200,000 Swedes, and smaller numbers of other nationalities farmed in the midwestern states. Their challenge of adjustment was greater and their effort to create elements of familiarity in their new setting commensurately more intense.

Unlike the majority of urban immigrants, rural immigrants competed directly with old-stock natives in the workplace. By most measures they did well, surprisingly well perhaps, given the handicaps of language and customs they brought to their work. Lack of familiarity with local institutions apparently kept Germans and Scandinavians from becoming land speculators and exploiting one of the prime opportunities available to farmers.[7] Some Germans also emphasized land ownership over other, more profitable economic objectives.[8] Language difficulties were undoubtedly handicaps in a spectrum of commercial relationships, but the problem is easily exaggerated. Communications skills were comparatively unimportant in nineteenth-century agriculture, and few immigrants were so isolated that they did not have access to an interpreter.

In retrospect, it is the similarities between native and immigrant farmers that stand out. Most Germans and Scandinavians brought substantial material resources and well-developed skills to their midwestern farm enterprises. They were not poor by the standards of their age; lack of land in their native countries rather than low incomes whetted their interest in the United States. For many Norwegians, American farmland "was a convenient solution to the scarcity of landed futures."[9] The disparity in land prices between rural Sweden and Wisconsin and Minnesota, an area similar in climate and appearance, attracted thousands of Swedes.[10] Landowners in effect traded their small farms in northern Europe for much larger farms in the upper Middle West, ensuring that their children could remain on the land. Landless immigrants, or those who had no claim on other family resources, could homestead, begin their careers as tenants or laborers, or, after the 1880s, buy cheap land in the vast cut-over area of northern Michigan, Wisconsin, or Minnesota. These were much less attractive prospects, however, and with the exception of irrepressible devotees of rural life (the cut-over counties had comparatively few Germans and disproportionate numbers of Finns), most poor German and Scandinavian immigrants joined the burgeoning communities of immigrant industrial workers in Chicago and other midwestern cities.[11] Thus, the immigrant stream divided: those who had adequate resources to buy good land opted for farm work, while poorer rural immigrants joined the larger movement from German and Scandinavian cities to midwestern urban centers.

Those who remained on the land invariably lived and worked in close proximity with relatives and former neighbors. The settlement patterns of Germans, Norwegians, and Swedes reveal "a remarkable exclusivity." In north-central and northwestern Ohio, western Wisconsin, northern Iowa, southern and east-central Minnesota, "whole counties were nearly filled by a single national group." In other places the area was smaller but the level of concentration equally great. "These communities were not only homogeneous at the national level; they consisted largely or exclusively of individuals from certain provinces, districts, or even parishes."[12] Though the statistical data is inconclusive, it is likely that the impetus toward segregation was greater among immigrants than among natives. Non-English-speaking immigrants had powerful incentives to remain in close proximity, and outsiders, either native or immigrant, often felt uncomfortable in the face of the alien influx.

The ethnic patchwork that developed in the settlement process and that had assumed semipermanent form by the 1880s was more than a curious and colorful feature of rural midwestern life (as it would be by the end of the twentieth century) or an example of the human predilection for familiar faces, social customs, and religious practices. It was also an essential feature of the labor system that characterized the rural Midwest, a way to reconcile the individualism of American farming with collective and community-based endeavors. There was no reason that Yankees, Germans, and Swedes could not pool their energies and resources for the common good. But in a competitive environment it was quicker and easier to turn to individuals who spoke the same language or dialect, who had reputations, and who depended on the good will of the group for their future well-being. Residential segregation was perceived as a prerequisite for material as well as social success.

In later years, as midwestern rural life came under attack from country lifers (and more effectively and permanently from literary "realists" such as Hamlin Garland), the bonds that held farmers and their families in a web of mutual interdependence grounded in work and social life were obscured and forgotten. The myth of individualism, isolation, and loneliness obliterated an essential feature of the rural labor system.

The Family Labor System

The pattern of individual autonomy within a larger social community was also characteristic of the work of the farm. Farmers, like urban artisans, placed a high value on personal freedom in the workplace. The wage worker was the lowest-status farmer, a subordinate who, regardless of age, was treated as a child and consigned to a child's duties. Yet autonomy had well-recognized limits. Farming was a group activity, requiring at a minimum two people, typically a man and a woman, and the optimum number was considerably larger. The widower or bachelor farmer employed a housekeeper; the widow consigned her fields to a son or a tenant. Couples whose children had left home often "retired" to a nearby village and lived off their rental income. Agrarian "individualism" took the family work unit for granted.

As a rule farm families divided responsibilities along traditional gender lines. Firsthand accounts of nineteenth-century farm life provide only the rarest instances of men cooking or caring for small children, or of women plowing or threshing. Immigrants from societies where women customarily worked in the fields, Sweden for instance, quickly adapted to the American way of production.[13] Typically wives managed the house and the activities that occurred therein, while husbands presided over the barn, fields, and forests. The exact demarcation was less arbitrary; women maintained the vegetable garden and the chicken coop, but not the orchards. Dairying was even more confusing. In New England men did the milking; in the South, women. Predictably in the Western Reserve, the first important midwestern dairy region, men took charge of the milking and care of the cattle. In southern Ohio, Indiana, and Illinois, women did the milking. In practice they often delegated these tasks to children or hired workers, male and female. At 7.5 minutes per cow, twice a day, 200 to 250 days a year, milking four cows (the midwestern average) was a formidable but infinitely tedious responsibility.[14]

The male-female demarcation line had other interesting subtleties. Regardless of who did the milking, butter and cheese making were women's work. Men were responsible for most commercial transactions, but women traded butter and eggs. Men maintained the privy, while women had charge of washing and bathing. One of the most important annual rituals, the hog slaughter, occurred outside and involved both men and women, including relatives and neighbors.

In short, the inside-outside dichotomy was a rough and occasionally misleading indicator of the division of duties between wife and husband. The vital distinction was not whether an activity occurred in the house, but whether it was essential to the family.[15] Wives consequently specialized in cooking and child care, while husbands devoted most of their attention to market crops. The overlap occurred in areas such as dairying, which were peripheral to the core endeavors.

The least well-documented area of midwestern farm work was the wife's activity. The majority of accounts, written by men, consist of platitudes about the drudgery of housework, the endless routine, the lack of a Sunday respite, and related themes that bear an uncanny resemblance to the urban writer's customary depiction of men's work in rural society. Apart from these poorly informed assessments, the midwestern farm home remains an improbable void.[16] Nineteenth-century industrialism brought a profusion of consumer goods, such as the iron kitchen stove, that made housework more challenging. Changing attitudes toward children, coupled with the economics of the midwestern farm, had similar effects.[17] The implications of these changes are largely unexplored.

Consider the wife's two most critical tasks, food preparation and child nurture. Though food preparation was a daily task involving the manufacture of many foods, as well as cooking and cleaning, it was hardly routine. An account of a southeastern Ohio farm at the turn of the century reports:

> . . . every autumn the fruit cellar shelves boasted row upon row of gleaming jars: fruits . . . vegetables . . . pickles and relishes . . . and jams and jellies. Potatoes, apples, onions, winter squash, butternut squash and pumpkins were stored in the cool cellar, as were crocks of sauerkraut and sausage. Wheat was taken to the mill to be ground into flour, an important item in a household where baked goods were a staple item.[18]

Apart from the flour and sausage, the wife was responsible for the harvesting and processing of all of these items. The hog slaughter (together with the pickling and smoking of meats and the manufacture of lard and sausage) and preparation of apple butter were other fall events that required one or more days of full-time effort. Holidays demanded careful planning, and the Sunday work restrictions of many Protestant denominations meant that Saturday food preparation often had to be for the entire weekend.

Child care was inherently less predictable. Indeed, the most demanding tasks, the care of newborns and the treatment of childhood diseases, frequently disrupted other activities. Long periods of convalescence in the era before antibiotics meant that the typical mother devoted more time to nursing than to any other activity except cooking. When the children were healthy, they demanded other types of assistance. Children were a valuable source of auxiliary labor (the alternative, a hired man or girl could command as much as a dollar a day plus board in the late nineteenth century), but only if they were properly trained and supervised. The wife was responsible for sons as well as daughters until the boys were old enough to do men's work. Boys characteristically cut firewood; pumped water; cleaned stalls; fed livestock; milked; tended vegetable gardens; and carried water, food, and messages to their fathers in the fields. Girls learned to cook, sew, and perform other household tasks and shared some of the laborious outdoor work with their brothers. Many mothers supplemented the schools and churches with literary, cultural, and religious training.

Other facets of the wife's role are less clear. The farmhouse was her principal workplace. Did she guide its evolution through the remodelings that characterized most midwestern farm homes? What distinguished creative homemakers from others? Wives developed reputations for their cooking, sewing, nursing, gardening, and children. There was informal competition (formal competition came at the end of the century as agricultural fairs introduced prizes for gardening and food processing). A daughter's skills or artistic accomplishments might compensate for the lack of a dowry. Good-quality butter and cheese and large eggs (and the wife's negotiating skills) directly affected the family's purchasing power at the neighborhood store. The issue of technological change in the home is addressed later, but it is clear that the quality of women's work materially affected the success of the farm family.

A final perplexing issue is probably more closely related to women's work than to men's. Despite the importance of children to the rural family and the large size of the farm family relative to its urban counterpart, fertility in the rural Midwest fell by approximately 50 percent in the nineteenth century. Farm wives of the 1880s and 1890s had one or two fewer children than their mothers. The obvious question of why has absorbed the energies of economists. The variable that has received the greatest attention and has performed best in the scholars' equations is "land availability," that is, the ability of farm couples to provide their offspring with land or the opportunity to acquire land. By the late nineteenth century, most of them had concluded that the era of cheap or free land was drawing to a close. They might be able to assist three or four children but not five or six.[19]

There is no record of individual parents making these calculations. There is, however, abundant evidence that pioneer farmers acquired more land than they could use, presumably to provide for their children; that real estate was an important topic in the discussions that occurred between the fathers of engaged couples; and that most landowning fathers provided land to their sons or sons-in-law through gifts, loans of money, or the mechanism of farm tenancy. There were many exceptions, such as the Germans who supposedly prized landownership above all else but did not limit fertility.[20] Noneconomic considerations were also important. Farm families, for example, were surely aware of the growing preference of urban couples for smaller families. Whatever the exact combination, the decline in rural fertility helped sustain the balance between workers and employment opportunities. The Midwest would have no surplus of underemployed farmers until well into the twentieth century.

The farmer's workday took him outside for most of the year and required arduous physical labor, even though the character of that labor changed in dramatic, often seemingly revolutionary, ways in the course of the nineteenth century. The most important change in the allocation of the farmer's time, however, had nothing to do with the larger economy or technological creativity. The passing of the frontier phase of midwestern farming meant that the farmer spent less time in the forest and more in the fields. By 1880 three-quarters of Ohio's forests had disappeared, and farmers began to bemoan the loss of timberland. By 1900 the deforestation of lands further west, together with the opening of new prairie lands had reversed the process in the less fertile, unglaciated regions of eastern Ohio.[21] The return of the hardwood forest to the eastern edge of the Midwest would continue, with accelerating tempo, through the century and symbolize the impact of competition on midwestern agriculture.

Land clearing nevertheless remained the most arduous and expensive task of the nineteenth-century farmer. One late-nineteenth-century study concluded that girdling trees on an acre of land cost $8 for labor and took nearly two weeks. Clear-cutting was initially more expensive and more time-consuming—$10 to $12 per acre and 16.5 to 20 days—but once the unusable wood had been burned, the field was ready for planting.[22] Since most midwestern farmers did the cutting themselves during the winter months, when opportunity costs were low, the time estimate was more relevant than the cash outlay. The most arduous work occurred in the early years of farming, but in most cases it never really ceased. Still, at some point the objective changed from land clearing to the acquisition of fencing, lumber, and firewood. The farmers who complained about deforestation at the beginning of the twentieth century were acutely sensitive to this transition.

After the trees had been cut, a major hurdle remained. Removing stumps was as time-consuming and expensive as cutting the forest, at least until the introduction of dynamite in the 1880s. Most midwestern farmers used explosives sparingly, relying instead on a team of horses or oxen to pull partially decayed stumps from the ground. (Beleaguered settlers in the northern "cut-over" areas discovered to their dismay that pine stumps did not readily decay.) As one authority concludes, "the task of clearing the woodland was a monotonous one of hacking, grubbing, and burning: it was a task not of a few years but of at least a generation."[23]

Even after these tasks were completed, the midwestern farmer spent much of his time during the winter and spring months in the forest and woodlot. In most areas the rail fence remained a common sight until the turn of the century. Barbed wire, invented in the 1870s and greatly improved by the 1890s, was a godsend to prairie farmers in Illinois and Iowa; for others it was a luxury that diverted scarce dollars from other uses.[24] The other near-universal activity of midwestern farmers was cutting and splitting firewood. A typical Iowa farmer devoted February to replenishing the family fuel supply, creating a woodpile twenty feet high.[25] Frontier farmers in Michigan, Wisconsin, and Minnesota often earned extra income by working in the pineries during the winter or by joining the spring log drives. In Isanti County, Minnesota, the principal "crops" were wheat and logs.[26] Even if we exclude such supplementary employment, the farmer in the forested areas of the Midwest probably spent a quarter of his time working with an axe and saw.

The eotechnic age of midwestern farming lasted through the nineteenth century.

The other hallmark of the late-nineteenth-century farm that distinguishes it from the mid-to-late twentieth-century farm was its diversity—a diversity that permitted a high degree of self-sufficiency and made economic success dependent on the efficient use of labor. At the time of the Civil War, most midwestern farmers produced corn, wheat, hay, oats, and potatoes. They also raised hogs, milk cows, beef cattle (most farmers favored, and continued to favor, dual-purpose breeds that were comparatively poor milk producers), horses, and less commonly, sheep.[27] A half-century later, the list was remarkably similar, though wheat and sheep had declined because of competition from specialized regions and horses had become popular because of the proliferation of horse-drawn machines.

Much of this production was for home consumption. The corn crop provided food for the hogs, cattle, and to a lesser degree, the family. Hay and oats were consumed on the farm, though every town was also a market. Potatoes, hogs, cattle, sheep, chickens, eggs, and most garden crops were primarily for home consumption. Surplus horses were readily sold or traded. The portion of the crop consumed at home depended on market conditions, the size of the family, and the family's preferences. Most accounts emphasize the family's commercial orientation. Yet relatively few farmers were prepared to wager their futures on a single crop. Liberty Hyde Bailey's highly successful farm near South Haven, Michigan, produced apples and peaches for the Chicago market but remained "a general farming enterprise . . . the kind of farm that produced much of what the family consumed as well as much for sale."[28]

Apart from these general considerations, land tenure and ethnicity influenced the farmer's choices. Tenants favored grain crops that were readily salable; those who developed an interest in livestock were usually preparing to buy their own farms.[29] The behavior of immigrants is more difficult to characterize. Most immigrants apparently adapted their farming practices more readily than other activities. The Scandinavian farmer who grew the same crops and raised the same livestock as his Yankee neighbor continued to speak his native language; celebrate traditional holidays; and defer to Lutheran clergyman, militant opponents of assimilation, on noneconomic issues.[30] Yet there were enough exceptions and variations to make generalizations dangerous.[31]

Regardless of the details, success depended more on labor than capital. Many prosperous midwestern farmers cut hay with a scythe or cradle, planted corn by hand, spread manure by pitchfork, and grew their own seeds. Their achievements were the results of good organization and management, especially the management of their time and energies. The rule of thumb in diversified midwestern farming was "When the crop work is demanding . . . 'do nothing today that can be put off till a later date,' and when work is not pressing 'put off nothing that can be done today.'"[32] Thus the importance of land clearing, stump pulling, fence building, firewood splitting, and construction in the months between November and April. Oats were planted in April, corn in May. The rest of May and June were devoted to cultivating the new corn. Hay was harvested in June or early July; oats and wheat in August and September. The farmer and his sons often joined local threshing crews in late summer. In the early fall they cleaned the barn and spread manure. Mid-October marked the beginning of the corn harvest, a particularly intensive period of hand work. In the meantime, they had sold livestock and slaughtered hogs. Diversity allowed the well-organized farmer to spread his work through the year; minimize expenditures for nonfamily workers and animal fodder; preserve the fertility of the land; and protect the family against catastrophic losses due to insects, disease, or drought. The biggest question mark was the farmer's health. Illness or injury upset the schedule and threatened the balance that sustained farm and family.

It is hardly surprising that most farm youths opted for careers in agriculture. Any boy who had grown up on a farm had at least rudimentary skills. Capital was not an insurmountable barrier. Numerous studies of midwestern-farm tenancy have demonstrated that it was usually a step on the way up the agricultural ladder, not a permanent state or, for more than a tiny minority, a step down. Midwestern tenants needed only a fraction of the capital that prospective owners did, and they obtained valuable on-the-job training.[33] In any case, agriculture offered farmers greater personal autonomy than virtually any other career, certainly any low-paying career. The activities of the husband, wife, and older children were interdependent, but the separate spheres of men and women, and the spatial dispersion of farm activity, meant that close supervision was impossible. Organization and management were based on common values and cooperation.

Despite these advantages, farming grew more slowly than the midwestern population in the late nineteenth century. The absolute number of farmers stabilized at the turn of the century and fell after 1910; the decline was most rapid in Indiana, Ohio, and Illinois, in that order. Only in Minnesota and Wisconsin did agriculture continue to attract more workers after 1910. Farming was attractive only as long as the farm was competitive and the agricultural ladder reached at least to the middle of the social order. By the late nineteenth century, however, land prices had become an obstacle to mobility in long-settled, fertile areas. Inexpensive, undeveloped land was available in the comparatively infertile counties of southern Ohio, Indiana, and Illinois and the cut-over regions of Michigan, Wisconsin, and Minnesota, but it demanded hard, unremitting toil. The opportunities that had encouraged poor boys to become laborers or tenants and had enticed northern-European immigrants no longer existed in many areas of the Midwest. Faced with this choice, many farm youths looked elsewhere.

They did not have to look far. At least three other career choices were available to rural children. The first was a rural, nonagricultural occupation. A study of rural life in Dane County, Wisconsin, listed fifty-seven nonfarm occupations, embracing nearly 10 percent of the county's rural "gainful" workers.[34] Most numerous were servants, housekeepers, and teachers, unmarried women who worked outside the home. The rural community also included construction workers; traders; professionals; and even a few industrial workers, employed in sawmills, cheese factories, and other plants that processed agricultural products.

A second and often more attractive option was to move to "town," to one of the villages that dotted every state and served the neighboring hinterland. Villagers had the advantage of easy access to the larger world while retaining their rural roots and family ties. Their living and working conditions, chronicled in Lewis Atherton's *Main Street on the Middle Border* (1954), struck many urban dwellers as backward and parochial. Yet most villagers could have taken city jobs at any time. They remained because of the economic and social attractions of village life. By 1920 they equaled the farm population and together equaled the population of towns and cities of 2,500 and more.[35]

Gradually the villages developed a permanent population of people who had been raised in town and were unfamiliar with farm work. The least successful of them earned wages that were lower than those of urban industrial workers. By the 1920s manufacturers of automobile parts and other labor-intensive products began to look upon them with growing interest.

The third choice was to seek one's fortune in the city. The ranks of those who opted for urban careers included John D. Rockefeller, Henry Ford, and other illustrious individuals, as well as many men and women of more modest achievements. Whatever their prospects or attainments, they had one thing in common besides their rural origins: they invariably sought, and usually found, white-collar rather than industrial jobs. Old-stock migrants became a small but notable fraction of the urban business community.

Community Endeavors

Regardless of the quality of its management, the farm family required additional labor at various times during the year. Some occasions were predictable: the hay and wheat harvests, the building of a barn, or the birth of a baby. Others, due to an illness or injury, for example, were impossible to anticipate. In either case midwestern farm families turned to a network of acquaintances for assistance. These informal groups, which originally had been synonymous with the ethnic clusters that appeared in census and tax records, gradually came to include other elements. They gave the family labor system substantial flexibility and ensured that most family members did not work or live in isolation.

The most obvious and least important of supplementary workers were those whose relationship was purely economic, akin to the urban employee. The hired man is a shadowy but ubiquitous figure in the history of midwestern agriculture: a young man without contacts or capital, an older man without ambition or enterprise, a villager down on his luck.[36] Most farm laborers were young and transient; either they saved their earnings and became tenants or they drifted to the villages or cities. In the meantime they lived with a farm family and performed the chores that family members sought to evade. In legend, at least, they devoted their free time to the farmer's daughters, particularly if the farm was prosperous and the parents seemed generous. The hired girl is more easily described. She was typically a teenager, employed for a few days or weeks to help with household chores or to baby-sit. She, too, lived with the family and received a small wage and board. However, she was not the equivalent of the hired man. Girls lived apart from their families but seldom were "adrift." Some of them undoubtedly moved to cities, but the majority returned to their homes and eventually became farm wives. Nor were they comparable to the domestics who worked in the homes of urban middle-class families. The availability of child workers and country "visitors" obviated the need for long-term domestic employees.

In addition to these individuals, drawn from the local population and often known to the employing family, there were seasonal laborers, who appeared for brief periods of intense labor. Nearly all of them were men. In earlier years, midwestern farmers had relied on skilled specialists to cut wheat and thresh grain. The reaper and mower eliminated the cradler, and the grain separator converted the barn from a workshop to a warehouse. By the 1880s, moreover, wheat was becoming the specialty crop of the plains states; Kansas, Nebraska, and the Dakotas became the center of the harvest labor market. Except for northwestern Minnesota, the Midwest was an area of comparatively small grain fields and local harvest workers.

Vastly more important were cooperative endeavors based on the barter of labor. Farmers and homemakers often joined relatives and neighbors in common endeavors. On occasions such as the hog slaughter, large groups worked together; more commonly, two or three men or women collaborated. A landmark study of a Wisconsin community, based on the journal of a prominent farmer, David Wood, explains:

They [farmers] depended on each other in building barns and houses, in marketing their products, and in planting and harvesting their crops. . . . [Wood's] journal leaves the impression that few of the men who stopped at the Wood farm left without making arrangements for some type of exchange. [Wood] kept careful records of all he owed or was owed by his father, sons, stepbrothers, and neighbors.[37]

A similar survey of Indiana farm wives discovered a "dense web of social and economic relationships."[38] The "bee," a term that connoted a combination of work and entertainment, gave formal recognition to this phenomenon.

Studies of midwestern rural life in the nineteenth century emphasize the frequency of contacts between individuals outside the nuclear family. Though the rural workday was from sunup to sundown, the pace was slow and irregular. Except on the busiest days of the hay, wheat, or oat harvest season—certainly no more than thirty or so per annum—the agricultural regimen permitted rest breaks, extended noon meals, trips to neighbors' farms or the crossroads store, and conversations with salesmen and others who found their way to the farmstead. Diaries of Western Reserve residents reveal an "extensive system of interaction." At least one family member left the farm every other day. One-fifth of the trips (or approximately three trips per month) were outside the township; the rest were local.[39] The Wood journals portray a Wisconsin farm family that had almost daily contacts with neighbors and friends.[40]

The irregular patterns of work and the mixing of work and social activity should not be confused with the persistence of preindustrial values. Ethnic clustering meant that most personal contacts were with relatives and other long-time acquaintances who could be trusted, or at least whose idiosyncrasies were known. Informal bargains and implicit understandings were commonplace. But farmers were no less aware of the economic value of their labor than urban workers. Diaries like David Wood's show that farmers kept detailed records of their assistance to friends, neighbors, and work rings. Reciprocity was the foundation of group work. The operations of the White Plains Threshing Ring, a group of Franklin County, Indiana, farmers illustrate this point. Members devised a "difference" system to equalize the contributions of small and large landowners. Farmers with smaller acreages received cash from their wealthier neighbors. The ring also spelled out the length of the workday, the duties of officers, and procedures for selecting professional threshermen to work with the ring. Until 1922 the captain assigned tasks to ring members. In later years a lottery, supplemented by individual bargaining, superseded the captain's authority. At the end of the harvest, the men met outside the local church to settle their "differences." Having completed their business, they joined their wives inside for cake and ice cream.[41]

Women were even more commonly involved in cooperative work arrangements. Unmarried women and women whose children were grown had more leisure time and greater freedom of movement than men of comparable age. Motherhood, the common experience of midwestern farm women and the most labor-intensive of all farm tasks, also encouraged joint activities. Visits to friends, grandparents, and aunts and uncles, with one or more children in tow, allowed mothers to vary their regimen and children to develop new friendships. Sewing likewise encouraged the sharing of materials and techniques. Abundant food supplies meant that guests could be accommodated with minimal expense and effort.

Jane Marie Pederson's study of rural hospitality in Wisconsin provides valuable detail. Women were the most frequent visitors and usually visited sisters, daughters, and aunts. In most cases they did not travel with their husbands and rarely visited members of the husband's family. This pattern had an economic basis: since the farm was likely to have been obtained through the husband's family, women tended to live closer to their in-laws and were likely to see them at church or in town. Visits to the wife's family usually required more extensive arrangements, recorded in diaries and newspapers. But even that fraction of the total was impressive. A community of 300 households left a public record of 20 to 50 intercommunity visits per week in the 1880s and 1890s; by the 1910s the total had risen to 60 to 100. One-quarter of the visits reported in the local newspaper in 1890 lasted a week or longer. By 1914 the total had risen to one-half, including a substantial number that were "extended" or "indefinite." Since the purpose of many "extended" visits was to nurse an ill relative, the visit was not necessarily a vacation. Regardless of purpose, visitors became part of the family labor system, participating in the routine of the home. Though "women's and children's place may well have been . . . in the home," Pederson concludes, farm families "did not seem to be overly particular about which home."[42]

Innovation in Agriculture

By the 1880s the work of the midwestern farm family reflected the same influences that were transforming the work of the factory and mine. Iron machinery and draft animals, especially horses, became part of the fabric of farm life, diminishing the value of age-old skills, creating new skills, extending the family's ability to produce, and forcing farmers to make decisions about their futures that would have been unimaginable a generation earlier. Yet the technological revolution in northern farming, a familiar chapter in agricultural history, was only part of a larger mosaic. Midwestern farmers of the late nineteenth century were probably no more aggressive than mid-Atlantic farmers in adopting new techniques, less vigorous than western farmers in mechanizing their operations, and less active politically than farmers of the

South and Plains. But they recognized the value of collective endeavors. By the end of the century, they approached the organizational revolution that would mark the "golden age" of the early twentieth century.

The most obvious changes in midwestern agriculture to anyone living at the time were the mechanization of field work and the substitution of horsepower for human labor. From time immemorial, farm work had been handwork; productivity had depended on the farmer's ability to utilize axe, adze, hoe, sickle, and other tools. Draft animals pulled plows, harrows, and wagons and assisted with threshing and other tasks, but the most notable feature of farm work was its profligate use of human skill and energy. The pioneer decades of midwestern farming coincided with the advent of steam power, the proliferation of machinery, and an acceleration in the pace of mechanical invention. Midwestern farmers consequently became avid consumers of new technologies. Oxen, too slow and immobile for the new machinery, gave way to horses; barns were redesigned to house machinery; and farm youths devoted much of their apprenticeship years to machine operations.

By the 1880s the typical midwestern farmer probably had a greater array of tools and machines at his disposal than any other worker. A diversified Ohio farm was likely to have, or have access to, the following: a riding or "sulky" plow, a disk harrow, one or more seed drills, a corn planter, a corn cultivator, a reaper, a mower, a hay rake, a hay fork, a windmill for pumping water, a wagon, and three or more horses. For a week or more in the late summer, it would also have a threshing machine and portable steam engine, together with a crew of operators and mechanics.[43] Most farms had other more specialized machines as well.

The mechanization of midwestern agriculture was not painless. As early as the 1830s, the advent of threshing machines provoked protests, occasionally violent, from men who devoted their winters to flailing wheat. More serious opposition appeared in the mid-1870s, when recession coincided with the appearance of the labor-saving twine-binder, a machine that substantially reduced the size of harvest crews. Strikes and terrorist acts punctuated the normally placid midwestern summer of 1878. Ohio, still an important wheat-producing state, was the center of the violence. As Peter and Jo Ann Argersinger report:

> In Fayette County . . . a wealthy farmer responded to a farmworker strike by announcing his intention to use his new self-binding reaper to 'do the work that formerly took a dozen men to do.' That night the reaper was destroyed by fire, an action attributed to resident 'desperadoes' in the neighborhood. In the Miami Valley, many farmers had their reapers and mowers burned at night, and one farmer, who had been repeatedly warned not to use his self-binder, even had his machine destroyed in the midst of harvest during the break for dinner.[44]

In response Ohio, Indiana, Michigan, and Minnesota farmers formed vigilante groups, mobilized public opinion in the defense of property rights, and less often, deferred the purchase or use of machines. As the economy improved in 1879 and fewer city workers turned to the countryside for employment, the crisis passed.[45] Thereafter there was little or no overt resistance to mechanization.

Technological change also was an important influence in women's work. An 1876 poll by the Ohio State Board of Agriculture provides a useful benchmark. Officials of county societies reported that substantial brick or frame structures—the imposing Victorian homes that still dot the Ohio landscape—had replaced the crude log or frame buildings of earlier years. Most farm homes had windmills, iron cook stoves, and kerosene lamps. Sewing machines were nearly universal. Many homes had factory-made washing machines, churns, furniture, and textile products—blankets, carpets, and curtains.[46] A survey of Indiana, Illinois, southern Michigan, or Wisconsin would have produced similar replies. The substantial midwestern farm home of the 1880s was nearly as comfortable as the middle-class urban home of that era.[47]

Midwestern farm families also recognized the importance of improving the institutional environment in which they lived and worked. Two groups of proposals attracted wide interest in the 1880s and 1890s. The first called for a revised and expanded public education system; the second, for political action to stimulate the farm economy and regulate the activities of merchants and processors. Neither resulted in significant changes. Educational reform threatened local control and did not directly address the future of the *farm* family, while the prospect of a farm-based political crusade evoked more skepticism than sympathy. They nevertheless underlined a receptiveness to organizational activity that would take more concrete and effective form in later years.

Farm families recognized the importance of publicly supported schools at an early date. By the 1830s all of the midwestern states had adopted legislation encouraging public education; by the 1860s all but Michigan required local elementary schools. Most legislatures did not spell out the character of the school system or the curriculum, but the results were remarkably uniform. Midwestern public education was locally managed, locally financed, and closely coordinated with the needs of the farm family, particularly the work of men and boys. The neighborhood school served a small, usually four-square-mile area so that no child had to walk more than a mile. Local residents employed the teacher, typically a teenage girl in the spring and fall and a young man in the winter, when the older boys attended. A few teachers were high school graduates; most had less-exalted credentials. An elementary education, supplemented by attendance at one or more of the teachers institutes that the state normal colleges operated during the summer, was typical. The curriculum emphasized reading; writing; arithmetic; and a smattering of history, geography, and science.[48]

The apparent contrast between the farmers' enthusiasm for public education and the decentralized and seemingly haphazard system that emerged impressed critics as a failure of public policy. The history of public education in the Midwest is largely the story of conflict over school "reform," spearheaded by urban educators who advocated consolidation, professionalization, and bureaucratic management. In the 1880s and 1890s, the reformers made little progress. Several states shifted to township control with generally unhappy results.[49] Indeed, after a brief experiment with township management, Iowa reverted to local control. By the turn of the century, it had more one-room common schools than any other state. It also had a highly literate population, suggesting that the problems of the common school were not as compelling as the reformers suggested.

The reformers' ideas were the core of an approach that was highly relevant to the urban middle-class worker but had little immediate value for the agricultural population. A common-school education provided essential skills at low cost, maximized community involvement in public education, and complemented the vocational training that students acquired at home. The best measure of its utility and flexibility, however, was the large number of late-nineteenth-century farm youths who had successful business and professional careers. The real deficiencies of the common school were not its casual organization or community-based management but its neglect of mathematics and science and its dependence on a comparatively dense rural population. Neither was a serious problem before 1900.

Whatever their opinions about public education, midwestern farmers were increasingly anxious about the web of commercial relations that seemed to draw them ineluctably into the world of urban business on disadvantageous terms.[50] Like their counterparts in other regions, they reacted by mobilizing economically and politically, creating another force for change in rural life. The best examples were the Patrons of Husbandry or Grange, which in its formative stage was almost exclusively a midwestern organization, and the farmers' alliance movement of the 1880s and 1890s. These organizations were part of the broader farmers' revolt that swept through the southern and western states. Yet the parallel between midwestern and southern and western farm movements is inexact and potentially misleading. The midwestern Grange, for example, declined as precipitously as it had grown, though not before its political agenda had been hijacked by commercial groups.[51] When it reemerged in the 1890s, it had a more pronounced emphasis on social and educational activity. In this guise it flourished.[52] The critical lesson of the abbreviated Granger crusade was not the farmers' failure to sustain a political effort; it was their skeptical attitude toward broad-gauge political campaigns and third parties.[53] Unlike the southern radicals of midcentury or the Populists of the 1890s, most midwestern farmers viewed politics as a mechanism for obtaining specific services.

Still, for a brief period in the late 1880s, it appeared that midwestern farmers might join hands with wheat, cotton, and tobacco farmers of other states in a broad-based interregional political movement. Low prices, antipathy toward "middlemen," and a belief that urban interests dominated government to the detriment of rural interests spurred the growth of the farmers' organizations throughout the Midwest. Like the labor movement of that period, the alliance movement was highly fragmented. In Illinois, where one in four farmers was involved in alliance activity by 1890, five organizations competed for members: the National (or Northern) Alliance, concentrated in the northern part of the state; the Farmers' Mutual Benefit Association, dominant in the south; the Southern Alliance, concentrated in the west; the revived Grange, which had its greatest strength in the central counties; and the Patrons of Industry, concentrated among dairy farmers along the Illinois-Wisconsin border. In Ohio the Northern Alliance dominated. In Michigan the Patrons of Industry overshadowed other groups. In every midwestern state the Grange was active.[54] As Roy V. Scott has noted, all of these organizations

> reflected the vague if often expressed desires of farmers to combine for mutual protection, all were heavily imbued with the myths of agrarian fundamentalism, and all evolved educational, social, economic, and political programs calculated to protect the farmer in an industrial society.[55]

Alliance groups advocated currency inflation, railroad regulation, greater democracy in government, and less often, women's rights, prohibition, and state expenditures for public education. They also encouraged a host of cooperative and educational activities. Alliance activities marked a new peak in rural sociability.

Despite the willingness of farmers to address their problems collectively, the midwestern alliance movement collapsed in the early 1890s. The immediate cause was disillusionment with the operations of the various organizations. Alliance-backed cooperatives were a particular source of discord. As much as farmers distrusted merchants and manufacturers, they were unable to provide consistently superior services for themselves. Most alliance cooperatives were in trouble by 1892. Rivalry between the competing groups also contributed to disillusionment. Most serious, however, was the alliances' inability to resist partisan political activity. Many alliance leaders were political activists, veterans of the Granger and Greenback crusades of earlier years, eager for new campaigns. Yet translating this interest into an effective political presence proved remarkably difficult. A convoluted battle over an Illinois Senate seat in 1891 was the single greatest blow to the midwestern alliance movement. Whenever alliance leaders attempted to mobilize farmers as voters, the results were similar. By 1892, when the People's party emerged as the political expression of the alliance movement in the Plains and South, the midwestern alliances were in disarray, and midwestern farmers abandoned any hope of a farmers' party. People's parties in Illinois, Wisconsin, and Ohio attracted virtually no farm support. Midwestern Populism was almost wholly an urban phenomenon, a minor chapter in the history of the Knights of Labor and the incipient socialist movement.[56] Most farmers of the 1890s voted Republican, albeit reluctantly.

In contrast to the noisy alliance effort, which had virtually no effect on the practice of farming or the activities of the farm family, a parallel movement to improve the operations of individual farms began to gain momentum in the 1890s. It, too, reflected the frustrations of farmers and sought to raise the incomes of farm families. It too looked to government for assistance. But its tone and approach were different, and its results were more profound. Because its impact was most evident in the years after 1900, it is treated in detail in chapter 4. It, rather than any of the innovations described above, would shape the fate of the rural Midwest in the following half-century.

2.

Industrial Workers, 1880–1900

A large and growing number of midwestern workers who were not farmers were involved in processing the Midwest's abundant resources and in other industrial activities. Many of these individuals operated steam-powered machinery and qualified for membership in the nineteenth century's best-known new occupational category, the factory labor force. Unlike farmers, industrial workers used tools and machines but typically did not buy or borrow them. They labored in groups, but as employees, rather than as members of family or cooperative work organizations. Nine of every ten were men, and the vast majority (the only significant exceptions were in clothing manufacture) had no workplace contacts with women. The manager, almost unknown in midwestern agriculture, was an essential figure in industrial work, and relations between managers and workers were an important and often highly visible feature of the operation of industrial enterprises. The workers' voice could be a creative or disruptive force.

Most industrial workers were also part of a family economy rather than a family labor system.[1] While members of the farm family worked together as a unit, members of industrial families worked separately, with little or no direct contact. Husbands worked in factories or mines. Children might work for the same employer but usually not under their fathers' supervision. Wives worked in the home, but in ways that would have seemed strange and undesirable to farm women. Their houses and families, on average, were smaller; their resources, including tools and implements, more limited; and their economic role more restricted and yet more difficult. Shopping took the place of most food production, and part-time jobs (cooking and cleaning for boarders and washing for outsiders were most common) supplemented the husband's and children's incomes. Wage labor was the hallmark of the family economy, and the number of participants was the best gauge of the family's well-being. Poor families had multiple workers, while more affluent families sent their children to school and reduced or eliminated the wife's wage-earning activities.

The most visible and fundamental difference between midwestern agricultural and industrial work, however, was in the workers themselves. Most farmers were old-stock Americans, while most industrial workers were immigrants or the children of immigrants. Even in rural industries immigrants predominated. This association was primarily a reflection of the uncom-petitiveness of industrial occupations. Some skilled male immigrants—con-struction workers, machinists, ironworkers, and pottery and glassmakers in particular—practiced their trades and earned high wages, but the majority filled positions that old-stock midwesterners rejected. Long hours, poor working conditions, regimentation, and insecurity made industrial work unattractive. The availability of immigrant workers also kept wages low relative to other occupations, reinforcing the social and cultural gulf between farm and factory.

The occupational distribution of ethnic groups was another measure of these relationships. The choices of immigrants who arrived before the 1880s, when inexpensive, undeveloped land was available, were not substantially different from the choices of old-stock midwesterners. In contrast, very few of the immigrants who arrived between the 1880s and 1900 became farmers. Opportunities existed, but they were opportunities in industry and, increas-ingly, in the cities.[2]

An Immigrant Labor Force

Economic growth in the Midwest in the decades from the 1850s to the 1880s created profound changes in the economic life of the region. Most notable was the rise of manufacturing and other industrial operations. Given the prosperous state of midwestern agriculture, as well as the attachment of midwestern youths to rural life, nonagricultural enterprises there faced greater labor constraints than in any other region. The problem was especially severe in the mining and forest-products industries, which were forced to attract employees to isolated, rural settings. Most industrial activity, however, was concentrated in urban areas and, increasingly, in the region's largest cities. By the 1880s Chicago was emerging as the world's leading industrial city, and Cincinnati, Cleveland, Detroit, Milwaukee, and Minneapolis were only relatively less important. Urban employers had little difficulty attracting young people to business or clerical careers. Jobs in construction and manufacturing were less appealing. Unlike New England shoe and textile makers, or South Carolina and Georgia textile producers, midwestern indus-trialists could not look to an economically depressed hinterland for employ-ees. Immigrants were an attractive alternative to expensive agricultural work-ers.

By the 1880s European immigration had become the most notable dynamic in the growth of the urban Midwest. Nearly four of ten residents of Chicago, Milwaukee, Cincinnati, Detroit, and Cleveland were foreign-born, matching the levels of New York and other eastern cities. The immigrants and

Table 2–1

Immigrants and Their Children in Midwestern Cities

| | *(Percentage of total population)* | |
	1890	*1900*
Milwaukee	86	82
Chicago	77	77
Detroit	77	77
Cleveland	75	76
Minneapolis-St. Paul	67	70
Cincinnati	69	61
Small cities*	52	51
All other Midwest	41	41

*cities of 25,000–100,000 population (21 in 1890, 32 in 1900)
Sources: U.S. Census, *Population*, 1890, tables 50, 51; 1900, tables 58, 78.

their children born in the United States made up more than half of the urban population of all of the region's largest cities and of most of its smaller urban centers. In the following years, as industrial opportunities increased, the ethnic character of the cities persisted, as table 2–1 indicates.

Most immigrants came in response to specific opportunities communicated through relatives and acquaintances. As Daniel E. Weinberg notes in his study of Hungarian migration to Cleveland:

> The eastside Buckeye neighborhood or westside Hungarian settlement in Cleveland were the immigrants' residential goals. They knew of them, the jobs available nearby, wage levels, and housing opportunities before leaving Hungary from "American Letters" and returning immigrants, and it was Cleveland, alone, to which these people were traveling. Indeed, even when unable to reach the city immediately upon entering the United States . . . these immigrants grasped the first opportunity to reach Cleveland.
>
> Reaching the city, immigrants found lively Hungarian neighborhoods . . . family or friends willing to house, feed, and assist them in becoming familiar with the area and acquiring a job.[3]

As the number of individuals from a village or region increased, ethnic boardinghouses, churches, social organizations, shops, and saloons followed. Though immigrant ghettoes, comparable to the black and Asian neighborhoods of East and West Coast cities, were a rarity in the Midwest, the typical immigrant group was socially and culturally cohesive, "a community which could live in almost complete autonomy—a city within a city."[4]

By the 1880s the costs of moving to the American Midwest had fallen dramatically. Trans-Atlantic transportation costs declined with the advent of steam-shipping and the proliferation of shipping firms. The costs of travel from the port of debarkation and of subsistence until a paycheck appeared were also comparatively low. The presence of relatives and former neighbors who promised assistance reinforced the sense of opportunity. While immigration remained more expensive than moving from the American countryside to the city, the costs were no longer a deterrent to ambitious men or women. When Alfred Nelson and Anna Johansson married in Chicago in 1906, supposedly having met on shipboard on the journey from Gothenburg in western Sweden, eleven of their thirteen siblings attended the ceremony.[5] For them and for many of their contemporaries, moving to Chicago, four thousand miles from home, was only slightly more adventurous and risky than moving to a European city.

In reality, of course, there were risks and dangers, as numerous accounts of individual suffering and tragedy attest. In 1912, the Illinois Immigrant Protective Society reported that 20 percent of unaccompanied female immigrants who left New York for Chicago never arrived at their destination.[6] Though the Society's accounting may have been defective, it emphasized the hazards that immigrants confronted, including the hostility of other ethnic groups and the criminal proclivities of supposed friends. But the greatest dangers were more mundane. The employment opportunity that looked so attractive from a distance was often less appealing on closer inspection. Even if a job remained promising, it could disappear at the first change in business conditions. Many immigrants found themselves jobless, impoverished, and forced to start over. In recent years urban historians have documented large-scale movements out of, as well as into, urban areas, confusing if not contradicting the customary conception of city growth. Although geographic mobility is difficult to interpret, it suggests a failure to find satisfactory employment.[7] The fact that low-skill workers were more likely to disappear from the records of a given community than higher-skilled industrial or white-collar workers is testimony to the difficulties that the most vulnerable newcomers faced.[8]

How do we reconcile the sense of an efficient labor market, conveyed in the testimony of immigrants, with evidence of transiency and the chaotic conditions, poverty, and distress that economists documented? Several features of the process of job seeking and recruitment may help. One was the employer's ethnic sensitivities. Although business and labor-market conditions influenced their behavior, most employers were highly selective. In Michigan, for example, small-town employers often rejected immigrants altogether in favor of more expensive, native workers with whom they were comfortable. In cities such as Grand Rapids and Detroit, employers hired immigrants but placed them under supervisors of the same ethnic heritage and made little effort to prepare them for more responsible positions.[9] Large cities also had growing numbers of firms owned or operated by first- or second-generation immigrants who offered newcomers an internal ladder to positions of greater pay and responsibility. Germans, for example, owned and operated most furniture factories and breweries and employed other Germans almost exclusively.[10] Most immigrant workers were unable to find such a niche, but there were enough instances of this form of mobility to spur them to continue their search, often in a new location.

It is also clear that the employment relationship was, by later standards, highly informal and impermanent. Employers customarily delegated personnel decisions, including the power to hire and fire, to first-line supervisors. This practice was a double-edged sword. Since supervisors first turned to family members, neighbors, or individuals recommended by neighbors, the foreman's power was a valuable resource for favored job-seekers. But it also led to abuses that ranged from bribes to the scandals associated with Italian padrones.[11] When workers became dissatisfied, the most common response was to quit and look elsewhere. Although many remained with a given firm for long periods, frequent job changes were the rule.[12] Mobility between jobs was related to mobility between cities, but neither form of movement necessarily meant success or failure.

Job changes enabled many workers to improve their wages and employment conditions, provided jobs were available. In many cases there were no jobs, or weeks or months of searching were required to find them. Frictional and seasonal unemployment together with disease and injury were major threats to workers' living standards in good times. The threat of unemployment dictated the family economy. Of course, in periods of cyclical unemployment, such as the mid-1890s, multiple wage earners were no hedge against disaster. The industrial family's dependence on a cash income made it highly vulnerable to downturns in the business cycle.[13]

While most immigrant blue-collar workers prospered by the standards of their home communities, they did not do well by American standards. Compared to white-collar workers and farmers, their earnings were low and unsteady. Most of them lived on the brink of poverty. In Michigan, for example, locomotive engineers, the highest-paid blue-collar employees, made less than bookkeepers, and machinists made less than janitors at Detroit's city hall.[14] The majority of industrial workers, who lacked skills, made considerably less. Their average annual earnings in the 1880s were about $250, or half the minimum middle-class income, too little to support a family.[15] It is not surprising that immigrants competed vigorously for public-patronage positions or looked upon a job in the police or fire department as mark of status.[16] For those who did not have the connections to move up through this route, the family economy provided a critical hedge against penury.

The work of the immigrant homemaker has received even less attention than that of farm wives. There were obvious variations based on family income and ethnicity. Wives of skilled workers were most likely to adopt the American diet of beef, fruits, and vegetables and relegate traditional dishes to holidays and celebrations. Some ethnic groups were also more receptive to American foods than others. (Italians and Jews were among the most resistant.) Regardless of such distinctions, many immigrant women took pride in skillful and economical food preparation.[17] But there were inevitable constraints. The mechanical revolution in middle-class cooking, which filled the fashionable kitchen with tools and utensils, "hardly touched" the working-class kitchen.[18] Working-class homemakers had to shop more often (because they did not have iceboxes) and devote more time to washing (because they did not have washing machines), cooking (because they could not afford modern stoves or many canned foods), and nursing (because of high morbidity and mortality rates in congested urban areas). Wives of unskilled workers also had to defer family-oriented tasks in favor of income-producing work. Daughters, relatives, and friends assisted, though formal "visiting" was difficult in the congested urban home, and the family goal of maximizing cash incomes reduced the amount of barter and cooperative labor. Relations between homemakers and boarders are largely a mystery.[19] Most social contacts occurred outside the home, one reason for the proliferation of ethnic clubs and societies.

Rural Industry

In the late nineteenth century, a small but growing number of midwestern industrial workers remained close to the land, toiling in forests and mines. One of the region's notable resources had been its magnificent pine forests, stretching from the western shore of Lake Huron five hundred miles through central Michigan, Wisconsin, and Minnesota. The clear-cutting of this vast area in a single generation made white pine the ubiquitous construction material of the late nineteenth century and the lumber camp a magnet for rugged male workers. Midwestern copper, iron, and coal created other opportunities. Keweenaw and Houghton counties in Michigan's Upper Peninsula dominated the copper-mining industry until the 1880s, and the area around Iron Mountain, Michigan, played a similar role in iron-ore mining, though it would soon be overshadowed by the new Vermilion and Mesabi Ranges of northern Minnesota. Southeastern Ohio, southwestern Indiana, northern and southern Illinois, and southern Iowa all had substantial bituminous coal fields by the 1880s. At the turn of the century, the Midwest accounted for one-third of bituminous production and nearly a third of all coal miners.

Operating in agricultural areas, often poor farming areas, logging and mining firms presumably should have recruited employees from the local labor force. In fact, most employees of logging and mining enterprises were immigrants. Because logging complemented the agricultural labor cycle and relied on skills that were widely diffused among the farm population, every midwestern camp had a handful of farm laborers and struggling mortgagees. But most of these men remained farmers, temporarily sacrificing their long-term prospects, dependent largely on their progress in clearing their own land, for desperately needed cash. Professional lumberjacks were typically Scandinavian immigrants who had learned their craft in the old country.[20] Mining had even less appeal. The confined and unpleasant environment, substantial risk of injury or death, and limited opportunity for advancement deterred most farmers. In southern Illinois, coal mining became a career option for the poorest farmers. More often the movement was in the other direction. In the Iowa fields, for example, the mines closed during the summer months, and many miners worked as farm laborers.[21]

Fortunately for employers, a ready supply of immigrants made it possible to increase output without competing for farm workers. Cornish immigrants predominated in copper and iron mining; English, Welsh, Scottish, Irish, and German workers, nearly all of whom had prior mining experience, dominated coal mining. At first employers favored them because of their familiarity with mining techniques. However, by the 1880s a substantial cadre of British managers and supervisors reduced the firms' dependence on veteran workers. Apart from a few critical tasks, such as shot firing, mining was semiskilled work; a few weeks of observation and learning-by-doing were sufficient to create a proficient miner or mine laborer. Employers increasingly turned to "new" immigrants to hold down wages and dilute the British tradition of trade unionism.[22]

Regardless of background, coal miners were highly mobile. Mines often closed after the most accessible veins had been exhausted, and even the most durable of them operated sporadically, depending on market conditions, the availability of transportation, and other variables. This feature of the industry dictated others: the owners' reluctance to spend money for safety; the company-owned towns (though less common in the midwestern fields than in other regions); the coal town's shabby appearance and lack of amenities; the ease with which employers fostered ethnic rivalries; the battles over seemingly minor irritants, such as the accurate weighing of coal; and the workers' predilection for formal organizations that would increase their market power and counter the employers' efforts to cut corners. In the rapidly growing, intensely competitive coal industry, unorganized workers were largely at the mercy of individuals who had strong personal and institutional interests in reducing labor costs.[23]

Lumberjacks were also typically transient, seasonal workers. They worked in the winter when the ground was frozen and logs could be moved by sled. Some of them started their careers in New England or the Adirondacks and ended them in the Pacific Northwest. Like miners, they worked singly or as part of a small group, and they enjoyed considerable freedom on the job. Further, their living conditions were exceedingly primitive. The "state of Maine" camps, which were common until the 1880s, consisted of a single large building with a fire in the middle, where the thirty to fifty camp residents slept, ate, and shared brief moments of relaxation. They slept on long bunks, "packed on their sides, all facing one way . . . as closely as a bundle of spoons. If one turned, all turned."[24] Family life was unknown, though the foreman's wife often served as a cook or laundress. In the spring, as the ice on the rivers melted, many "jacks" joined the log drive, an even more arduous and dangerous undertaking. Others headed for mill towns to find a sawmill job for the summer and celebrate their freedom. Their revels made Muskegon, East Saginaw, and Bay City, Michigan, the "toughest towns on the Great Lakes." Muskegon's Sawdust Flats was an area of "unspeakable whoredom and violence." Bay City's Catacombs "developed such a reputation for whoring, murder, and robbery, it is impossible for the modern-day historian to distinguish fact from fiction."[25]

Copper and iron miners, on the other hand, were among the most sedentary of midwestern workers. Mine owners recruited Cornish immigrants in the 1840s and 1850s to develop the first copper mines; a half-century later their sons and grandsons held a disproportionate share of supervisory jobs. At the Soudan mine, the first of the Vermilion Range operations, the labor force at the time of the mine's closing in 1962 consisted of second-, third-, and fourth-generation miners.[26] Geographical isolation was one reason for the miners' persistence. But compared to other mining jobs, and to most urban positions, the work of the Michigan and Minnesota mines was attractive. Calumet & Hecla and Oliver Mining, the major employers in Michigan and Minnesota respectively, were among the most paternalistic of mining firms, and the Michigan mines were safer than those of the Rocky Mountain West. Despite a surplus of single men and conflicts between the old and new immigrant groups that coexisted in the typical mining town, northern mining settlements were communities of families with a spectrum of social organizations and activities.

Coal mining was arguably the simplest and most tumultuous of the region's rural industries. Both characteristics arose from the abundance of coal and the ease with which it was extracted. Hand methods prevailed.

Miners worked with picks and shovels, simple explosives, and horse- or mule-drawn carts. They had to judge the character and quality of the mineral and extract it safely and expeditiously. And like other miners, they often worked in near total darkness. Production management was negligible because of the dispersed character of the work and the difficulty of moving underground. Mining thus remained labor-intensive; two-thirds or more of total costs were typically wage costs.

Two other specific factors largely explain the timing and intensity of the miners' militancy. The first was the mine owners' aggressiveness in replacing them with cheaper workers, especially during labor disputes. This threat was foreshadowed in the Hocking Valley in 1873, when mine owners imported five hundred black strikebreakers from Memphis, Louisville, and other southern cities. Threats from the strikers persuaded a quarter of the newcomers to defect, but the others remained in a fortified camp and eventually broke the strike.[27] Thereafter, racial tension would distinguish the mining communities of southern Ohio, Indiana, and Illinois from the Michigan and Minnesota mining communities.[28] The second factor was a catastrophic decline in miners' wages and living standards after 1893. Coal miners suffered more than most industrial wage earners during the depression of the mid-1890s. Wage cuts and unemployment reduced their real wages by one-quarter and their earnings, relative to those of factory workers, by one-third.[29]

Loggers and copper and iron miners, on the other hand, were parts of complex economic and technological systems that featured large business units and sophisticated engineering (the Soudan mine was a half-mile deep by the turn of the century, while the neighboring Mesabi Range featured the largest open-pit mines in the world and the largest excavating machines anywhere). Yet their actual work often resembled that of the coal miner. Apart from sawmill workers and mine employees who worked above ground, operating steam engines, rock-crushing machinery, or giant steam shovels, loggers and miners performed their tasks with simple hand tools. Pneumatically powered drills, introduced in the northern mines in the 1870s, saved time and energy but required two operators who controlled the drill's speed and use. Forty years later mine owners substituted a one-man drill that provoked widespread protests. Even more troubling, however, was the simultaneous elimination of the "runners," who carried messages and tools and performed other menial tasks. This innovation displaced the miners' sons and reduced family incomes.[30] In the copper mines, the most restive employees were the trammers who loaded cars and pushed them to the mine hoists.[31] Even affluent and progressive companies such as Calumet & Hecla did not introduce electrically powered equipment until after 1903.

In theory, production management in the mines was simple, straightforward, and authoritarian. A general superintendent presided over a mine captain and several assistants who in turn presided over shift foremen, responsible for twenty to forty miners, laborers, and other employees. In the Quincy operation of the 1880s, eighteen managers, including ten foremen, managed a labor force of four hundred.[32] Each man controlled the destiny of his subordinates. In practice, however, only the individuals at the top of the hierarchy, responsible for the financial performance of the mine, were closely supervised. The other employees enjoyed a high degree of personal freedom and autonomy. The obvious reason was the difficulty of supervising men who worked individually or in small groups in almost total darkness and whose activity was so deafening that oral communication was impossible. Ensuring responsible behavior was not difficult. Piece-rate systems of wage payment, often based on a "contract" between the worker and the foreman, forced the miner to match the output of other men performing similar tasks.

The engine of change in midwestern forestry was the locomotive, which began to be used in Michigan as early as the 1870s. Warm winters were the initial stimulus to railroading, but the depletion of the forests adjacent to lakes and rivers left loggers with little choice but to devise a new transport system. Railroads made it possible to cut trees year-round, gradually ending the seasonal character of the industry and making the river drives obsolete. By 1900 both Chicago and Milwaukee, the major wholesale centers, received more lumber by rail than by water. Railroads also encouraged the migration of sawmills from river and lake ports to forest areas and the production of finished lumber products and paper. Of greater importance to the lumberjack, they gave the larger companies a decided advantage. Larger operations, in turn, led to specialization. The "jack-of-all-trades" became a scaler, teamster, log driver, barn man, saw fitter, road foreman, or cook.[33] The logging camps became semipermanent industrial communities, with frame bunkhouses and dining facilities. By the early twentieth century, model camps, such as the Hines Lumber Company at Loretta, Wisconsin, with painted buildings, electricity, and steam heat, set a new standard of luxury in midwestern forests.[34]

New mining technology had a more immediate and decisive effect. The spread of open-pit operations in Minnesota (especially after the opening of the Mesabi Range in 1893), eliminated the traditional miner with his lantern, drill, and blasting powder. In open-pit mines, a crew of twenty to thirty laborers, headed by the steam shovel operator, performed the essential tasks. The steam shovel, and the other highly mechanized transport and loading systems that the huge Mesabi operations encouraged, made the mine more like a railroad yard or factory; machines did the work while the workers, from the most to the least skilled, attended and maintained them.[35]

Urban Industry

As dramatic as the growth of the forestry and mining industries was, it paled alongside the expansion of urban industry. By the time of the Civil War, the Midwest had become part of a northern manufacturing belt, largely on the basis of urban industry.[36] In the following years midwestern manufacturers eagerly adopted new products and processes that reinforced their position. They kept labor costs low by adopting labor-saving technologies and hiring immigrants. By 1900 they had created a flourishing manufacturing sector and a foundation for the dramatic changes that followed in the early twentieth century.

The single most notable feature of midwestern manufacturing before 1880 was the relative insignificance of textile production, a reflection of the dominant position of New England and the mid-Atlantic region (and later the Southeast). The absence of a substantial textile industry meant that the Midwest did not experience an abrupt shift to large-scale factory production, similar to that of the Northeast in the early nineteenth century and the Southeast after 1880. It also meant that an important stimulus to the employment of women and children was missing. Until the end of the century, the typical midwestern factory worker was a male immigrant, German in heritage, trained in a traditional craft, and able to apply that training in his new setting.

In an important study of antebellum industry in Philadelphia, Bruce Laurie and Mark Schmitz have classified types of industrial establishments. "Artisan workshops" did not use water or steam power and employed few than 6 workers. "Small manufactories" did not use water or steam power but employed 6 to 25 workers, and "large manufactories" employed 26 or more workers. "Small factories" used water or steam power and employed no more than 25 workers, while "large factories" relied on water or steam power and employed 26 or more workers.[37] The distinguishing feature of the factory, then, was machinery that required more energy than an individual could supply. This did not mean that other plants relied exclusively on hand tools; the foot-powered sewing machine, one of the most sophisticated machines of the age, was the basis for many manufactories. But there was a qualitative difference. As steam engines became more efficient and reliable (water power was not important in the Midwest after midcentury), power-distribution systems based on shafts and belts improved, and wood- and metal-cutting machines proliferated, the potential of the factory became obvious. Factory owners inevitably shifted their focus from the worker, the productive mechanism of the artisan shop and the manufactory, to the machine and the relations between machine activities.

To date, the most thorough study of the evolution of Midwest manufacturing in an urban setting is Robert V. Robinson and Ann-Maria Wahl's
examination of Indianapolis. Using Laurie and Schmitz's categories, they
report the following distribution of workers:

Table 2–2
Distribution of Indianapolis Workers
(Percentage)

	1850	1880	Men	Women	Children
			1880		
Artisan workshops	18	8	84	12	4
Small manufactory	32	18	81	16	3
Large manufactory	27	8	67	27	6
Small factory	20	9	88	6	6
Large factory	4	57	86	8	6

Source: Robert V. Robinson and Ann-Marie Wahl, "Industrial Employment and Wages of
Women, Men, and Children in a 19th Century City: Indianapolis, 1850–1888," *American
Sociological Review* 55 (December 1990): 916–17.

In Indianapolis, as in other cities, factory production grew rapidly after 1850,
accounting for two-thirds of manufacturing employment by 1880. But the
transition occurred in a dynamic economic environment; greater opportunities
for factory owners and workers did not mean reduced opportunities for
nonfactory producers. In most industries, workshops and factories coexisted.
The absolute number of workshops in 1880 was eight times greater than in
1850, and the number of workers was six times greater. Artisans also became
factory production managers, foremen, or skilled workers. In the decentralized
nineteenth-century factory, foremen enjoyed substantial powers, including the
power to employ subordinates and choose tools and techniques. Adaptable
artisans could enjoy a rewarding career in such a setting.[38]

Not all artisans found these choices inviting. Histories of industrial life in
Chicago, Detroit, Cincinnati, Milwaukee, and other midwestern cities note a
growing defensiveness among German artisans who dominated the traditional crafts.[39] Their immediate concerns were increased competition and
technological obsolescence. Probably as important, however, was a nagging
sense of decline as they saw factory owners and supervisors command larger
incomes and poorly trained workers produce commercially successful products with the aid of machinery. Their unease was an important impetus to the
resurgent labor movement of the 1880s.

Although the scale of manufacturing operations increased with the advent of factory production, the factory of the 1880s was by later standards a modest enterprise. The "large" factories in table 2–2 employed 26 or more individuals. In the 1870s only 67 of 2,500 Cincinnati industrial plants had 100 or more employees.[40] Only 45 of 919 Detroit plants employed 100 or more workers in 1880, and only 7 employed more than 300 workers.[41] Even the largest plants, moreover, were congeries of shops, often semiautonomous in operation and direction. Steam power and power distribution via shafts and belts made expansion difficult, but the real obstacle was the owners' limited outlook. Only gradually did they perceive the relationship between productivity and organization. Contemporary insurance maps of industrial plants typically show clusters of buildings devoted to different activities. Some of them, such as foundries, were segregated for good reason; others, simply because no one thought of a factory as more than a group of workers gathered around a central power source.

Yet even at that time a more sophisticated conception of the factory was beginning to emerge. In the 1880s and 1890s this development had no particular association with midwestern industry. However, the rapid growth of industries that made iron and steel products and depended on complex fabricating and assembly techniques alerted some midwestern industrialists to the possibilities of superior organization. By the early twentieth century they would play a leading role in the spread of new ideas and techniques.

We can see the origins of this process in the operation of the carriage and wagon industry in Cincinnati, its midwestern center in the late nineteenth century.[42] In the 1890s U.S. Commissioner of Labor Carroll Wright used it as an example of an industry that had been transformed by the advent of iron and steel machinery. In the 1860s carriages had been made with hand tools; by the time of Wright's study, they were made almost entirely by machines. Six men had taken 200 hours to perform the 64 operations required to manufacture a single carriage in the 1860s. Thirty years later 116 men took just 40 hours to perform 72 operations. The labor cost per carriage had declined by 80 percent, though the workers' real wages had risen more than 50 percent. As the industry evolved, the most versatile of the artisans became supervisors, and inexperienced men were trained to operate the complex wood- and metal-cutting machines. The operatives were able to work faster because the machinery provided them with superior materials, precisely cut and prepared. An 1886 account of one Cincinnati carriage maker found that production "proceeded so routinely that management could concentrate on other problems."[43] The dramatic contrast between hand and machine methods, and the obvious importance of finance and marketing, encouraged an illusion of routinized operations that could be managed by subordinates. But as more and more producers introduced machinery, the competitive advantage of machine operations declined. What had seemed routine and automatic in the 1880s would appear haphazard and even "chaotic" a decade later. The new perception was common to all industry at the end of the century, but it had special significance in industries (such as carriage building) that assembled finished goods from many separate components.

Although the industrial future of the Midwest would be closely associated with products like carriages, two other types of manufacturing deserve attention because of their concentration in the region, their role in the rise of the factory, and ultimately their contributions to the history of twentieth-century labor unrest and union organization. The first was the iron and steel industry, a comparative newcomer in the 1880s. Ohio had a substantial charcoal iron industry in the south-central Hanging Rock area, and there were iron fabricators in every large city well before the 1880s. But the iron industry had been concentrated in eastern Pennsylvania until the Bessemer and open-hearth processes revolutionized steel manufacture. High-grade ore was essential for steel making. To most manufacturers the Great Lakes shoreline was the best compromise between accessibility to markets and the Michigan and Minnesota mines. After 1880 notable concentrations of steel mills appeared at Cleveland, Milwaukee, and, above all, Chicago. The new mills were notable examples of capital-, energy-, and management-intensive production—what twentieth-century observers would call mass production. They also symbolized the shift from "manipulative" to "diagnostic" skills in production systems based on heat and chemical processes.[44] From the workers' perspective they were the region's preeminent employers of unskilled laborers, who moved materials and performed a host of menial, auxiliary tasks. Heat, dirt, danger, and long hours, especially in the continuous-process departments, made steel-industry jobs anathema to all but the least-competitive workers, increasingly eastern-European immigrants. Iron and steel employment in the Midwest rose from 31,000 in 1880 to 64,000 in 1900, just before U.S. Steel's massive Gary, Indiana, works signaled the industry's new concentration at the southern end of Lake Michigan.

Unlike steel manufacture, meatpacking was a venerable midwestern industry that had grown with the region's diversified agriculture. Until the 1870s processors concentrated on pork, which they salted or smoked. Their two biggest obstacles, shortages of salt and coopers, had been overcome by midcentury; Cincinnati became "Porkopolis," and other cities had extensive operations. The advent of the refrigerated railroad car in the 1870s transformed the industry: Chicago became its center, dressed beef became its principal product, and large firms with plants adjacent to the Chicago stockyards dominated the industry.[45] Within the plant, two features of the production process stood out. The first was the so-called disassembly line. It dated from the Cincinnati packing houses of the 1830s and consisted of lines of workers who cut up the hog, piece by piece, with each worker responsible for a single task. Since the publication of Sigfried Giedion's *Mechanization Takes Command* (1948), the disassembly line has often been portrayed as an antecedent of the assembly lines of the twentieth-century automobile plants. The comparison is misleading. The early packing houses were classic examples of manufactories. Packers increased production through a minute division of labor but did not use power machinery until the 1850s. Gradually they introduced mechanical devices such as steam-powered conveyors to carry carcasses between work stations, and the manufactory became a factory. But meatpacking remained a comparatively backward industry, technologically and organizationally primitive by the standards of the steel and machinery factories of the late nineteenth century.

The second notable feature of meatpacking, poor working conditions, also emphasized its primitive character. Slaughtering and processing were inherently disagreeable because of the blood and gore and the razor-sharp knives, cleavers, and axes that the workers used. Employers, large and small, did little to improve conditions. Their indifference ultimately provoked moves for government regulation—particularly after the publication of Upton Sinclair's classic, muckraking novel *The Jungle* (1906)—but another immediate effect was equally important. Meatpacking, like steel, became dependent on immigrant labor. In Chicago, German and Irish workers predominated in the 1870s. Although they continued to fill many of the skilled positions, other immigrants soon outnumbered them. By the early twentieth century, Poles dominated the Chicago plants. The low-skill, repetitive nature of the work and the offensive atmosphere ensured a constant succession of individuals and groups.[46]

Technological innovation was equally important in nonfactory industries, though its impact on the character of work was no more predictable. In construction, for example, it produced new building materials; new occupational specialties associated with the introduction of iron and steel, water, gas, and electricity in urban structures; and a constantly changing mix of factory-made and site-made components. Plumbers found that the decline of their traditional work, installing lead pipe, "was counterbalanced by the need to learn new skills to be able to install complex systems of plumbing."[47] But if the industry seemed to be in turmoil, the work continued to require skilled, responsible individuals who could work with minimal supervision. Workers continued to move back and forth between wage-earning, supervisory, and entrepreneurial roles, and machinery had little impact on production except in road, bridge, and skyscraper construction. In most cities Germans and Scandinavians dominated the construction trades, though Italians became increasingly common after 1900.

David Gordon, Richard Edwards, and Michael Reich have argued that the last quarter of the nineteenth century marked the beginning of a long period of "homogenization" in industrial labor, as semiskilled machine operators became more numerous.[48] Though the experience of the Midwest would just as readily support the opposite contention, that of growing diversity in occupations and skills, Gordon, Edwards, and Reich have emphasized a theme that often appeared in late-nineteenth-century labor publications. Craft workers often saw themselves locked in a desperate struggle with an incongruous alliance of rapacious employers and opportunistic immigrants. The future looked bleak. In retrospect it would be easy to dismiss their complaints as hypocritical or misguided, except that they paralleled the emotional protests of farmers and manufacturers during the same period. What these groups shared was a sense of growing insecurity as local monopolies gave way to regional, national, and, in the case of industrial labor, international competition. Farmers responded with alliance activities and appeals to government. Manufacturers formed cartels and other combinations. Craft workers created unions and attempted to influence wages, working conditions, and recruitment policies. The career of Eugene V. Debs, the Terre Haute, Indiana, union leader and socialist politician, typified the worker's anxious reaction to economic change. Debs's growing sense of estrangement was an important stimulus to his political activism.[49]

Dissatisfied industrial workers had several options. They could quit their jobs or "exit" and look for something better. This was the usual choice, no less important because it typically left no record and received little publicity. Job changes were effective antidotes to abusive supervisors, poor working conditions, and in some cases, low wages. Presumably the loss of capable employees prompted employers to improve conditions. But the ameliorative process was slow and inexact. To deal with specific problems or change the economic or political setting, "voice" was necessary. Voice embraced the informal organization of the workplace, more formal organizations such as labor unions, and external efforts to influence employment conditions through economic or political action. While anyone could quit, an effective voice required cooperation and organization, one reason that histories of workers' voice in the late nineteenth century are mostly histories of skilled workers like Debs. Voice was most effective in prosperous times, when labor was in comparatively short supply and employers sought to create an environment attractive to employees. On the other hand, it provoked strong and usually hostile reactions in good times and bad. Voice and struggle went hand in hand, as the experiences of industrial workers in the 1880s and 1890s emphasize.[50]

The Midwestern Labor Movement

Industrial workers, like farmers, grasped the value of collective action to address grievances, monopolize a trade, or enhance their position in society. They also had many models to guide them. They could look to the American labor movement of the Civil War era, to dissident political movements such as the Grange, or to the worker-oriented political parties of northwestern Europe during the 1870s and 1880s. Not surprisingly, in view of the ethnic and occupational diversity of the industrial labor force, their response was eclectic. They devised a series of organizations that operated with varying degrees of success. By 1890 the contours of the twentieth-century labor movement were visible. This story, like the story of farm protest that paralleled it, is much more than an account of midwestern workers. But unlike the region's farmers, who operated on the periphery of the agrarian protest movement, midwestern industrial workers were at the center of the urban labor upheavals of the late nineteenth century.

The stimuli to these events included a recession in 1883–1884 that revived memories of the depression of the 1870s, the mounting frustrations of craft workers, public policies that were strongly anti-union and conducive to violence, the rise of the Knights of Labor, and the growth of a socialist and anarchist subculture in cities with a large German population. The most active and vocal participants were craft workers of northern-European background. The fragmentary evidence that survives suggests that both the Knights of Labor and the independent trade unions consisted mostly of English, Irish, and German immigrants and their children.

The turmoil and violence of the late 1870s had left a legacy of bitterness and a handful of labor and socialist groups that grew to unprecedented membership levels and significance by the mid-1880s. What accounted for this development? The state of the economy was obviously a factor. After a revival that began in 1878 and featured employment and wage increases, a recession in 1883–1884 brought new rounds of layoffs and wage reductions. By the fall of 1884 there were thirty thousand unemployed in Chicago, overwhelming the city's relief agencies. Many of the city's skilled workers were destitute; the less skilled suffered proportionately more.[51] Reports from other midwestern cities were distressingly similar. Yet economic conditions improved in 1885 and remained buoyant for more than eight years. Worker organizations reflected this pattern. The Knights, for example, grew rapidly until 1882 or 1883, remained stable until 1885, and experienced a spectacular membership surge in 1885 and 1886. Other unions grew rapidly in the late 1880s and early 1890s. Increased employment opportunities were a prerequisite for union growth, though they did not explain the character of that growth.

Where it existed, collective bargaining was simple and direct. The International Molders Union represented skilled foundry workers at the McCormick Company, Chicago's largest industrial employer from 1862 to 1885. During that period, as Robert Ozanne explains:

> Wage settlements were oral and of no set duration. . . . One side or the other opened "bargaining" by unilateral action; the employer generally by effecting a wage cut, the union by presenting a citywide ultimatum to all foundry employers calling for a wage increase by a certain date. Managements that failed to comply were generally struck, though compromises were sometimes achieved.[52]

At other organized companies—the Chicago meat packers, the John Deere Company of Moline, and the Minnesota Iron Company of the Vermilion and Mesabi Ranges, for example—the process differed only in detail.[53] More formal union-management relationships existed in the pottery industry of East Liverpool, Ohio, and in the railroad, iron, and glass industries, but they were exceptions to the general pattern. Ad hoc collective bargaining contributed to dramatic fluctuations in union membership. Success typically produced a flood of new members; failure, a comparable exodus. Confidence about the future, especially a sense of immunity from reprisal, was essential. By the mid-1880s midwestern workers became convinced that they could organize without penalty.

Union membership rose dramatically in 1885 and 1886, thanks in part to the success of the Knights in well-publicized disputes with the Gould railroads. The capitulation of many employers in 1886 to demands for an eight-hour day with no reduction in pay—the celebrated "shorter hours" campaign—had a similarly exhilarating effect in Chicago, Cincinnati, Detroit, Milwaukee, and other midwestern cities. No one knows how many individuals joined unions, but the total was substantial; in Detroit, for example, membership nearly tripled in eight months.[54] For a few months, the labor movement embraced a majority of skilled workers and a substantial minority of the less skilled. The exodus dated from the Haymarket disaster of May 4, 1886, and continued at an accelerating pace in the following months as organized workers lost strikes and employers returned to the ten-hour day. By the end of the decade, the Knights had virtually disappeared. Craft unions fared better, but they, too, lost many members.

These events not only had dramatic effects at the time; they also help explain a process that occurred again in the late 1910s and in the mid-1930s. A growing economy shifted the labor-market balance in the worker's favor at the same time labor activists provided an appealing rationale for collective action. The result was rapid union growth and the emergence of an institutional workers' voice. But that was only the beginning. The other distinguishing features of this period were efforts to organize alternative institutions (consumers cooperatives and independent political parties in particular) and to enlist unconventional, primarily low-skill workers as union members. These controversial activities created growing opposition among unorganized workers, permitting employers to enlist allies and counterattack. Labor activism ultimately threatened the new organizations.

The Knights' appeal, reformist and inclusive, was the catalyst for the upsurge of the mid-1880s. It combined demands for political reform with campaigns for individual and collective self-help. Coupled with the prospect of higher wages and better working conditions, it had the potential to attract workers who had never thought of themselves as union members and, in many cases, would not have been welcome in existing craft organizations. In 1886 the Illinois Bureau of Labor Statistics conducted a survey of union members in Chicago. German immigrants constituted almost one-third of the total; followed by native-born whites, including the children of immigrants (20 percent); Irish immigrants (17 percent); and Scandinavian immigrants (10 percent). No other ethnic group was numerically significant. When individual union memberships were taken into account, an additional distinction appeared. German immigrants made up 36 percent of trade union membership and 21 percent of the Knights' membership, while native-born workers were 16 percent of trade union membership and 34 percent of the Knights' membership. This disparity reflected the Knights' appeal to low-skill employees, including the upwardly mobile children of new immigrants.[55]

Other midwestern cities and towns provide similar examples. In Detroit the Knights attracted the city's labor activists and eclipsed the Socialist Labor Party in mobilizing a "subculture of opposition."[56] In Dubuque, Iowa, they created a "mass labor movement" that included many low-skill workers (one-quarter of all union members in 1886) and women (one-fifth of the total).[57] The Knights' many "ladies' locals" included the "Our Girls Co-Op" garment-workers assembly in Chicago, the Martha Washington underwear-workers assembly in Indianapolis, the Good Will Assembly of domestic workers in Shawnee, Ohio, the Joan of Arc mixed assembly in Toledo, and an assembly of Cincinnati shoe workers that dominated the local industry.[58]

Clearly the Knights appealed to many workers, including many native-born workers. These individuals were attracted to calls for higher wages, the eight-hour day, cooperation, and attacks on business monopolies. Had they lived in the countryside, they probably would have joined the Grange and been active in the alliance movement. Their careers as unionists were generally short-lived because of employer opposition, haphazard organization, and the difficulties of operating a successful cooperative, but their presence in the labor movement emphasized the importance of ideas, and idealism, to a mass movement.

Most accounts of the dramatic collapse of the Knights, and the retreat of the labor movement as a whole, emphasize defective leadership in the management of the strikes and the alienation of public opinion, symbolized by the Haymarket Square violence. The subsequent campaigns of labor leaders to curb the strike powers of local unions and to avoid association with violence reflected their perception of the labor movement's self-destructive potential. But these were not the only reasons for the decline of the Knights and the unions. The willingness of employers to sustain losses to punish their employees was as important as the unions' miscalculations. Even more decisive was the partisan role of the state, not only in curbing strikers' powers but also in utilizing police and militia forces in a way that maximized the likelihood of violence.

By the 1880s the role of city, state, and national officials in labor disputes had become anti-union in practice if not in theory or intention. The readiness of Chicago politicians to use police and militia against strikers during the turmoil of the mid-1870s had caused much bitterness in working-class neighborhoods. The influence of the anarchist International Working People's Association in the Chicago labor movement was a measure of this disillusionment. So, too, was the growth of the Lehr-und-Wehr Verein and other paramilitary groups that prepared to return the blows and shots of police and soldiers.[59] Elsewhere the situation was similar. During the great sawmill strike at Bay City and Saginaw, Michigan, in the summer of 1885, mill owners turned to Governor Russell Alger, a mill owner himself, after local officials, all members of the Knights of Labor, insisted on neutrality. The governor rushed to Saginaw with five companies of militia and browbeat the mayor and sheriff into a more helpful posture. Thomas Barry, a prominent Knight who was directing the strike, was arrested six times. With the governor's assistance the mill owners were able to hold out and ultimately defeat the strikers.[60] There were exceptions, such as the Hocking Valley coal strike of 1884–1885, in which the Ohio National Guard played a neutral peacekeeping role, but they were infrequent.[61]

Police and militia violence was a critical element in the debacles of May 3–4, 1886, that undermined the Knights and the labor movement. The immediate prelude to the Haymarket incident was a police assault on a mob attacking nonunion employees leaving the McCormick works. After witnessing the beatings and shootings, which left two dead and many injured, the anarchist August Spies issued an inflammatory call for a protest meeting the following night at Haymarket Square. At the conclusion of that meeting, a large contingent of police officers, led by a notoriously anti-union official, suddenly appeared and began to clear the area. One of the anarchists, probably a man named George Schwab, threw a bomb at the police. One officer died from the blast; three others were shot and killed in the ensuing melee; three others died from a combination of bullets and bomb fragments; an eighth officer died two years later from injuries that included bullet wounds.[62] Although the police and public blamed unionists and anarchists for the killings, there was no evidence that anyone in the crowd shot an officer. Schwab was apparently the lone assailant, and his bomb killed only one officer. The others died from police bullets.

News of the Haymarket riot had a catalytic effect. Socialists, anarchists, and union leaders were arrested in many cities. Most of the eight-hour strikes collapsed. Ohio's governor sent the National Guard to Cincinnati in response to antisocialist hysteria.[63] In Milwaukee troops fired into a crowd outside the Bay View works of the North Chicago Rolling Mill Company, killing five and wounding many others. After near-riots the day before, the plant had closed, and Knights of Labor leaders began a concerted campaign against violence. The prospects for a peaceful settlement were good until news of the Haymarket killings arrived. When a crowd of a thousand gathered outside the closed factory on May 5, the governor ordered the soldiers to fire.[64]

In the aftermath of the eight-hour strikes and the Haymarket and Bay View violence, union groups sought to reverse the prevailing pattern through the ballot box. Forty percent of the local labor parties associated with the Knights of Labor operated in the Midwest.[65] In Chicago the union party elected seven assemblymen and five judges. In Milwaukee a People's party, organized by the Knights, won control of the city government in November, 1886. Loosely affiliated with the agrarian political movement, the Milwaukee party drew its support from German and Polish neighborhoods where the Bay View shootings had been most unpopular. Cincinnati unions formed a United Labor Party the following year. With a sweeping program of labor reform and the support of the city's diverse and often fractious labor groups, the ULP had broad appeal. In April it narrowly lost the mayoral race but elected nine of twenty-five city council members. It commanded more support than any third party in the city's history. In more than a dozen other midwestern communities, ranging from Ohio to Iowa, the Knights elected mayors and other public officials. Activists argued that these victories or near-victories were the first steps in the political mobilization of the urban working class. But they were mistaken. The Milwaukee party lost after one term, and the Cincinnati party never again mounted a significant challenge to two-party domination of the city government.[66] In other cities, the decline was equally precipitous. Republicans and Democrats typically combined forces to overwhelm the labor independents. By 1890 the workers' political efforts had succumbed to ethnic and political divisiveness and opposition from entrenched politicians.

The Knights and the conception of organization they championed declined rapidly in the late 1880s. Strike defeats in Bay City and elsewhere accounted for some membership losses. The collapse of the Knights' cooperative enterprises dispirited other workers. Public opposition was also a factor. In Dubuque the Knights had seven assemblies and more than 2,500 members in 1887 but only one assembly and several hundred members in 1890. There had been no major strikes or other confrontations during the intervening years. The hostility of the town's established leaders was sufficient to intimidate most workers, including virtually all of the unskilled.[67]

Ethnic and occupational distinctions were also influential among Knights who had organized as conventional unionists. Seven hundred and fifty employees of the Laughlin and Junction steel company of Mingo Junction, Ohio, organized a local assembly and negotiated contracts in 1886 and 1887. The skilled workers, approximately one-third of the total, soon became dissatisfied with the Knights' diverse structure and solicitude for the less skilled. In 1887 they invited the Amalgamated Association of Iron and Steel Workers, the industry's craft union, to organize a lodge at Mingo Junction, precipitating a major test of the Knights' ability to hold skilled industrial workers. For a month the battle raged; at one point the Knights' leaders tried to recruit strikebreakers to replace the AA members. When these tactics failed, the Knights were driven from the plant. They had not "come to grips with the issues central to the skilled workers" or erased the "desire for status distinctions between the skilled and less-skilled workers."[68]

Other skilled workers followed the example of the Mingo Junction employees. The formation of the American Federation of Labor, in Columbus, Ohio, in December 1886, symbolized the tendency of skilled workers to emphasize their own interests. The history of the Chicago carpenters union provides a more direct measure of the change. On the eve of the eight-hour campaign, the Chicago carpenters had been led by men whose principal interests were economic and political reform. The events of 1886 excited organized and unorganized workers alike, greatly increased union membership, and provoked a series of structural and tactical changes in the Chicago labor movement. Local carpenters unions formed a United Carpenters Council to coordinate activities, elected new leaders who emphasized aggressive bargaining for wages and other benefits, and joined other construction workers to create a Building Trades Council to negotiate with contractors. By 1890 the Carpenters had become exponents of militant collective bargaining.[69] If they were less idealistic and less interested in the fate of other industrial workers, that seemed a small price for what they had achieved.

The depression of the 1890s intensified the problems of industrial workers at the same time it undercut the possibility of successful organization and negotiation. By the fall of 1893 many mines and factories had closed. Layoffs had cost half of Chicago's factory workers their jobs; carpenters union officials reported that only 20 percent of their members were working.[70] From the Mesabi to the grimy mill towns of Ohio's Mahoning Valley, the situation was similar. Indeed, the severity of the distress stimulated a series of innovations that distinguish that period from earlier periods of economic collapse and anticipated many features of the twentieth-century economic and social order. The era's experiments in government activism and self-help, many of which had a midwestern setting, have been extensively documented elsewhere. The decade's political crusades have received even more attention. We have already examined the limited inroads of Populism among midwestern farmers. Among industrial workers, Populism had its greatest appeal among coal miners, especially old immigrants who confronted rising competition from new immigrants. In Illinois coal towns, the presence or absence of new immigrant communities largely determined the size of the Populist vote.[71] Although the dissidents fared poorly, a sweeping protest vote decimated the Democratic party and provided a foundation for subsequent divisions in the now-dominant Republican party and for new third-party efforts by disaffected workers.

The depression also had a permanent impact on the labor movement. It obliterated the midwestern remnants of the Knights of Labor and with them the dream of an all-embracing organization that transcended industry and skill. On the other hand it encouraged craft and skilled factory workers to organize in close-knit units that could survive the fluctuations of the economy. It also encouraged some of the century's most notable and violent strikes, as unions and desperate workers resisted labor-market competition.

Coal mining was the center of the strike movement. Strikes, with or without the backing of the United Mine Workers (formed by a merger of miners unions in 1890), became the most dramatic way to resist the downward spiral of wages and employment. There were at least 271 in the four midwestern coal-mining states between 1887 and 1894 and many more between 1894 and 1897. The largest strike, called in the spring of 1894 to protest wage cuts, threatened to paralyze what remained of the regional economy. Widespread violence alienated the public and led to a crackdown on the strikers. As the strike collapsed, UMW membership also plunged. But the UMW did not go the way of the Knights or of the American Railway Union, whose unsuccessful strike against Pullman and the railroads during the summer of 1894 attracted more attention.[72] In 1897 the UMW led another series of strikes that had a vastly different outcome. Victory enabled the UMW to become the stabilizing force in the industry, reducing competition and raising wages to unprecedented levels.[73] The creation of the Central Competitive Field, embracing western Pennsylvania and the Midwest, ended the turmoil of the 1890s and established the UMW as the largest and most formidable American union.

If the volume of union activity in the 1880s and 1890s was a reflection of the workers' desire to create conditions and opportunities that farmers took for granted, the level of conflict was a measure of their employers' hostility to labor organization.[74] These were among the few unchanging features of midwestern industrial relations in the following years, as organizational and technological innovation transformed the work of industrial employees and an increasingly militant and sophisticated urban working class sought to duplicate the farmers' successes in enlisting government support. In the 1890s, however, there was little reason to assume that the future of industry would differ from the pattern of the late nineteenth century. On the contrary, a careful student of the census data would have pointed to the region's offices and stores as the fastest changing, most promising workplaces. White-collar work, labor-intensive, unmechanized, and in many respects old-fashioned, ironically offered opportunities unknown in agriculture or industry.

3.

White-Collar Workers, 1880–1900

Nearly one midwestern worker in five in the 1880s had no direct involvement in the work of farms, factories, mines, or logging camps. A heterogeneous mixture, they included rich and poor, prominent and obscure individuals, and a large majority of the region's women who worked outside the home. Two groups stood out: the producers of services, the majority, and a small but fast-growing minority of managers and other office workers from the region's large industrial firms. In the 1880s the most prominent of the service producers, merchants, bankers, attorneys, clergymen, and other profession-als, were the regions' most distinguished and wealthiest citizens. By 1900 they were increasingly overshadowed by the executives, a transition epito-mized by the career of John D. Rockefeller, the merchant-turned-industrial-ist. Together these two groups formed the region's business elite, easily recognizable in the workplace by their fashionable attire. This elite included most of the workers who made more than $500 per year, the threshold of the middle class, and a large majority of those who made more than $2,000, the threshold of real wealth.[1] Middle- and upper-class white-collar workers and their wives also dominated the region's political and social institutions, setting standards for taste and refinement. As John F. Kasson explains, they understood such "necessities" as "frequent bathing and meticulous groom-ing," the "increasingly specialized furnishings and functions of different rooms in a stylish household," the management of servants, and the appropri-ate behavior for business and social functions.[2]

Apart from the growing prominence of men like Rockefeller, the most important changes in the world of white-collar and service work involved comparatively inconspicuous individuals. Although less obvious and less important than the mechanization of agriculture or the application of steam power to manufacturing, these changes made the office, the store, and, to a lesser degree, the home a different institution by the turn of the century.

White-Collar Work: Stability and Change

The evolution of the business community in the Midwest reflected changes in the larger economy. The number of white-collar workers grew more rapidly, proportionately, than either of the major occupational groups, became more distinctive in appearance, and became more technically sophisticated. Yet it is likely that a Rip Van Winkle who awoke in 1890 and made his way to a typical business office or store would have been less impressed than if he had visited a midwestern farm or factory. Rather than massive steam engines, large and noisy machines, and armies of employees, he would note the somewhat larger size of the office or store and the piles of papers, letters, reports, and memos. If perceptive, he might also notice that white-collar workers spoke grammatical English and that many of them performed their tasks with the aid of tools and even machines. More likely, he would simply note the presence of female employees in many offices and stores.

In earlier decades, business activity had not been so clearly defined outside the largest cities, and the merchant or industrialist was often indistinguishable from his neighbors. In Trempealeau County, Wisconsin, for example,

> there was often a community of interest between the merchants and storekeepers on the one end and the producers of commodities—the millers, brewers, and artisans engaged in the leather, building, metal, and clothing trades—on the other. Moreover, there was a marked tendency to shift from one type of business to another. . . . [3]

As the economy grew, however, business activity matured, and the changes that had occurred over a half-century in the Northeast were compressed into a decade or two. By 1880 all but the smallest towns had a cadre of specialists: bankers, insurance agents, brokers, undertakers, barbers, innkeepers, stable operators, and retailers who specialized in foods, clothing, hardware, and other consumer products. Most of these firms were small; their proprietors had adapted to a changing economy by developing a profitable niche. But because they were specialists, they were rarely important as employers. If they succeeded, they typically added partners, not employees. Apart from the bank, which required a literate, trained staff, most workers who were not owners or part-owners were laborers. In that respect, the typical midwestern business of the later nineteenth century resembled the typical farm. Still, anyone who analyzed the Main Street firm with some care would have found many indications of a world of large organizations, novel technologies, and new forms of work. The factory-made goods that lined the store shelves were an obvious example. The department stores—clusters of specialty shops under a single roof, not large general stores—were another. Most telling was an omnipresent figure: the railroad-station agent or district superintendent who personified the link between the town and the outside world.[4]

If specialization was one response of the business community to growth and competition, professionalism was another. The growth of medical, legal, and other professional groups had similar effects everywhere: the new organizations standardized services, reduced competition, raised fees and salaries, offered practitioners a source of identity, and assured the public of reasonably efficient service. A bloody 1884 Cincinnati riot over an apparent miscarriage of justice spoke to the need for more professional, as well as more honest, legal procedures.[5] Professionalization was also a powerful stimulus to formal education, helping transform the region's land grant universities into clusters of professional schools. But this trend was most easily observed from afar. In 1900 most doctors, lawyers, teachers, clergymen, and nurses performed the same kinds of services in the same way they had a quarter-century before.

Who were the people that one would likely meet in an office or store of the 1880s? Studies of midwestern business provide more detailed views of the white-collar elite than of any other group. A survey of eleven hundred prominent Chicago executives, for example, found that 84 percent were native-born. Approximately half of that group had been born in Chicago and the Midwest; a slightly smaller percentage was from the Northeast. Virtually no one came from the South or West. Of the 16 percent who were foreign-born, the largest groups were from Britain, Germany, and Scandinavia and had arrived in the 1860s and 1870s.[6] A similar division characterized the Detroit elite at the turn of the century.[7] Seventy-eight percent of Cleveland's late-nineteenth-century iron and steel manufacturers, and 81 percent of Youngstown's, were native-born.[8] Most of the immigrant merchants and executives were Canadian or British; among the iron and steel makers, over 90 percent shared a British heritage.

The relative homogeneity of the midwestern business elite reflected several factors, including the importance of communication skills and mastery of English.[9] It was also an example of the ethnic clustering that resulted from informal recruitment activities. Most of all, it was a reflection of the process by which young men prepared for white-collar careers. Since that process would change swiftly and drastically after the 1880s, it deserves special emphasis.

The business-elite studies provide the information in Table 3-1 on the occupations of elite members' fathers. The Chicago data are for men who were at least twenty years old in 1880. The Cleveland and Youngstown data are for those who held responsible positions in the iron and steel industry in the late nineteenth century. As time passed, Chicago's elite became more like that of Cleveland and Youngstown, with more and more business leaders drawn from white-collar families. But even before 1880 the trend was clear:

Table 3–1
Fathers' Occupations
(Percentage)

	Farm	Blue-Collar	White-Collar
Chicago*	33	9	57
Cleveland	2	13	84
Youngstown	14	7	79

* Includes only those individuals born between 1820 and 1860.
Sources: Joyce Maynard Ghent and Frederic Cople Jaher, "The Chicago Business Elite: 1830–1930. A Collective Biography," *Business History Review* 50 (Autumn 1976): 303; John N. Ingham, "Rags to Riches Revisited: The Effect of City Size and Related Factors on the Recruitment of Business Leaders," *Journal of American History* 63 (December 1976): 628–31.

most executives had followed their fathers into a business or profession. Those who had not were usually the sons of farmers who had sought their fortunes in the city. Even in the iron industry, comparatively few executives were sons of the artisans who had dominated the industry's earlier history.

The vast majority of elite men began their careers as apprentices in offices and stores, as office boys or clerks, working for a small wage and the opportunity to "learn the business." They performed menial tasks and in return were trained and given the imprimatur of the man or firm under whom they served. Business training had three bases: double-entry bookkeeping, commercial law, and finance.[10] Each industry also had its own particular specialized knowledge. By the 1880s and even more obviously by 1900, technical knowledge had become a barrier rather than a hurdle, creating the basis for more systematic and impersonal education. Apart from such knowledge, the apprenticeship was supposed to inculcate values or "character" and to permit the executive to evaluate the apprentice's personal qualities. Punctuality, diligence, honesty, good manners, and personal charm were as important as technical acumen.

Given this approach to business education, it is clear why comparatively few sons of industrial workers became members of the midwestern business elite. Educational deficiencies excluded many of them. The expectation that apprentices operate in the same social milieu as the executive and customer closed the door to others. With a limited number of openings and many aspirants, most firms chose boys who had personal ties to members of the firm. Though it was not impossible for the factory worker's son to find a position, the obstacles discouraged all but the most diligent and aggressive young men.

Several unrelated factors undermined this system in the late nineteenth century. The first of these was the increasingly technical character of business, which made the informal apprenticeship unnecessary or inappropriate. In large private bureaucracies, such as railroads, clerks were specialists who had little need to learn railroading in general. Railroads hired literate young men for clerkships and promoted from within; a broader background was not necessary. Although executives subscribed to the vision of a job ladder that extended from the lowliest white-collar position to the president's office, most clerical workers had too little exposure to workings of the firm to climb it. Even a middle management position might be out of reach.[11] Those who did serve business apprenticeships faced a different problem. In the design and engineering departments of railroads, mines, and large manufacturing companies, where technical work was increasingly based on an understanding of chemistry, physics, and mathematics, on-the-job training was inadequate. Apprentices gave way to university graduates. Mechanical and mining engineering, which reflected the rise of science-based technologies in industry, burgeoned in the 1880s and 1890s. In commercial enterprises the informal approach persisted, though employers increasingly sought entry-level employees with more theoretical business training.

The second factor that undermined the informal apprenticeship was the gradual rise of the high school in the 1880s and 1890s. High school graduates were almost as rare as university graduates in the 1870s. High schools were too expensive for small towns and rural areas and too exclusive for most urban youths. Even in the largest cities they seldom enrolled more than a few hundred students. Of those only a minority remained through the twelfth grade. As late as 1890 only 8 percent of Ohio secondary students and 6 percent of Wisconsin secondary students graduated.[12] The contrast between the high school curriculum and the educational requirements of most industrial jobs seemingly guaranteed that high school enrollments would remain low. Sensitive to these problems, professional educators lobbied vigorously to extend secondary education to smaller towns. They also devised a variety of solutions for the "boy problem" (the high drop-out rate among boys) and the embarrassing tendency of high schools to become increasingly female at each grade level.[13] Manual and vocational training, designed largely for boys, received much attention, energy, and resources, despite little evidence that it kept boys in school or provided meaningful skills. What was almost wholly overlooked was the significance of the academic curriculum for middle-class boys and the commercial curriculum for girls.

Although the relationship between the high school and the recruitment of managerial employees has received little attention, business biographies and company histories indicate that most executives were high school graduates by the early twentieth century. Secondary education was a valuable asset for the minority whose parents could afford to take a longer and more expansive view of their prospects. During the 1880s and 1890s high school superseded the informal apprenticeship. Men who had graduated from high school in the 1870s and 1880s and had become employers by the turn of the century were even more likely than their predecessors to favor high school graduates for entry-level jobs. Yet the transition was fitful and uneven, and many firms, especially family-operated establishments, were unaffected. While high schools taught communications skills, mathematics, and science, they did not provide technical training for potential executives. This shortcoming made the high school a transitional institution. It provided the best available vocational education for prospective white-collar workers in the years between the decline of the informal apprenticeship and the growth of business education in urban and state universities, which combined academic and technical training. For girls, including many daughters of immigrants, it had a larger and more permanent role.[14]

Technology and Management

Compared to agricultural or industrial work, the distinctive features of white-collar work were its labor-intensive character and higher pay. These attributes were concomitants of the growing separation of manual from nonmanual labor, of production from management, and by 1900, of management from ownership. Executives bore greater responsibility and received higher pay. Their subordinates, including clerks and secretaries, also worked in an unmechanized setting and earned higher money wages than most farmers, miners, and factory workers. Their comparatively advantageous situation helps explain the ideological cohesiveness of the white-collar labor force despite wide disparities in incomes and authority.[15] Yet office work was in flux. New technologies, unimpressive by the standards of farm and factory and almost unnoticed in contemporary society, increased the productivity of the office and the potential power of the manager and raised issues reminiscent of those that confronted workers in factories and mines.

All of the revolutionary technologies of the nineteenth century affected the work of the office by encouraging expansion, greater competition, and a continuing search for efficiency. But the machines and processes that had the greatest impact on day-to-day activity were comparatively modest. The telegraph and telephone proved to be relatively unimportant except in the railroad and brokerage industries. Telegraphy was too expensive for all but the most important or perishable information, and the telephone, a feature of most offices by the 1880s, was useful primarily for informal or preliminary contacts. Both devices were most effective for internal communications between offices, factories, or other units of large organizations where personal contacts and written statements were not necessary. On the other hand, a series of modest devices that transformed clerical work and created the stenographer and secretary were of substantial importance.

The essential tools of the mid-nineteenth-century office were the steel pen, the letter press, and the pigeonhole desk.[16] All were passé by the 1890s. The pen enabled the clerk and bookkeeper to prepare correspondence and record the results of financial transactions; the letter press permitted handwritten letters to be copied quickly and cheaply. After the development of aniline inks in the 1850s, it could make two reasonably legible copies of any document. The pigeonhole desk allowed an executive to keep important correspondence and other written information close at hand. Convenient in a small firm, especially one with a single office and a small staff, it could not accommodate a large volume of communications. By the 1880s many executives had supplemented it with box files, which enabled them to maintain a larger number of records in systematic order.

Each of these devices gave way to new, more sophisticated technologies in the late nineteenth century. The typewriter was by far the best known and most important of these innovations, as many students of office work have noted. Invented in the 1870s and improved in the 1880s, it had become ubiquitous by the turn of the century. Because a skilled typist could type at least three times as fast as a skilled clerk could write, the typewriter greatly reduced the cost of preparing letters and other documents. Yet this reduction in labor costs was only the first of many economies. The typewriter also revolutionized copying; the introduction of carbon paper enabled each typist to make as many as ten copies of every document without additional effort. Carbon paper was cheaper than traditional copying paper and eliminated one of the major jobs of the office boy. Together with the mimeograph machine, which the A. B. Dick Company successfully introduced in the late 1880s, it introduced an era of low-cost copying. More copies in turn created a demand for improved filing systems and led to the development of vertical file cabinets in the 1890s.

By the turn of the century, the work of the office had become mechanized, standardized, and increasingly routinized, as the volume of activity and the productivity of the labor force increased. It is tempting but misleading to compare the office to the factory. Office machines were hand-operated; no office, however large or routinized, required a fraction of the power that the average manufacturing plant required. Typewriters were more expensive than pens but cheaper than most industrial machines. Moreover, with the possible exception of the mimeograph and the dictating machine, which also appeared in the 1880s, office machines were passive instruments. There was nothing comparable to the machinery of a refinery or steel mill, which dictated the worker's pace. Finally, the machine operator in an office was more likely to be a woman than the machine operators in most industries and was, like the clerks who preceded her, comparatively well paid.

The growth in the number of female white-collar workers was a reflection of the changes that affected clerical work, not just the advent of the typewriter and other office machinery. The increase in firm size, the obsolescence of the informal apprenticeship, and the growing pressures to contain administrative costs all contributed to the transformation of clerical activity. The typewriter forced employers to think about these issues. Since it required a novel skill, specialized training, and a break with traditional practice, it encouraged the reorganization of office work. The promise of additional savings in wage costs was a bonus few could resist.

There is no record of conflict over the decision to employ women, in part because the change usually occurred over several years. Typically a firm hired a "typewriter" and, satisfied with her work, added others as male clerks left or the volume of business grew. Occasionally men were discharged, but in most cases the transition was gradual and peaceful. Since the two groups performed different tasks and men continued to hold the more responsible, better-paying positions, male clerks could argue that only office boys and low-skill specialists had been displaced.

The other major reason for the seemingly effortless transition was the availability of female candidates who were both technically capable and accommodating. By the 1870s single, educated women had begun to take positions as clerks in government offices and as public stenographers. From their perspective the work was respectable, interesting, and better paying than most female occupations. Employers were pleased with their diligence, cooperativeness, and comparatively low wages. Typing was a logical extension of this activity. The catalyst in the growth of the female labor force, however, was the proprietary business college, which was the principal mechanism for training clerical workers until the turn of the century. In Chicago, for example, the number of such colleges rose from five in 1880 to twenty-eight in 1890.[17] Their growth was initially a response to the increasingly specialized and technical character of clerical work in large firms; as late as the 1890s, two-thirds of the students were men. But the schools quickly recognized the potential of typing and stenography. By the turn of the century, they emphasized clerical training for a predominantly female student body.

Public high school officials were much slower to grasp the potential of clerical education, despite their preoccupation with vocational education.[18] In Chicago the school system first offered clerical courses in an evening extension program. Day classes followed at the turn of the century. The city's business leaders wanted more emphasis on clerical training, including a separate clerical high school for boys. School officials, who opposed a separate institution, decided instead to offer typing, stenography, and other business courses in academic high schools. Again, their effort failed. "Instead of keeping boys in school," they "inadvertently created the opportunity for more women to take commercial courses."[19] By the early 1910s most evening students were enrolled in commercial courses. By that time the high school commercial curriculum was the one notable example of successful public vocational education.

Lisa Fine's reworking of an 1892 report of the Illinois Bureau of Labor Statistics helps explain the appeal of white-collar work to Chicago women. Table 3–2 compares the earnings and expenditures of Chicago female factory employees with those of two groups of white-collar employees, clerks (including store clerks) and stenographers. Most of the factory workers were young, single, and part of the family economy. Room and board (usually the daughter's contribution to her family) accounted for 60 percent of their expenditures, and they spent modestly for clothing and recreation. In comparison, clerks earned more and spent more, especially for clothing. The contrast between clerks and stenographers was even greater. Indeed, compared to their *male* contemporaries, Chicago stenographers were well paid. They earned one and a half times as much as unskilled male workers, nearly as much as molders and machinists, and two-thirds as much as skilled construction workers in 1890. Their earnings were comparable to those of carpenters or bricklayers who lost a day of work per week, a common occurrence.[20] Typically unmarried, stenographers could afford much higher living expenses than female factory workers or male workers with dependents. They could live independently and spend freely on clothing and recreation. And they had

Table 3–2

Earnings and Expenditures of Chicago Women Workers, 1892

| | *(Female factory workers' average = 100)* | | |
	Factory	*Clerks*	*Stenographers*
Earnings	100	131	210
Total Expenses	100	118	175
Clothing	100	144	222
Room/Board	100	105	162
Other	100	142	198

Source: Adapted from Lisa Fine, *The Souls of the Skyscraper: Female Clerical Workers in Chicago, 1870–1930* (Philadelphia: Temple University Press, 1990), p. 43.

opportunities to meet men in business positions and possibly secure an even more comfortable future. From the employer's standpoint, women were an inexpensive source of skilled labor. From the worker's perspective, typing and stenography were the one assured route to middle-class living standards. It is not surprising that in many midwestern cities the pressure for high school commercial courses came from students and parents, not from teachers and administrators.

Table 3–2 also underlines the dangers of generalizing about the character of office and other white-collar work. The range of earnings between clerks and stenographers was as great as the range between semiskilled and skilled workers in industrial occupations at the turn of the century. No employer (or worker) would have confused the responsibilities of a clerk with those of a stenographer. In a few large firms, such as Sears Roebuck, Montgomery Ward, and some insurance companies, stenographers performed routinized tasks and were subject to intense and intrusive supervision.[21] But these companies also paid lower wages and undoubtedly attracted the least-competitive commercial graduates. In women's work, as in men's work, a high positive correlation existed between pay, responsibility, and personal autonomy. Stenographers represented one end of a new spectrum of occupations, file clerks and switchboard operators the other. The private secretary had no more in common with the telephone operator than the bricklayer did with the factory laborer.

By the end of the century, the work of the business office had become highly specialized and technical. Offices had become larger, more office workers were employees rather than proprietors, and more workers devoted their attention to the internal operations of the firm, as opposed to relations with suppliers or customers. Women were more evident, but immigrants were not; the arrival of the female clerical worker did not affect the social gulf that separated white-collar work from industry.

Other Service Employees

In contrast to the farm, factory, and office, most service industries changed little, if at all, at the end of the century. The fundamental dynamic was the economy: as it grew the demand for services kept pace, accounting for substantial employment increases and opportunities for large groups of low-wage employees. Most service workers, like most office employees, worked for small, family-operated firms. Their work was cleaner, less dangerous, and less likely to be interrupted by seasonal or business changes than the work of farmers or industrial employees. Its prime attraction, however, was the prospect of a partnership or proprietorship. Because there was so little obvious change or drama associated with these jobs, they received little attention. The following comparison of department store employees and domestic servants, two of the best-documented examples, suggests the possibilities and limitations of such employment.

The department store clerk and domestic servant of the late nineteenth century were both products of urban growth and the burgeoning of the middle classes of American cities. The department store was a midcentury marketing innovation that spread from New York and other eastern cities to the Midwest in the 1860s and 1870s. Located in the downtown business district, convenient to railroad stations and other public transport, the department store offered middle-class shoppers variety, bargain prices, and a range of services and attractions that the traditional merchant could not provide. To pay for the services, as well as the ornate building and newspaper ads that publicized the store, labor costs had to be minimized. Savings were achieved by reducing the labor required for each sale and by employing low-wage employees. Attractive displays, glass counters, signs, and other merchandising techniques helped minimize the worker's role. Promises of steady work, promotions from within, and, increasingly, nonwage benefits attracted employees, despite low wages. As competition between department stores increased, proprietors turned increasingly to young women to fill sales positions.[22] They also hired legions of ten- to thirteen-year-old boys to carry money and merchandise between the selling floor and the store's commercial centers. By the turn of the century, department stores were among the leading employers of teenagers. Marshall Field, the largest Chicago store, had two thousand employees by 1880 and more than ten thousand by 1900, probably making it the largest midwestern employer in a single location. Although an exact accounting is impossible, half or more of Field's employees were minors.[23]

Child labor helped keep costs low but also threatened to endanger the store's relationship with its middle-class clientele and to open it to charges of exploiting defenseless workers. There was no way to eliminate these problems apart from hiring higher-priced adults, but it was possible to finesse them. To maintain an acceptable level of service, merchants instituted strict rules of behavior on the selling floor, introduced training programs to enable unskilled employees to act more like traditional clerks, and inculcated loyalty to the store. The favored means to this end also confounded the stores' social critics. Welfare work, nonwage benefits that included educational and recreational programs, savings and insurance plans, paid vacations, and other related services not only made the store attractive to employees but also enabled merchants to argue that they provided a superior environment to the working-class home and the average public school. The store became an engine of social mobility. Marshall Field, J. L. Hudson in Detroit, and others turned a perplexing problem into a public relations triumph. In the process they helped popularize the idea of employee benefits as an inexpensive way to achieve goals that wage increases alone would not ensure.

Domestic service had also emerged at midcentury from the earlier tradition of the "hired girl" (a tradition that persisted in rural areas) as upper-middle-class homes became larger and more difficult to manage.[24] By the 1880s most middle-class families had at least one full-time, live-in servant, and the housewife had become a supervisor as well as a worker and shopper. Except in the largest homes, which had cooks, gardeners, drivers, and other specialists, servants were generalists. Their usual tasks included cleaning, food preparation, and baby-sitting. Washing and ironing were typically done by specialized laundresses, usually in their own homes. Ninety percent or more of servants were women, in most cases young and unmarried.[25] In eastern cities domestic service was largely an Irish occupation, a product of immigrant poverty and a tradition of service in Ireland. In midwestern cities the Irish servant was less common. German and Scandinavian families favored servants of their own nationality, and many native-born girls worked as domestics. Some of the natives were rural girls who had been attracted to the bright lights of the city only to find that "typewriters" had to have extensive training.[26]

Compared to other regions, however, domestic service was not popular in the Midwest. The number of servants was low compared to the Northeast, and the ratio of servants to families in midwestern cities was significantly lower than in eastern and southern cities. The ratio also varied within the region; Minneapolis, for example, had one and a half times as many servants per family as Cleveland in 1880 and 1900.[27] These variations partly reflected European traditions. To Swedes service was "respectable" and "lucrative; "to Italians, a stain on a family's and a daughter's reputation.[28] Intercity differences were also a measure of the availability of alternative employment opportunities. The number of female factory employees per capita in Cleveland was approximately one and a half times that of Minneapolis, almost exactly the reverse of the ratio of servants to families in the two cities. There were good reasons to select even lowly factory jobs over domestic service. Long, irregular hours, isolation, and the capricious behavior of employers made service unattractive. An association with crime and prostitution was another deterrent.[29] Some men supposedly refused to court servants because of their low status. Whenever other low-wage jobs became available, the supply of servants declined.[30] The department store, the business office, and the high school ultimately spelled the end of domestic service as it had been known in the nineteenth century.

Despite these drawbacks, domestic service compared favorably with many unskilled jobs, especially the positions available to men. The rising affluence of the middle class meant that jobs were always available. Though tedious, the work was comparatively undemanding. Ingenious servants cut corners, did as little as possible, and maximized their free time. Because they received room and board, they could save their wages or spend them on leisure activities. Above all, service was temporary, a way to live semi-independently before marriage. Most servants were younger than twenty, and few were older than twenty-five. Older, married, or widowed women without capital or skills were typically laundresses who worked in their own homes. As demand grew, more domestics became day workers who lived apart from their employers.

A turn-of-the-century observer might have concluded that the servant's work had changed less in the preceding quarter-century than virtually any other job and was unlikely to be very different in the future. That would have been an accurate assessment but a poor prediction. In fact, domestic service would change as much in the following quarter-century as most industrial occupations. Associated with radical differences in the demand for and the supply of labor, the transformation of domestic service was a symbol of the post-1900 innovations that fundamentally altered the employment patterns of the nineteenth century.

Part II

Workers in a New Economy, 1900–1930

After 1900 the Midwest rapidly acquired the economic and social structure that would prevail for the next three-quarters of a century and distinguish it from other regions. The basis for this development was the pattern outlined in part I, particularly the parallel growth of farm and factory in the regional economy. Twentieth-century organizational and technical innovations reinforced the comparative advantage of midwestern agriculture and manufacturing and the attractiveness of farm and factory careers. However, the social impact of these changes differed. In the countryside the most notable changes affected the relations between farmers and institutions external to the farm; the family labor system and the networks of neighborhood contacts that had emerged in the middle decades of the nineteenth century were largely unaffected. Innovations in industry, on the other hand, continued to stimulate employment and earnings growth and immigration, but they also created new occupations, redistributed workers within the industrial sector, and redefined the significance of skill and autonomy in the workplace. Chapter 4 examines the innovations that enlarged the roles of farm and factory in the midwestern economy. Chapter 5 summarizes the efforts of urban workers to ensure that their voices would be heard in the new economy.

4.

Revolutions in Production and Work, 1900–1930

During the first third of the twentieth century, the Midwest became a center of innovative activity that directly or indirectly affected nearly every worker. Organizational and technological change transformed the work of the farm and factory, creating new and challenging environments for those who had or hoped to have careers in agriculture and industry. By the 1910s midwestern boosters pointed to the world's most modern farms and manufacturing firms as evidence of the region's dynamism. Critics replied that innovation too often had been detrimental to the quality of work life. Yet neither defenders nor detractors fully grasped the significance of the changes. The pattern of the 1910s was to be the pattern of the twentieth century. The transformation of farm and factory focused the attention of midwesterners, preempting other possibilities, and reinforced the cultural gulf between country and city. Indeed, because of a third group of innovations, which began outside the region and gradually transformed the work of the home, the distinction between country and city became even more acute than in the nineteenth century.

The Rise of Scientific Agriculture

Since midcentury most changes in farm work had resulted from the mechanization of hand tasks and the growth of urban markets. Although these forces continued to be important influences in midwestern agriculture, they were overshadowed by the rise of rural social engineering, which sought to make agriculture more productive through the reform of farm operations and rural institutions. The effects of these activities were probably greatest in Wisconsin and Iowa, which receive disproportionate attention in the following account. They provide a yardstick for measuring the transformation of midwestern agriculture before the 1930s, when market conditions reinforced the reformers' work.

63

By 1900 most of the institutions that would serve as vehicles of change operated in the midwestern states. They were expressions of a long-standing interregional movement to enlist government in the promotion of commercial farm operations and included the U.S. Department of Agriculture, state agricultural experiment stations, and, most notably, the agriculture colleges of the land grant universities. The outstanding feature of these institutions at the turn of the century was their isolation from the work of the midwestern farm community. The problem was initially the meagerness of their intellectual resources; the experiment stations, for example, "were created before there was an adequate base of knowledge for them."[1] More important, as scientific knowledge grew, was the absence of an effective mechanism for communicating that knowledge to farmers. The early histories of the colleges were stories of clashing cultures, as professors and administrators who emphasized research and professional development confronted farmers who demanded solutions to immediate problems. W. A. Henry, the unconventional dean of agriculture at the University of Wisconsin until 1907, was one of the few university officials who tried to address the problem. Clad in overalls, Henry could "spit tobacco juice with the best of them."[2] But there were few Henrys. Indeed, his successor, Harry L. Russell, a city-born scientist who was most comfortable in the presence of business executives, symbolized the gap between country and college. Wisconsin farmers viewed him with suspicion.

Class and cultural differences exacerbated what, in reality, was a comparatively simple problem. There is no evidence that agricultural administrators and professors became less patronizing after 1900. In fact, as the automobile and electrically-powered machinery made middle-class city life more interesting and appealing, they became more convinced of the backwardness of the countryside. Typically products of prosperous farm families, they had sought to escape the physical labor and intellectual confinement of farming through higher education.[3] They now approached their work with renewed fervor. Evidence that the growth of agricultural productivity had slowed was the last critical ingredient in the emergence of the country-life movement. To their delight, they discovered that a substantial minority of midwestern farmers had become receptive to their scientific, if not their moral, analyses.

What had changed? The scientists had developed a practical mechanism for disseminating their ideas. Its origins lay in the farmers-institute movement that began in Michigan in the 1870s, spread to Ohio in the 1880s, and encompassed the other midwestern states by the 1890s. The institutes were typically two or three day meetings featuring lecturers from the state's experiment station, agriculture college, and other scientific institutions, as well as dinners and social events.[4] After 1900 the institutes' popularity grew rapidly in the South and West but especially in the Midwest. The number of meetings tripled, and attendance nearly quadrupled between 1900 and 1914.[5] Institutes customarily emphasized crop and livestock issues, but they included cooking schools and other activities that addressed the woman's role as well. As the institute movement emerged into the broader country-life movement, it spawned a variety of clubs for rural women and children that became permanent features of rural life.

The most influential figure in the midwestern institute movement was Perry G. Holden. A graduate of Michigan Agricultural College, Holden became a specialist in corn breeding as a faculty member at the University of Illinois in the late 1890s. After a brief stint at a seed company, he went to Iowa State College in 1902 as professor of agronomy and made his mark as a popular lecturer to farm audiences. Holden's aggressive efforts to take the college to the farmer, through regional experimental farms and traveling short courses, evolved into an institutionalized extension program, sponsored by the state, that other states quickly copied. In 1912 he joined International Harvester as head of its new extension department and presided over a private endeavor that rivaled the most ambitious state efforts. Holden was best known for his campaigns to convince farmers to raise soil-conserving alfalfa hay. The first was in Kent County, Michigan, in 1913:

> In the course of the five-day affair Holden and a dozen other experts moved about the county by automobile, stopping at prearranged spots for meetings with farmers and often for demonstrations in the fields. Night sessions were held in the country towns. Everywhere the lesson was the same. Alfalfa was the ideal crop; it could be grown easily; and farmers growing it could expect to see their operations become more profitable. In all, over 6,000 Kent County farmers heard the message in one or more of the thirty meetings held during the campaign.[6]

If Holden's work dramatized the educational possibilities of agricultural extension, the demonstration farm, pioneered by a transplanted Iowan, Seaman Knapp, provided a refined mechanism for diffusing the experts' ideas. The success of demonstration farms in Louisiana, Texas, and other cotton states spurred a movement to place extension agents in every farm county. In the Midwest the Council of the North American Grain Exchanges and other mercantile groups were particularly influential. Julius Rosenwald of Sears Roebuck offered $1,000 to any county that set aside funds to support an agent. In 1914 Congress adopted the Smith-Lever Act, adding federal government subsidies. At that time there were over a hundred county agents in the midwestern states, providing a "firm foundation" for the federal-state effort that followed.[7]

The common thread that ran through the campaigns for scientific agriculture was the leadership of nonfarmers. Scientists, government officials, and business executives were responsible for virtually every feature of the extension campaign. Farmers were not oblivious to this fact. The transparently self-interested activities of International Harvester and other businesses provoked opposition in many quarters. The role of agricultural scientists was only marginally less controversial, even after they began to offer more "practical" advice. Though agricultural extension brought together the agricultural bureaucracy and the farm family, a combination that would ultimately be a powerful stimulus to change in the rural Midwest, it was easy to overlook its significance in the 1910s because it was closely related to, and often impossible to distinguish from, the broader, urban-based campaign for rural renewal. Only later, after the country-life movement had declined, was it clear that the techniques but not the biases of the urban reformers had found a responsive audience in the Midwest.

The ideology of the country-life movement was as imprecise as its membership. It included nostalgic agrarianism, assumptions about the decline of rural institutions, and fears about an increasing imbalance between rural and urban society. The theorists, social scientists, and business and government representatives who espoused these ideas had little in common except for an interest in change; a national organization of country-life advocates did not appear until 1919, long after the movement had peaked. The catalytic agent was the growing body of statistical data that seemed to document rural decay: population losses, increasing tenancy, low educational expenditures, poorly qualified rural teachers, and abandoned churches. Although the data was consistent with presumptions of a regressive and declining countryside, they would also have sustained more sanguine interpretations of the transition to urban society. The country-life critique was primarily a reflection of urban anxieties.[8] Many individuals who identified with it were no less alarmed about the state of urban institutions.

Apart from advocacy of scientific agriculture, the feature of the country-life movement that had the greatest salience to the work of the farm family was an effort to modernize rural schools. Like earlier education critics, the country-life reformers sought to broaden the curriculum, raise academic and professional standards, lengthen the school year, and create high schools. To achieve these goals, they proposed to consolidate rural school districts and transfer control to professional educators. Farmers continued to oppose these proposals because of their cost and antirural bias.[9] Consequently, the pace of consolidation was slow and fitful. In Ohio, where rural interests confronted a burgeoning urban population, the one-room schoolhouse had virtually disappeared by 1920. In Wisconsin, it proved to be more durable despite growing state assistance for transportation, school construction, and administrative expenses.[10] In Iowa there was little consolidation before 1913 or after 1920, when the collapse of the rural economy undercut support for public programs. Only in the 1930s and after did the high school become the focus of community activity in many rural areas.[11]

Farm resentment over school consolidation extended to the curricular changes that accompanied school reorganization. Country-life advocates hoped to raise academic standards and make education more useful. They sought to supplement traditional vocational training with scientific agriculture and home economics, its female equivalent. Their goal was a more productive, prosperous, and, above all, modern rural labor force. In theory, scientific agriculture would percolate up from the schools at the same time it trickled down from the extension services.[12]

In reality the curricular changes were exceedingly modest. Several legislatures required instruction in agriculture, and progressive school administrators introduced home economics, but the effects were negligible. In areas where dairy farming and other specialized activities dominated the farm economy, reorganized schools provided useful technical instruction and won public approval. Elsewhere educational reforms were less successful. In Wisconsin, for example, only 100 of 6,500 rural schools taught cooking and sewing in 1915.[13] But if curricular reform did not fulfill the expectations of country-life advocates, it did reinforce the work of the extension services. Teachers promoted extracurricular activities such as corn clubs and often served as de facto assistants to county agents. They and their programs became another link in the chain that connected government and the midwestern farm.

The potential of the country-life movement was greatest in Iowa, Minnesota, and Wisconsin, where the farm population was large and other occupational groups were politically weak. Each of these states had a substantial extension organization by 1914; each had a substantial progressive movement; and each had a large contingent of politically active farmers. The Wisconsin experience was most significant and distinctive because of the large role of dairy farming in the state's agriculture. Unlike the majority of grain and livestock farmers, dairy farmers had long recognized their dependence on state-sponsored research and education. The work of university researchers such as Stephen Babcock had been instrumental in creating the state's cheese industry and other opportunities for milk producers.[14] Scientific agriculture promised even greater benefits in the future. The astute management of Dean Russell strengthened the relationship between the farmers and the state. Sensitive to farmers' suspicions, Russell excluded private businesses from extension activities and employed only mature, experienced men who could speak the farmers' language.[15] The state's grain farmers, generally poorer than the dairymen, and advocates of cooperative marketing remained aloof, but the dairy-state alliance was a significant force in state politics by 1910.

Under Governor Robert M. La Follette and his allies, Wisconsin farmers became the basis of a formidable political movement that created an "agriculture service state" and defined progressivism at the state level. La Follette's contribution was to extend the dairy-state alliance to other farm groups and to a substantial fraction of the state's industrial workers. He succeeded where others failed by shifting the tax burden for this activity to the state's manufacturers via a state income tax, enacted in 1911.[16] By the eve of World War I, the pattern was clear. The state taxed manufacturers to finance agricultural research, extension activities, and other services, such as the regulation of agricultural products. Labor legislation and similar urban-oriented services ensured the support of organized labor and neutralized manufacturers' complaints that high taxes crippled industry.

In Wisconsin and in other rural states, the most important single development of the 1910s was the growth of the county agent system. Two features of this process stand out. First, agents increasingly confined themselves to technical advice, jettisoning the rest of the country-life program. Few male agents had the time or inclination to promote school reorganization or participate in social groups apart from farm bureaus, the voluntary (later membership) organizations that mobilized support for extension activities. The bureaus were essential to the agent's success, even his survival in most counties, and invariably attracted leading commercial producers. Agents were inevitably drawn into political alliances with the most affluent farmers. Both trends—the emphasis on technical assistance and the agent's dependence on the richest farmers—gave the extension program an unintended but important bias.

Second, World War I mobilization gave the extension program a substantial boost. Under the mobilization legislation, the number of agents and other extension employees grew rapidly, and they assumed new duties. In 1917, Iowa had 24 agents; by 1919 the total had grown to 100, or one for every county, plus 41 home economists and a staff of 50 extension employees at Iowa State College. In addition to their prewar activities, agents organized farm labor bureaus and helped allocate seed and fertilizer. Home demonstration agents briefly revived the promise of the country-life movement by promoting food conservation, canning and drying techniques, and gardening clubs. By 1918 the extension service had "permeated every corner of the state."[17]

By 1920 state activism had added a significant dimension to midwestern agriculture. To all but the most acute observers, the farmstead and the work of the farm family were unchanged. Farmers and farm wives operated much as they had at the turn of the century, children still attended one-room schools in most states, and market towns continued to be the focus of rural economic and social activity. But farm families now had access to systematic technical knowledge and assistance on a range of subjects. This change also encouraged them to think more expansively. If government could operate effectively as a research and development agency, could it not also influence the larger environment in which farmers bought and sold?

Two developments of the World War I years help explain the farmers' answer to this question. During the mid-1910s, North Dakota farmers created the Non-Partisan League to oppose urban business interests. The NPL captured the state's Republican party and spread to neighboring states, including Minnesota. The NPL platform called for a variety of state enterprises, cooperative-marketing institutions, regulation of competing private firms, and higher taxes on urban businesses. In effect it proposed an exaggerated version of the La Follette formula. In Minnesota it won a substantial following among grain farmers who shared their neighbors' antipathy to railroads, elevator operators, and millers. But farm support, mostly in the Northwest, was not enough to control the Republican party or win elections. In 1919 the NPL concluded an alliance with the State Federation of Labor, then at the peak of its power in the Twin Cities. Though it produced no leader of La Follette's stature, the farmer-labor coalition came close to victory in the 1920 elections and elected Henrik Shipstead to the U.S. Senate in 1922. Thereafter, it declined, though the Farmer-Labor party persisted and, like Wisconsin's Progressive Republicans, displaced the Democrats in the state's two-party system. Its platform, calling for an expanded agricultural-service state and labor legislation, remained largely unchanged.[18]

Among the factors in the decline of the NPL was the severe postwar recession, which began in mid-1920 and featured a dramatic deflation in raw materials prices. Rural areas that had experienced the greatest price increases in the preceding inflationary years now suffered the greatest distress. The average value of farm land and buildings in Iowa, which had risen to nearly twice the midwestern average by 1920, fell by one-third as grain and livestock prices declined. The crisis in Indiana, Illinois, and Minnesota was only marginally less severe. On the other hand Wisconsin farm values declined by only one-tenth, and Michigan farmers, who had barely noticed the wartime boom, were virtually unaffected by the postwar collapse.[19] Farmers who had borrowed to buy land at inflated prices were most vulnerable as incomes declined and mortgage and interest expenses remained unchanged. Yet even prudent farmers had taken advantage of the inflation to make down payments on automobiles, trucks, implements, and household appliances. The farm crisis of the early 1920s was essentially a debt crisis. Midwestern farm bankruptcies quadrupled in 1922 and doubled again in 1923.

Regardless of their attitudes toward the NPL, many farmers blamed merchants and other "middlemen" for their economic problems and looked to government for solutions. Yet railroads, merchants, and processors had no obvious role in the deflation. The culprits included the international economy; the U.S. government, which had bid up farm prices and failed to curb inflation; and the farmers themselves. NPL candidates did reasonably well in Minnesota and Progressive Republicans swept Wisconsin in the 1920 elections. But as the crisis deepened and foreclosures multiplied, farmers became disillusioned. Political activists increasingly turned to a different group of agricultural boosters, who focused on the operations of national and international markets.

Advocates of farm "parity," who dominated discussions of agricultural problems during the following decade, sought to raise farm incomes through indirect government price-fixing. Closely identified with Iowa publisher and Secretary of Agriculture (1921–1924) Henry C. Wallace and Illinois implement manufacturers George Peek and Hugh Johnson, the parity campaign drew much of its grass roots support from the state farm bureaus. In the 1920s farm activists backed the congressional McNary-Haugen bills and won substantial interregional support. Ultimately their proposals proved to be too controversial; critics charged that they would raise the cost of living for nonfarm consumers and curtail international trade. Nevertheless, the parity crusade was an impressive demonstration of the organizational and political skills of midwestern farmers and their allies.[20]

The war years effectively introduced another innovation that reinforced the effects of scientific agriculture. By the mid-1910s many midwestern farmers had automobiles for family use but continued to rely on horses for farm work. Although gasoline tractors appeared with the first automobiles, they had little appeal until the mid-1910s. Heavy, clumsy, expensive, and prone to break down, they found a niche in the West, where they were used to plow large, flat, and comparatively dry fields, but they were rarely used in the Corn Belt. Beginning in 1917, however, changes in tractor design created new opportunities for midwestern farmers. The Ford Motor Company's Fordson, introduced in 1917, was the first inexpensive tractor. Though it could do little more than pull a plow and was unsafe, it underlined the potential of farm mechanization in the automobile era. In the following decade manufacturers introduced major improvements: the "power take-off," which enabled the tractor engine to power implements; the all-purpose tractor, designed to cultivate row crops; the power lift, which simplified turning; and the pneumatic tire.[21] As a result the number of Illinois and Iowa farms with tractors rose from 18 to 31 percent and 17 to 29 percent respectively between 1925 and 1930.[22] By the latter date the tractor was becoming a fixture on prosperous farms in the most fertile areas.

The decision to buy a tractor was a critical one for midwestern farmers. Tractors allowed them to complete tasks quickly and efficiently, freed land formerly devoted to hay and oats production (three to five acres per horse), reduced the time spent in the fields and barn, and fostered new mechanical skills. The principal drawback was the purchase price, which even after 1917 was equivalent to the cost of a lifetime of horses. Tractors also required new or redesigned implements and purchased fuel. They were less adaptable than horses for some purposes (such as the corn harvest) and were not suitable for hauling goods to town. Most farmers kept some of their horses as a safeguard after purchasing a tractor, decreasing their savings. The precise benefits depended on the size of the farm and the mix of crops.[23] In any case, tractors required greater cash outlays and more market-oriented activity. Like scientific agriculture, they encouraged farmers to be more businesslike in perspective and behavior.

The Triumph of Industry

At first the differences between midwestern agriculture and industry appear to have been a striking feature of the regional economy. Agricultural production and productivity grew slowly between 1900 and 1930, while manufacturing production and productivity grew rapidly. Average farm size barely changed while the region's largest factories became the world's largest industrial plants. The rural labor force became more native, while the industrial labor force became more diverse. Farmers formed political movements that dominated states such as Wisconsin and Minnesota, while industrial workers enjoyed only sporadic success in the political arena. But these contrasts obscure as much as they reveal. The key to change in both sectors was an elite that applied new knowledge to production. In agriculture it consisted of scientists and administrators who promoted the results of biological and chemical research and the techniques of urban business firms. In industry it was a new class of managerial employees who approached their responsibilities in a scientific spirit.

The most visible symbol of industrial innovation was the giant factory, the plant with more than six thousand employees in a single location, which became a feature of the midwestern industrial landscape after 1900. In 1900 there had been fourteen such establishments in the United States, three of which (Armour & Company, Deering Harvester, and Illinois Steel's South Chicago plant, all in Chicago) were located in the Midwest. A decade and a half later, a dozen Detroit-area auto plants were that large, not to mention a score of other midwestern factories producing steel, tires, glass, and assorted machinery. In all, they accounted for at least half of all large American industrial plants, including the largest ones.[24] Size in itself meant little. Some large facilities (the Armour and Swift plants in Chicago) were lumbering behemoths; others (Ford's Highland Park plant and U.S. Steel's Gary works) were the most modern manufacturing plants in the world. Data on economic performance suggests that most midwestern industry, and the industries characterized by large plant size in particular, had more in common with Ford than Armour.[25] Size was an imperfect but useful reflection of the dynamism of midwestern industry.

The transformation of midwestern manufacturing occurred in an era of industrial consolidation, when mergers created multiplant combines that were as large, in terms of sales, investment, or employment, as all but the largest railroad companies, the big businesses of the nineteenth century. Many midwestern companies were part of this process: Standard Oil, long a symbol of combination, was a Cleveland company until the 1890s; International Harvester, one of the best-known products of the turn-of-the-century merger movement, was exclusively a midwestern firm; and U.S. Steel, the greatest of the "trusts," had extensive operations in the Great Lakes states. Other examples abound. Yet the largest and fastest-growing midwestern firms, notably those associated with automobile production, were new. Most of them dated from the 1890s or later and had grown largely or wholly through internal expansion. They were also different from the archetypal nineteenth-century firm that emphasized quality and service and dominated an industrial niche.[26] They were devoted to expansion and run by professional managers. Organization and efficiency were their watchwords.

The most striking example of the new role of the manager and internal management was the extraordinary popularity of "systematic management" in the years after 1900. Systematic management encompassed a variety of efforts to improve coordination, internal communications, and managerial controls. It was an outgrowth of the increasing size and speed of industrial operations and the emergence of a new generation of industrial managers, university-trained engineers who saw the factory as a well-organized machine. The hallmark of systematic management was the introduction of managerial systems, which took the place of the ad hoc measures that had evolved in the nineteenth century. Though advocates used neutral terms like "coordination" and "integration," their innovations had important social implications. They expanded the authority of the top executives, made middle managers more accountable to their superiors, diminished the ad hoc powers of first-line supervisors, and reduced the autonomy of skilled production workers, the final level of authority in the turn-of-the-century factory. The shift to systematic management, usually in response to increasing competition or larger-scale operations, was seldom painless. A conflict between new- and old-style executives at the Illinois Central Railroad in the late 1880s was a harbinger of the disputes that would characterize the growth of midwestern industry.[27]

Although systematic management in theory could affect everything that happened within the firm, practitioners emphasized management accounting systems, which tabulated operating costs; production systems, which coordinated the flow of materials and the operations of machines; and personnel systems, which guided the management of employees. The experience of several notable midwestern firms suggests the importance of systematic management for work and workers in industry.

By the turn of the century, midwestern employers were increasingly sensitive to the alien and often alienated character of their labor forces. The turmoil of the 1880s, the conflicts of the following years, such as the coal and railroad strikes of 1894, and a modest union revival in the late 1890s were obvious influences. More decisive for large-scale manufacturers were the growing number of eastern-European, non-English-speaking job-seekers; the seemingly chaotic movement of workers as a result of quits and discharges; the growing need for experienced, literate workers; and the public outcry over the employment of women and children in industry. Systematic-management theorists emphasized the desirability of wage incentives to win employee cooperation, but many employers recognized that additional measures were desirable. Welfare work had been common among firms that operated in rural areas or employed large numbers of women, such as Calumet & Hecla, the large Michigan copper company, and Marshall Field, the Chicago department store. But they had few imitators and many critics who condemned their activities as paternalistic, demeaning, and hypocritical. Welfare work nevertheless became the foundation of a new, systematic approach to labor problems.

The most important event in the rise of the new labor management was the creation of a labor department at the National Cash Register Company of Dayton, Ohio, in 1901. John Patterson, president of NCR, had introduced systematic production management and an ambitious welfare program, mostly for his female employees, in the 1890s. A 1901 strike against a tyrannical foreman graphically illustrated the limitations of these initiatives. In response, Patterson discharged the foreman and strikers, embraced the open shop (unions, which Patterson had not opposed, had struck in sympathy with the molders), curbed the welfare program, and established a labor department. The labor department had responsibility for hiring and firing, resolving grievances, promoting safety, training supervisors for their new, more circumscribed roles, and administering the remaining welfare activities. It became a prototype for the personnel departments that appeared in the following years.[28]

Midwestern industry played a major role in this development. At the turn of the century, the Cleveland Chamber of Commerce vigorously promoted the work of Patterson and like-minded industrialists. The McCormick family and the National Civic Federation made International Harvester an exemplar of the new approach in Chicago and Milwaukee.[29] The Ford Company's sociological department, introduced in 1914, was another well-known example. Procter & Gamble, Armco Steel, and Western Electric's Hawthorne works appeared on many lists of notable innovators. The industrial boom of the late 1910s made virtually all executives aware of the advantages of systematic personnel work. During that tumultuous period, large corporations continued to provide most of the impetus to the personnel movement.

At the turn of the century, a prominent engineer and systematic-management pioneer, Frederick W. Taylor, had combined the diverse features of systematic management into an appealing package; added stopwatch time study, which he had developed in the 1880s and 1890s; and promoted the amalgam as a comprehensive, scientific approach to production management. Though Taylor's promotional activities were highly successful, he had less success winning acceptance of scientific management per se, which many executives considered overly costly and bureaucratic. Of those who attempted to introduce the Taylor system, the managers of the Joseph & Feiss Company, a Cleveland men's-suit maker, probably made the most ambitious and determined effort. Their experiences are particularly valuable because the company relied on labor-intensive hand methods and simple machines that were available to all suit makers. It depended on its novel organization to achieve ambitious business goals.

Richard A. Feiss, the company's part-owner and factory manager from 1905 to 1926, was imbued with the new managerial vision. He also faced an intriguing challenge: how to expand the output of a standardized, inexpensive product while keeping costs low. Feiss established a central planning department to coordinate the flow of materials; reorganized operations to minimize the movement of materials; subdivided each job to encourage specialization; used time studies to determine the time necessary for each operation; introduced bonuses to encourage workers to maintain output; and redesigned chairs, tables, and other equipment to reduce fatigue. The results amazed observers. One visitor reported that "the operatives work with a smoothness, rapidity, and precision that are astonishing."[30]

Feiss's efforts to control his employees led to additional innovations. At first he tried to impose a variety of rules and restrictions. In 1909, when he also cut the piece rates of the most highly skilled workers, many of them struck. Like Patterson a few years before, Feiss was shocked. Realizing that his work was flawed and his achievement incomplete, he began an ambitious effort to enlist the employees' cooperation. He introduced benefits such as a cafeteria and health insurance and hired an employment manager, Mary Barnett Gilson, to administer the company's welfare programs. A social worker and scientific-management devotee, Gilson spearheaded a vigorous campaign to improve the employees' skills and lives. Like Feiss, she sought to control and direct them; "there is no facet of life we did not touch," she recalled.[31]

For individual employees, Feiss's and Gilson's innovations meant increased opportunity and greater regimentation. Workers could learn more and earn more. Female employees received special training and counseling and, if successful, promotions to supervisory posts. There was probably no better workplace for young immigrant women. Yet Feiss and Gilson were social engineers, not democrats. They expected the employees to react positively and to cooperate. Feiss aggressively fought the Amalgamated Clothing Workers when it tried to organize his employees. Gilson was no less assertive, though her campaigns against cosmetics, fashionable clothing, and parental controls were apparently less successful.

Joseph & Feiss prospered as long as the market for its suits remained strong. However, by the mid-1920s its rural midwestern market began to shrink as farmers became less dependent on village stores and simple, utilitarian products such as Joseph & Feiss suits. As the company's sales declined and production fell, Feiss's organization became an expensive luxury. In 1925, with losses mounting, the other executives rebelled. They forced Feiss, Gilson, and most of their subordinates to resign, cut back many benefit programs, and devoted more resources to marketing.[32] Feiss's career ended on this sour note. Better than any other midwestern executive, he had shown that improved organization could transform industrial production and industrial labor, though his success was short-lived and his reputation clouded by the turmoil that brought his work to a close.

In the meantime other midwestern manufacturers combined features of systematic management with new technologies to create mass production operations. In the auto, tire, and glass industries, as in the late-nineteenth-century steel and match industries, the introduction of capital-, energy-, and management-intensive technologies increased production, reduced unit costs, enlarged the manager's role, and made careful, systematic operations more important than ever. The effect on the shop floor was as disruptive as it had been in the late-nineteenth-century steel industry. Familiar skills disappeared and new skills emerged. A larger percentage of employees became machine operators. Managers became more influential and the foremen less influential. In most cases some form of personnel management became a necessity.

Mass Production: Automobiles

The production of automobiles began in the late 1890s and grew rapidly after 1900, especially after the introduction of the Model T Ford in 1907. As competition intensified (nearly 500 of 600 pioneering firms had failed by 1910), automobile and automobile-parts production became highly concentrated in the Great Lakes States, notably Michigan, Ohio, and Wisconsin.[33] As Detroit became the industry's center, parts makers also clustered in the

Detroit region or nearby cities—Milwaukee, Toledo, Akron, Cleveland, and many smaller communities. Auto and auto-parts production increasingly became midwestern activities.

The automobile's influence was a result of its popularity and mechanical complexity. Even a simple vehicle like the Model T consisted of ten thousand parts, each of which required many separate operations. Early producers were typically assemblers of purchased parts. As Ford and other mass producers revolutionized the industry, manufacturing and manufacturing technique became increasingly important. The last producer to operate chiefly as an assembler, the Durant Company, failed in the mid-1920s. By that time the overriding managerial challenge was to make enough components to control production and costs but not so many that the firm became inflexible. Thus there were two midwestern auto industries: the famous and visible one, clustered around Detroit, and the less well known industry of parts makers, concentrated along the shores of Lake Michigan and Lake Erie. Some parts manufacturers, such as the tire and glass makers, were themselves mass producers. Many others competed by keeping labor costs as low as possible.

The industry catalyst was the Ford Company, founded in 1903. Until the early 1910s Ford obtained most of its components from Detroit-area parts suppliers, notably Dodge Brothers, which made engines, transmissions, and front and rear axles, and Briggs, which made bodies. After Ford decided to concentrate on a single inexpensive vehicle for the middle-income market, the company began to make more of its parts. In 1910 Ford built a vast new plant in the Highland Park area of Detroit. In the Highland Park machine shops, it installed thousands of machine tools, many unique in design. Specialized metal-cutting machines permitted Ford to do what only a handful of manufacturers, concentrated in the New England armaments industries, had done previously: to create parts so nearly alike that they could be used interchangeably. Ford managers organized production sequentially in order to reduce handling, inventory, and indirect labor. In 1913 they developed moving assembly lines and, in 1914, doubled the pay of unskilled workers with the famous "five-dollar day." At the same time, Ford managers introduced cost-accounting and production-control systems and a rudimentary personnel operation, the sociological department.[34]

Although the chassis assembly line attracted the greatest attention and became the symbol of mass production in the auto industry, it was no more significant than the other Ford innovations. The greatest savings resulted from manufacturing components at the Highland Park plant; the machine shop, not the assembly department, was the key to Ford's success. Assembly lines, on the other hand, had limited applications. They were not initially installed in the company's regional assembly plants, which proliferated as

Model T sales grew, and were not used to assemble the all-important vehicle bodies, which were made in more conventional fashion at Briggs or other supplier plants. Not until the 1930s did body assembly lines appear in American auto-body plants.[35]

What effect did mass production have on the Ford labor force? Certainly it increased employment opportunities for large numbers of workers (Highland Park employment peaked at more than thirty thousand in the late 1910s), including large numbers of low-skill workers. Men who had been able to find only ill-paid, disagreeable tasks now became well-paid machine operators.[36] Many of those who crowded the Ford employment office in 1914 had traveled long distances, including a large number of Upper Peninsula miners who had been on strike since the previous fall.[37] For many years Ford sustained its reputation as a place of opportunity by hiring workers who were unwelcome elsewhere—handicapped, African American, and Mexican laborers, for example.[38] Successful applicants overwhelmingly filled positions that required little training or experience.

But was there also a qualitative difference in the Ford labor force? Was its composition different from that of other large factories? Did mass production and the growth of a large semiskilled labor force mean that a smaller number of skilled workers was required? The answers to these questions are less obvious than many observers have assumed. Stephen Meyer has recently examined the Ford labor force in the pre–World War I years. His data, drawn from fragmentary payroll records, are summarized in the 1910, 1913, and 1917 columns of table 4–1. The 1935 data are based on a study of employment data from the River Rouge plant, which became the principal Ford facility in the 1920s. By 1910 Ford had integrated backward to produce engines and other essential parts and had moved most of its operations to the Highland Park plant. Still, its operations were in transition. None of the changes was complete, and the moving assembly line was still several years in the future. Thus it is not surprising that the 1913 and 1917 data show additional changes in the Ford labor force or that the 1935 data show still more variation.[39]

What does table 4–1 indicate about mass production in the auto industry? Clearly, it documents the emergence of a vast labor force of low-skill employees, though the proportion of semiskilled and unskilled workers, even in 1917, was not exceptional. Textile mills and meat-packing plants had similar proportions of skilled and unskilled workers. But table 4–1 also emphasizes the persistence of the skilled group. As the Ford operation expanded, the number of skilled workers did not decline. On the contrary, it grew; only the proportion changed, and that change was not consistently downward. Mass production provided opportunities for both groups. This did not mean that all skilled employees prospered. Technical innovations constantly changed the demand for particular skills, boosting or diminishing the importance of individuals and groups.

Yet table 4–1 tells only part of this story. The data for 1917 and 1935 clearly understate the role of the specialists because they are only for Highland Park and the Rouge respectively. Beginning in 1909 Ford's regional assembly plants used parts shipped from the Detroit factories. These plants were comparatively small and restricted to final assembly operations, yet the largest of them, like the Kansas City plant, employed over two thousand workers in the 1920s.[40] On the other hand, the advent of the closed automobile in the mid-1920s greatly increased the number and role of the skilled labor force in the mass production plants, a fact that industry observers and historians, preoccupied with the chassis assembly line, have almost wholly overlooked.[41] The number of body workers was not inconsiderable; General Motors' Fisher body division, for example, employed about 40 percent of all GM workers in the mid-1920s.[42] Many of these workers were carpenters, painters, and upholsterers. The steel body gradually eliminated the wood workers but created opportunities for tool and die makers, welders, and others. Although manufacturers gradually simplified and routinized body work, they did not succeed in introducing an assembly line for more than a decade.[43] Even then the annual model change kept small armies of tool and die makers occupied.

What of the other auto manufacturers? Though the record is fragmentary, it is likely that Ford's innovations spread rapidly. Certainly most producers were aware of Ford's activities and were eager to introduce changes that promised to improve their operations. Large-volume manufacturers—companies that made fifty thousand vehicles per year—presumably had the most to gain. There were four (besides Ford) in the 1910s: General Motors,

Table 4–1
Ford Labor Force
(Percentage)

	1910	1913	1917	1935
Foremen	7	N/A	7	4
Skilled	30	28	17	30
Specialists	27	51	60	50
Unskilled	36	21	16	17

Sources: Stephen Meyer II, *The Five Dollar Day: Labor Management and Social Control in the Ford Motor Company, 1908–1921* (Albany: SUNY Press, 1981), pp. 46, 48, 50, 51; Ford Archives.

Dodge, Willys, and Studebaker.[44] General Motors' most important production manager, Walter Chrysler, was familiar with Ford's innovations and undoubtedly introduced many of them at Buick, though the details are obscure.[45] After breaking with Ford in 1914, the Dodges began to manufacture cars under their own nameplate. Their Hamtramck plant was "completely rearranged and retooled at great expense," and large quantities of "highly specialized machine tools" were purchased.[46] The situation at Willys is less clear. On the other hand, Studebaker apparently did not follow Ford's lead until the 1920s.[47] In general it appears that Ford's competitors introduced assembly lines at an early date but were slower to adopt the other innovations. They had good reasons for caution. Ford's reliance on highly specialized machinery was costly and committed the company to long production runs. Most manufacturers opted for a more flexible, evolutionary strategy. Regardless of their conservatism, the advent of the closed car in the early 1920s and the all-steel body in the early 1930s required them to make large investments in stamping machinery and dies and to surrender much of the flexibility they had preserved in chassis manufacture.

Ford's distinctiveness as an employer was also short-lived. Employment departments became common in the mid-1910s and the five-dollar day was eroded by inflation. Apart from an aggressive Americanization program, Ford did little that was novel after 1914. Indeed, the company became increasingly reactionary and repressive, as systematic management gave way to bureaucratic in-fighting, intimidation, and prejudice. The worst abuses involved low-level supervisors and dissident workers. By the early 1920s the leader's mantle had passed to GM, which had corporate and division engineering staffs devoted to plant design, layout, machine operations, and time and motion study.[48] GM's E. K. Wennerlund was a leading developer of incentive wage plans, especially for machine tenders and assembly line workers.[49] GM was also a leader in personnel management. In the 1920s a host of inconsistent practices gave way to a more systematic approach and company-wide standards in personnel policy. The meager evidence available on the activities of the other automakers indicates that they took their cues from GM, not Ford.[50]

Mass Production: Tires

In the meantime the demand for auto components encouraged midwestern suppliers to adopt mass production technologies. The best-known example was the rubber industry, increasingly devoted to tire production and concentrated in Akron, near the auto centers. The cluster of technical innovations that transformed the manufacture of tires reflected a process common to other industries. Each new machine or engineering change, introduced in expectation of reduced unit production costs, created "internal compulsions and pressures" that demanded more mechanization, reorganization, and investment. The "compulsive sequences" continued for more than a decade, eliminating all but the most able and aggressive producers. No single technical breakthrough unlocked the industry's potential for high-speed production; nor did any individual or firm dominate. The advent of mass production was a "cumulative process resulting from a vast number of successive small changes."[51]

The results were impressive. The single most striking feature of mass production was its labor-saving character. Employment in the Akron plants peaked during the post–World War I boom and then declined. Boris Stern, who studied tire manufacture in the early 1930s, reported substantial reductions in the labor force in each major step of the manufacturing process. The largest reduction occurred among the laborers, the unskilled workers who pushed, pulled, or carried materials and parts between machine operations. In small, primitive, turn-of-the-century plants, machine operators had moved their own materials. As the plants became larger, managers hired laborers to take over these subsidiary tasks. The development of labor-saving machines and fast, versatile conveyors brought the era of hand transportation to an end. Stern wrote that the most notable feature of the plants he studied was "the effective utilization of all types of conveyors. . . ."[52] By the mid-1920s they linked every step from the crude rubber warehouse to the tire storeroom. The effect was a "great reduction in the labor force as well as a very large increase in the average man-hour output of the plant." The elimination of laborers probably accounted for half or more of the job losses between the 1910s and 1930s. A guide to employment in the industry prepared in the late 1930s does not mention laborers. A detailed accounting of the B. F. Goodrich labor force at the same time lists only a handful of individuals who performed what remained of the laborers' duties. They ranged from 4 to 7 percent of the labor force in several plants.[53]

Mass production also reduced the physical demands of tire production. Early-twentieth-century observers agreed that the most notable feature of tire manufacture was its back-breaking character. The work was most arduous in the assembly room and in the curing room or "pit," the two largest departments. Before 1920 the difficulty of performing this work restricted many jobs to a physical elite of young, muscular men. Employers imposed informal height and weight requirements. "Let's see your hands" was the employment manager's first question to a prospective employee.[54] He expected visible evidence of hard, physical labor. The new technology gradually but profoundly changed this situation. William State's 1909 tire-building machine, the first major breakthrough, enabled the individual builder to quintuple his output, improve quality, and avoid much of the fatigue of hand building.

Succeeding innovations had similar effects. In the mid-1930s, Clifton Slusser, vice president for manufacturing at Goodyear and an industry veteran, claimed that all jobs were "white collar" by comparison with the 1910s.[55] Another measure of change was the growth of the female labor force in the 1920s. In the Akron plants, which employed practically no women in the tire departments before 1920, the total reached 20 percent by 1930.

As the work became less laborious, it became more demanding in another sense. The new machines were expensive and could operate faster than any individual could work. To spread their investment over the largest possible product, managers placed as many employees as possible on piece rates and used time and motion study and frequent rate cuts to raise the norm and eliminate the slowest operatives. These methods gave the industry a reputation for ruthlessness and insensitivity. "They just run the life out of a man," charged one worker, summarizing the consensus. The fast pace encouraged informal resistance, worker-imposed earnings limitations, and internecine warfare between time-study men and production workers. Rate cuts accounted for virtually all of the strikes that occurred during the 1920s and 1930s.[56]

Mass production also altered the balance between worker and foreman. In 1910 tire workers worked primarily for the foreman. As machinery costs increased and worker protests underlined the costs of haphazard shop management, manufacturers responded with industrial-engineering techniques to ensure optimum utilization of the new machinery and personnel management to combat absenteeism, turnover, and unrest. Besides achieving most of their immediate objectives, they decreased the supervisor's authority and enhanced the workers' influence. Thereafter, workers' entitlements grew slowly but steadily.

Finally, mass production contributed to a subtle but significant development outside the factory. Contemporary observers often emphasized that midwestern industry had outstripped other regions because of the creativity of men like Ford and Harvey Firestone, not the availability of raw materials or other "natural" factors. In Detroit, Akron, and hundreds of other cities and towns, industrial executives embraced this analysis and its implications. They formed exclusive service and social clubs and devoted their spare hours to community-uplift causes. Their wealth was important, of course, but their organizational skills were even more critical. By the 1910s every community had a handful of individuals, a small elite within the larger business community, who were vital to the success of any community enterprise and overshadowed the merchants, professionals, and clergymen, not to mention the public officials, who had shared such decision-making powers in the past.[57] The famous community studies of the following years, the Lynds' *Middletown* (1929) and *Middletown Revisited* (1935), Alfred Winslow Jones's *Life,*

Liberty, and Property (1941), and August B. Hollingshead's *Elmtown's Youth* (1949), document the influence of the elite and the mounting resentments that it inspired.

Innovation in Offices, Stores, and Homes

In the late 1910s, Mary Gilson had sought to reorganize the office staff at Joseph & Feiss and erase the social distinctions that separated blue- and white-collar employees. To her dismay she found that her support quickly evaporated.[58] Had she gone to Ford, Goodyear Tire, or any of the other fast-growing midwestern corporations, or indeed to the agricultural-experiment stations and state universities, she likely would have faced a comparable situation. The revolutions in production and work were revolutions of farm and factory. Not only did they enhance the attractiveness of agriculture and industry, they overshadowed other avenues and possibilities. White-collar and service occupations were virtually unaffected.

Why did managers disregard or reject the possibility of reorganizing production in offices and stores? In fact, they did not, except in a relative sense. The creation of big businesses in manufacturing and distribution, the inclusion of production and distribution within a single firm, and the emergence of hierarchies of managers all encouraged organizational innovations that reduced costs and enlarged the prospects of managerial employees.[59] By the early twentieth century, Chicago was the center of the mail-order-catalogue business, which had developed the largest private service-sector organizations outside the railroad industry. Sears, the industry leader, was not only one of the region's largest employers, but an exemplar of rationalized organization. Managers carefully organized purchasing, order processing, billing, and employee activities to achieve high-speed, low-cost operations. The company's size, complexity, and orderliness made it resemble a factory.[60] But Sears and the other mail-order houses were oddities, like the business offices of large railroad companies. Office staffs, even in the largest corporations, were still comparatively small, and personal relationships prevailed in most offices and stores.

Recent studies of white-collar workers have documented the introduction of systematic management in offices, department stores, and large telephone exchanges.[61] In most cases, however, the changes were consistent with Mary Gilson's experiences. Many of them, such as the close supervision of telephone operators or the introduction of typing pools, were simply examples of traditional "drive" methods and did not involve the introduction of management systems. Others affected only the most routine and menial office activities—the design of forms, the routing of reports and memos, filing, and similar tasks. This type of organizational innovation was appropriate only in the largest offices and would probably affect no one higher than the office manager. The product of the office was only marginally affected.

Most important, managerial initiatives in offices and stores focused on labor issues. Recruitment, training, benefit plans, and related activities were of special importance in labor-intensive service institutions. They also reflected the new sophistication of management reform in the post–World War I era, as consultants and executives transcended the earlier reformers' preoccupation with production standards and wage incentives. But these activities were seldom part of a larger approach. In department stores, for example, executives introduced employee training and other personnel measures and made some effort to organize the selling floor but little else.[62] Stockrooms were poorly organized, often chaotic; inventory controls and cost systems would have embarrassed any factory manager; and purchasing remained in the hands of semiautonomous buyers.[63] For most store owners, managerial innovation was a way to improve the efficiency of employees, not the efficiency of the organization.

One reason for this bias was the absence of labor-saving technological innovation. The most important new office machine of the 1910s and 1920s was the electric calculator, developed by the Burroughs Company of Detroit. It and other machines that manipulated numbers were commonplace in the 1920s, but their effects were limited to bookkeeping and accounting activities. They improved the performance of clerical workers, but they did not change the character of production. The typewriter continued to define office work. With the telephone, the duplicating machine, the vertical file, and the calculator, it provided a stable technological foundation for early-twentieth-century office work. A business college graduate of 1900 and a high school commercial graduate of 1930 each began their careers with similar skills.

The prevailing complacency was also related to the availability of a seemingly inexhaustible supply of inexpensive skilled labor. By taking advantage of the pay differential between men's and women's work, the prejudice against married women working outside the home (which reduced the number of more highly paid career employees), and the willingness of high school administrators to expand their commercial curricula, managers were able to contain clerical labor costs and avoid, or at least postpone, organizational innovation. The rapid growth of the female labor force after 1900 reflected a willingness of parents, especially native-born parents, to permit unmarried daughters to work outside the home. In the 1910s this change, together with a buoyant economy, the expansion of urban business activity, and the spread of secondary education, led to a "massive movement" of women into white-collar jobs.[64] The labor shortages of the war years undermined whatever opposition remained and made female clerks "a significant presence in offices everywhere."[65] The experience of the midwestern states essentially reflected the national pattern.

With some allowance for personal and institutional idiosyncrasies, two variables explained the substantial differences that remained between industries. Businesses whose customers were disproportionately female—retail shops, including department stores, were prime examples—were the first to hire women. By the 1920s most retail employees in Cleveland, for example, were female. Industrial firms that employed women in their factories also were likely to hire women for clerical positions. Conversely, banks, railroads, and accounting firms, as well as foundries and steel mills, with overwhelmingly male clients and employees, were slow to introduce women in their offices.[66] By the late 1920s, however, these distinctions had faded; the combination of high skill and low-cost proved irresistible to all but the most hidebound employers.

A similar pattern appeared when the issue of married clerical workers arose. By the 1920s most city stores did not force women to leave their jobs when they married. Department stores were particularly tolerant, in part because they sought experienced part-time employees. One study of Chicago department stores reported that most clerks were married. Manufacturers, who had rarely rejected married women for factory jobs, were also comparatively flexible, while bankers and insurance executives were more rigid.[67] By the mid-1920s the growing number of married women who worked in offices and stores began to raise questions about the female attachment to the home. Studies of office workers indicated that many employees enjoyed their work and did not do it simply for money. Indeed, the majority had husbands whose earnings were sufficient to support a family. Working outside the home gave them a sense of exhilaration; they were "free souls and women of the world."[68]

The growth of female employment had other repercussions. By 1920 many firms had banned tobacco chewing and smoking in offices, instituted rigorous dress and behavior codes, and remodeled their offices to make them comfortable and attractive, more like the living rooms of the middle-class homes.[69] They also expanded their benefit programs, giving greater emphasis to educational and recreational activities, paid vacations, and other measures that appealed to single, transient, middle-class employees. These changes enhanced the appeal of white-collar work. Together with the personal autonomy characteristic of white-collar work and the pay and status gradations that created informal job ladders in the office, they reinforced the disparity between clerical work and other occupations open to young women. By 1920 there were twenty times as many high school students in commercial programs as in 1890. A large minority were the children of immigrants; in Chicago two-thirds of commercial students were immigrants or children of immigrants.[70]

Some of the advantages of office work extended to lower-paid, less-prestigious occupations as well. As public dining grew in popularity during the early twentieth century, many restaurants substituted waitresses for waiters to reduce labor costs. The labor shortage of the World War I period and Prohibition, by breaking the link between the restaurant and alcohol consumption, removed additional barriers to the employment of women in food service. By the 1920s waitresses were among the most independent female workers. Their pay depended largely on tips, a form of piece rate dependent on the quality of their work. Waitresses responded to their ambiguous social role by creating a colorful, protective subculture, with distinctive language, standards of behavior, and mechanisms for mutual support. Within broad limits set by the restaurant proprietor and the customer, they enjoyed substantial autonomy.[71] Despite long hours and uncertain earnings, waitresses seldom considered industrial employment.

The most significant change in women's work, however, reinforced traditional roles and perspectives. Between 1900 and 1930 homemakers became the potential beneficiaries of technological innovations that affected virtually everything they did. The problem was that the new devices, household machines powered by electricity, required access to electric power and a large initial investment. Farm wives were not eligible because of the high costs of extending electric service into the lightly populated countryside. But the majority of urban women were also unable to take immediate advantage of the new technology. By the 1920s most working-class homes had electric lights, the one advance that nearly all city dwellers, however rich or poor, considered essential. The electric iron, vacuum cleaner, and radio also had become popular by that time. They were comparatively inexpensive and of unquestioned utility. Electric washing machines, refrigerators, and other large appliances, on the other hand, were found only in affluent homes. They were newer, less dependable, and more expensive luxuries for the rich and near-rich.[72] By 1930 the contrast between the affluent city home and the poorer city home was greater than ever. The contrast between the affluent city home and the farm home, rich or poor, was even more striking.

The impact of electricity was therefore greatest in homes that relied on domestic servants to do most of the housework. Wealthy families bought appliances for their servants' use.[73] Middle-class families were more likely to view the new machines as labor saving and their purchase prices (and electric bills) as substitutes for servants' wages. The cash savings must have been slight until the mid-1920s, when mass production lowered appliance prices. But the technologically sophisticated family eliminated the "servant problem" and gained an additional room or two. Since family members, principally the wife, also had to do more of the unpleasant work of the home, the transition would have been protracted except for the World War I industrial boom. By ending immigration, raising blue-collar wages, and opening many industrial jobs to women, the boom made servants expensive and, for many families unwilling or unable to pay higher wages, unobtainable. The ratio of servants to families in midwestern cities fell dramatically in the late 1910s. The decline of immigration in the 1920s was an unforeseen bonus to appliance makers.

Middle-class families rapidly adapted to the new order. Architects and contractors built smaller homes to offset the costs of electrical wiring and to simplify cleaning. Home economists redesigned kitchens and bathrooms to ease the housewife's labor. Dinner parties gave way to dancing and other less labor-intensive entertainments. Nevertheless, some surveys suggested that housewives devoted as much time to housework as they had in the pre-machine era.[74] As a result the most important effect of these changes may have been the emergence of a new type of domestic servant, the part-time "cleaning lady." In Muncie, Indiana, for example, only one-third of affluent women had full-time servants by the mid-1920s. Fifty-six percent had part-time servants, and only 10 percent did all the work themselves.[75] Part-time servants lived in their own homes, worked for a cash wage, and were generally older, married women. In cities such as Milwaukee and Chicago, they were likely to be black women.[76]

On farms and in factories, offices, and stores, then, the character of work, and in many instances the type of worker, changed between 1900 and 1930. The innovators included elites motivated by visions of an orderly and productive world and employers who discovered more congenial routes to low-cost production. This account of their activities has largely omitted the contributions of the workers themselves. But as even the most conventional histories of the era suggest, workers were not passive observers of economic change. They, too, influenced the early-twentieth-century workplace and helped shape the midwestern economic environment. We examine the nature of that influence and some of its effects in chapter 5.

5.

Urban Workers in a Revolutionary Era, 1900–1930

While agricultural renewal went hand-in-hand with farmers' efforts to protect themselves from the potentially adverse effects of innovation, industrial workers operated in a different and less manageable setting. By enhancing the competitiveness of midwestern industry, systematic management and mass production created opportunities for hundreds of thousands of workers. Most of the jobs were in cities and continued to be filled by European immigrants or, after the outbreak of World War I, migrants from the American South. Technological and organizational innovation thus sustained the nineteenth-century pattern of immigration and labor recruitment. But it created new opportunities as well. Industrial employees continued to rely on exit and voice to improve wages and working conditions but found the voice option increasingly attractive. After 1900 workers could exploit the informal organization of the shop floor, take advantage of the new personnel systems, reconsider the labor movement, or look to the political arena. All of these possibilities involved risks, but given the availability of jobs, the price of failure was comparatively low. In fact most workers became more prosperous *and* more assertive after 1900. They, too, played a significant role in shaping the new economy.

The Urban Magnet

During the first third of the century, the midwestern labor market changed in undramatic but fundamental ways. The proportion of rural workers steadily contracted. Farm employment stabilized at the turn of the century and then fell in the 1920s, as more farm children chose nonfarm occupations and the most vulnerable farmers abandoned the countryside for village life. Agriculture fell from 32 percent of paid employment in 1900 to 20 percent in 1930. The decline of rural industry was much sharper. Forestry and mining continued to grow after 1900 and even flourished during the industrial boom of the late 1910s. But the postwar recession initiated a painful adjustment process that underlined the region's growing competitive disadvantage in raw materials production. Table 5–1 provides an overview of the contraction. Job

Table 5–1
Industrial Employment, 1900–1930
(Percentage)

	Rate of Growth		Share of Total Industrial Employment	
	1900–1920	*1920–1930*	*1900*	*1930*
Forestry	90	-48	1	<1
Mining	86	-159	7	4
Copper	5	-29	<1	<1
Iron	118	-38	<1	<1
Coal	103	-39	5	3
Manufacturing and construction	157	12	91	96
Big city*	197	20	31	45
Other	95	6	60	51

*cities of 100,000 population
Sources: U. S. Census, *Population*, 1900, tables 93, 94; 1920, tables 15, 18; 1930, table 4.

losses were not primarily intergenerational, as they were in agriculture. Fortunately, displaced miners and lumberjacks had other possibilities, including urban industry. By the late 1920s the auto and tire industries, to cite only two, employed large numbers of former miners.

No less notable were changes in the supply of labor. In 1900 most midwestern industrial cities had large German, British, and Scandinavian populations, though Italian and Slavic communities were common to mining and steel-mill towns. The growth in urban industrial employment between 1900 and World War I coincided with declines in northwestern-European immigration and increases in southern- and eastern-European immigration. The turn-of-the-century tendency toward ethnic diversity became a marked trend by 1914. Table 5–2 summarizes this change.

Immigration continued to reflect economic forces—the push of poverty, population growth, and limited opportunities in Europe and the pull of the American economy. But the distribution of immigrant workers depended on other factors. First, of course, was the attitude of employers toward ethnic diversity. Since most of them continued to delegate hiring to first-level supervisors, they left little evidence of explicit policy making; in general the market reconciled the employer's desire for cheap labor and the worker's desire for employment. However, employers influenced this process by promoting members of particular groups to supervisory positions, enabling them to hire family members and acquaintances. Big-city employers continued to be more tolerant than small-city employers. All of Chicago's major manufacturing areas, for example, had become new immigrant residential enclaves by the early twentieth century. A similar phenomenon occurred in Detroit and Cleveland and, to a lesser degree, in other midwestern cities.

Some small cities also developed large eastern-European immigrant populations. Most of them, such as Granite City, Illinois, and Youngstown, Ohio, were steel towns. The steel industry's insatiable demand for low-wage labor gave those communities a distinctive character. In Lorain, Ohio, for example, the arrival of the steel industry and an influx of Hungarians and Poles redefined the word "foreigner":

> Previously "foreigner" had been differentiated. The Germans were called German, the Irish Irish, and the English English. After 1895 "foreigner" became a generic classification for anything that smelled of garlic, wore a shawl on the head, or spoke a language other than German. . . . To some it was a term of contempt; to others it was synonymous with "exotic."[1]

At least as important as employer policies were the immigrants' ideas about the desirability of particular occupations. The concentration of British and German immigrants in specific occupations reflected income-maximizing strategies based on prior training or occupational experiences. A much smaller proportion of twentieth-century immigrants had marketable skills or exposure to the types of jobs available in a modern city. As a result, noneconomic factors assumed a larger role in their decisions. Family obligations, gender expectations, religious customs, and other cultural preferences, documented at great length in the histories of ethnic communities, influenced immigrant choices. Once a pattern had emerged, it rarely changed. Soon employers began to assume that Italians, Poles, or Hungarians were suited to particular types of work.

Table 5–2
Old Immigrants* in Midwestern Cities, 1900–1920
(Percentage of total foreign-born)

	1900	1920
Large cities**	74	47
Small cities***	84	49

*northwestern Europe plus English-speaking Canadians
**Chicago, Detroit, Cincinnati, Cleveland, Milwaukee, Minneapolis, St. Paul
***1900: 29 cities with 25,000 or more residents, excluding the large cities; 1920: 8 cities with 100,000 or more residents, excluding the large cities
Sources: U.S. Census, *Population*, 1900, table 35; 1920, table 11.

The divergent employment experiences of Italians and Poles, the two largest new immigrant groups in the Midwest, illustrate this process. Both consisted of agricultural laborers who brought little to their jobs. Both favored the region's largest cities and tended to live in relatively homogeneous neighborhoods.[2] Both developed cultural, educational, and philanthropic institutions and became forces in local politics. They also differed in many particulars, such as their attitudes toward the role of the church in secular affairs. But they were most different in their employment choices. Poles favored large-scale manufacturing; in many big-city factories they dominated semiskilled and unskilled jobs. In the Chicago meat-packing industry, they outnumbered other ethnic groups by 1910; in Detroit auto factories, they held more foundry and assembly line jobs than any other group by 1920; in virtually all of the region's steel mills, they were the dominant ethnic group. Even in Milwaukee, which had proportionately fewer opportunities for unskilled industrial workers, Poles held most low-skill jobs.[3] Italians, on the other hand, preferred nonmanufacturing occupations. In many cities and towns they dominated construction and personal services.[4] When they did take factory positions, they favored the clothing and textile industries over steel mills and foundries.

Table 5-3, based on Olivier Zunz's sample of 4,300 Detroit workers, provides a quantitative measure of these preferences. It compares the experiences of Poles and Italians with other groups, including American-born children of Irish immigrants. A score of 100 for any occupation was the citywide mean for all groups. A lower score indicates that a group was underrepresented in a given occupation; a higher score, that it was overrepresented.

The data on Irish Americans provides additional perspective on immigrant preferences. Though the unskilled (those who were most like their parents) favored some poorly paid jobs over others, Irish Americans as a group preferred the occupations that old-stock natives chose. As the economy grew and they acquired skills, they collectively began to resemble their better-established neighbors. Indeed, in Detroit old-stock whites, Canadians, English, Irish, Germans, and their children, all had similar occupational profiles. They were concentrated in white-collar and skilled, industrial positions, in contrast to the Poles, Italians, Hungarians, and Austrians.[5] Judging from the scattered information available on Chicago, Milwaukee, and other cities, this pattern was common throughout the region.

Apart from local variations, there were two notable exceptions, Jews and African Americans. Because of the hostility of other groups, they were excluded from most factory jobs and many white-collar positions. In Detroit they had the lowest representation of any groups in skilled and semiskilled wage labor. With few exceptions they lived in poor, ethnically homogeneous neighborhoods. Yet their occupational profiles were highly dissimilar. Jews

Table 5–3
Ethnic Employment in Detroit, 1920
(100 = citywide mean)

	Poles	*Italians*	*Irish Americans*
Professional	14	0	247
White-collar, small business	27	65	121
Craft	83	275	0
Skilled, semiskilled industrial	117	86	91
Skilled, semiskilled service	38	144	203
Unskilled industrial	261	185	39
Unskilled service	103	155	93

Source: Adapted from Olivier Zunz, *The Changing Face of Inequality: Urbanization, Industrial Development, and Immigrants in Detroit, 1880–1920* (Chicago: University of Chicago Press, 1982), pp. 340–41.

were concentrated in entrepreneurial activities, while blacks were even more highly concentrated in unskilled industrial and service jobs.[6] In Chicago and Cleveland, Jews also worked in the clothing industry. And in all cities differences between German Jews and later arrivals from the Russian empire created additional distinctions that do not appear in the quantitative data.[7] The black experience, on the other hand, was distressingly uniform. The Midwest's small African American population faced increasing labor-market competition as racial consciousness became more acute and eastern-European immigrants sought jobs. Black barbers, waiters, and other craft workers were notable victims, as were teamsters, hod carriers, and railroad-track workers.[8] The decline of domestic service in the 1910s and 1920s reduced other opportunities.

The concentration of industry and immigrants in midwestern cities had other implications for community life and governance. One was the persistence of ethnic and religious isolation. Chicago's Poles typically "clung to old Slavic peasant traditions" despite their daily exposure to American institutions.[9] Most eastern-European immigrant communities achieved virtual "institutional completeness."[10] Working-class churches, schools, social organizations, and commercial establishments typically served a single minority. The potential for community or class-based activities was obviously limited.

For many immigrants the workplace provided the most frequent and important contacts with outsiders. It is not surprising, then, that it often became the starting point for enterprises that promised to transcend ethnic parochialism. Two developments of the years before World War I, the growth of the labor movement and of class-based political parties, exemplified this development.

Workers' Organizations, 1900–1915

The economic recovery of the 1890s marked the beginning of a new era of worker activism. With a few exceptions, skilled manual workers of old-immigrant background were leaders of this activity. Although they employed the protest language of nineteenth-century radicals and of European socialists, they were less ambitious than the Knights of Labor and many European contemporaries. Except in the coal and brewing industries, for example, they seldom tried to organize low-skill employees. Their more limited approach reflected economic and cultural considerations together with a shrewd practicality, given their employers' opposition to formal organization of any type and readiness to exploit skill and ethnic divisions in the labor force. The workers' successes were indications of their market power, organizational skills, and compelling sense of injustice.

The outlook of turn-of-the-century skilled workers has been the subject of sensitive analyses, some of which have focused on midwestern employees.[11] They suggest important similarities with the region's farmers. Market forces had created a more impersonal and competitive order, depreciated the value of familiar methods, and threatened the security of individuals and groups. The challenges came from above and below. The rise of big business and the new managerial systems threatened the status of skilled employees. At the same time, the expansion of the white-collar labor force, with its comparatively high pay, economic security, and perquisites set new and higher standards for economic achievement in urban society. The influx of eastern-European immigrants, on the other hand, increased economic competition and threatened the character of community life.[12] Though the newcomers were wage earners, too, their poverty and ignorance distorted their perceptions of workers' interests.

The old immigrants' reactions depended on local conditions, but two tendencies were notable. They organized in the workplace to take advantage of the buoyant economy, protect themselves from aggressive bosses, and prevent further erosion of their status. They also organized politically, often as socialists, to improve municipal services, ameliorate the effects of urban growth, and protect themselves in an increasingly competitive world. In practice these activities were closely related and interdependent. Union activism was most likely to be successful in the largest cities, while political activism most often succeeded in smaller cities and towns.

The experiences of Chicago, Milwaukee, and Detroit illuminate the role of the union in the midwestern metropolis. Chicago was the best illustration of a pattern that Gerald Friedman has detected in other regions.[13] The labor upheavals of the 1880s had alerted big-city politicians, mostly Irish Americans, to the desirability of cross-class alliances. In the 1890s they attracted middle-class citizens with low taxes and building-trades workers with judicious expenditures of public funds. By the early 1900s, Chicago construction workers enjoyed high wages, the eight-hour day, union recognition, control over public construction jobs, and regulations that insulated them from the larger labor market. In return, carpenters, bricklayers, and other building-trades officials worked closely with Democratic and Republican politicians.[14] In practice they became almost wholly absorbed in collective bargaining and jurisdictional conflicts. After a bitter 1900–1901 lockout, occasioned by contractors' efforts to curb sympathy strikes, their relations with Chicago employers were peaceful until World War I.[15]

The privileged position of Chicago's construction workers was often detrimental to industrial employees. With a secure political base, Chicago politicians could disregard other workers. Occasionally their indifference or hostility provoked potentially dangerous reactions. During a 1902 teamsters strike, for example, police efforts to maintain order inspired a brief antigovernment, antiemployer alliance of old and new immigrants and even white-collar workers.[16] But that was an exception. Outside of construction and a few other crafts, the open shop prevailed. Factory workers, who had few friends at city hall and little influence in the local labor movement, probably faced the greatest obstacles.[17] An apparent breakthrough occurred in 1903 when a coalition of unions at Deering Harvester forced the new International Harvester management to sign its first labor contract. Three of the dozen unions represented semiskilled or unskilled workers, including one, the twine workers, that was all female. Their unwieldy structure was one reason for the company's decision not to renew the contract the following year.[18]

Even more impressive was the growth of packinghouse workers organizations. The return of prosperity and a weakening of employer hostility gave employees their first real opportunity in a decade. Between 1900 and 1904 the Amalgamated Meat Cutters enlisted fifty thousand Chicago workers, principally skilled employees but also many eastern-European immigrants, African Americans, and women. The skilled butchers dictated the structure of the union. Locals were based on skills or occupations (Cattle Butchers, Casing Workers) and coordinated through a city-wide council. This arrangement protected the position of the skilled—about 20 percent of the total— but hindered factory-based unity and union discipline. By 1904 local disputes, including several short strikes, had antagonized the employers. When union leaders demanded a wage increase, they found the packers adamantly opposed and determined to eliminate them. In the ensuing strike the union was unable to win any concessions and gradually disintegrated. By 1905 the meat-packing industry was almost wholly unorganized.[19]

However impermanent and inconsequential its impact on wages and working conditions, the packinghouse workers organization was notable because it transcended ethnic and occupational lines. There were other Chicago examples, including a few that flourished after initial successes. The men's-clothing workers' victory over Hart, Schaffner & Marx, in a major strike in 1910–1911, was a landmark in the organization of Chicago clothing workers and the rise of the Amalgamated Clothing Workers of America.[20] In general, however, factory workers fared badly. Chicago was thus a union bastion and an open shop stronghold, a symbol of labor power and labor parochialism. A modest effort to expand city services under Mayor Edward Dunne in 1905–1906 collapsed under an avalanche of ethnic and partisan bickering.

Although building-trades organizations were prominent in the revived Milwaukee labor movement, their successes did not come at the expense of factory workers or result from political divisions. The most obvious difference between Chicago and Milwaukee was demographic: Milwaukee's population was more than 50 percent first- or second-generation German. The only other large ethnic group was the Poles, with more than 20 percent of the population. Though German-Polish tensions were a deterrent to political unity, the most important divisions in Milwaukee's working class were within the German community. A second difference was the relative absence of large-scale industry. The city's largest employer was Wisconsin Steel, whose south-side works, a magnet for Polish immigrants, employed fewer than four thousand on the eve of World War I.[21]

At the turn of the century, Milwaukee's labor movement experienced a vigorous revival. By 1899 there were 70 locals (up from 52 in 1890) and 20,000 members; three years later there were 105 locals and 23,000 members.[22] Although the city's traction company remained resolutely open shop, and many foundry and machine shop operators subscribed to their national trade associations' anti-union policies, Milwaukee employers generally were more flexible. Equally important, the Federated Trades Council successfully brought the Building Trades Council under its jurisdiction in 1907, ending the political bickering that had long beset union activities. The unions' most glaring weakness was their failure to make inroads among the Poles, who saw them as German, craft-oriented, and aloof.

The Milwaukee workers' most important asset was Victor Berger, an Austrian-immigrant publisher and socialist politician who dominated the city's political life from the 1890s to the 1920s. Berger's rise began in 1892, when he gave up teaching to devote himself full-time to politics. By the turn of the century, he had made his *Wisconsin Vorwaerts* (and later the *Milwau-kee Leader*) the organ of the FTC and the Wisconsin State Federation of Labor. Berger proved to be a superb editor and tactician. In 1899 he engineered FTC endorsement of the new Social Democratic Party. In subsequent years the two organizations became an "interlocking director-ate." Almost every socialist activity "was underwritten by the FTC in some way."[23] In 1900 the socialist mayoral candidate received 5 percent of the vote; in 1904, 27 percent; and in 1910, 40 percent and victory in a three-way race. In 1912 a Republican-Democratic fusion ticket defeated the socialist incum-bent, but in 1916 Berger's associate, Daniel Hoan, won a narrow victory. Buoyed by Berger's organization and a reputation for honest and aggressive leadership, Hoan was reelected seven times, serving until 1940. Berger himself was elected to Congress in 1911, 1918, and in the 1920s.[24]

Though dependent on German unionists, the Milwaukee socialists adopted policies that cut across ethnic lines. They created a city-owned transit system, municipal coal yard, public bath, and public employment-office system that, with state assistance, became a model for other cities and states. Their substantial contingent in the state legislature, composed almost exclusively of trade unionists, became a component of the coalition that pushed through workmen's compensation and other progressive measures.[25] Perhaps the best measure of the socialists' perspective, however, was their approach to the south-side Polish community. There they faced the opposition of Polish clerics, who were closely allied with the Democrats in resisting state regula-tion of parochial education. Yet they persevered. By 1920 Polish voters typically favored socialist and progressive Republican candidates, a change that reflected the political maturation of Polish voters as well as the appeal of the socialists' program.[26]

Detroit represented the opposite end of the spectrum of urban labor activity. In the 1890s the Detroit labor movement remained comparatively healthy.[27] A Republican reform mayor, Hazen G. Pingree, introduced a series of measures that anticipated Milwaukee's socialists and other midwestern progressives by a decade.[28] With the return of prosperity at the turn of the century, union organizing accelerated: membership doubled between 1901 and 1903. But at that point union gains slowed and the movement gradually withered. By the 1910s the Detroit labor movement was confined to the building trades, where it operated at the sufferance of local contractors. It had little influence on Detroit politics and little contact with the city's miniscule socialist movement.

The decline of organized labor in Detroit reflected several factors. The most obvious problem was the formation of the Employers Association of Detroit in 1903. A powerful and efficient open shop organization that specialized in blacklisting union members, the EAD spearheaded anti-union campaigns in the following years.[29] The booming auto-based economy and the high-paying jobs that it created—and the perception, reinforced by the five-dollar day, that this situation was exceptional and dependent on the employers' generosity—may also have deterred organization. However, the critical and ultimately insurmountable challenge to early-twentieth-century unionists was the influx of eastern-European immigrants. Detroit manufacturers often overlooked the union affiliations of their skilled employees. If they had attracted more immigrants with industrial experience and union backgrounds, they might have overlooked their associations too, as Milwaukee employers did. But the divisions and tensions that accompanied the growth of the labor force provided employers with a bonus that they were happy to accept. By forsaking the Chicago and Milwaukee models for the open shop, Detroit employers adopted a potentially risky course that paid off only as long as they remained vigilant and inflexible.

The dangers were greater because of the absence of municipal services that might have blunted the harsh edges of city life. Detroit became a city for opportunists, a place where one went to make money. But suppose the opportunities ended? By the mid-1910s Detroit had attracted a radical underground of Wobblies and socialists, analogous to the socialist and anarchist groups that had flourished in Chicago in the 1870s and 1880s. The radicals' presence and ambitions underlined the risks inherent in the employers' approach.[30]

Other midwestern cities fell somewhere between Chicago, Milwaukee, and Detroit. Cleveland resembled Chicago, an ethnic mélange that grew up around the local steel industry, a group of successful machine tool makers, and a vigorous commercial sector. After 1900 its labor movement embraced construction and skilled industrial workers. The most notable difference was the municipal government, which was dominated by a progressive mayor, Tom L. Johnson, a wealthy executive who had assembled a coalition of reformers and workers and made Cleveland another example of activist government. Johnson's betrayal of his labor allies in a 1908 traction dispute presaged the end of his administration and of union influence in Cleveland government.[31] Toledo, Ohio, on the other hand, more closely resembled Milwaukee, though its new immigrant population and its factories, including the Willys automobile company, were larger. In the late 1890s an unorthodox manufacturer, Samuel M. Jones, created a coalition of unions and reformers that elected him to three terms as mayor. Jones and his supporters made Toledo known for innovative public services.[32]

Smaller cities and towns often grew as fast as the metropolitan areas, creating opportunities for a new generation of industrial workers. With the exception of steel and mining towns, however, they attracted fewer immigrants: the less cosmopolitan atmosphere and the hostility of many small-town employers were effective deterrents. As a result old immigrants and old-stock natives filled supervisory and skilled positions, as they did in the cities, but old-stock natives, drawn from the neighboring villages, filled many less-skilled jobs as well. While every plant had its Italian, Czech, or Polish employees, old-stock natives predominated at Ball Brothers of Muncie, Indiana; John Deere of Moline, Illinois; and Hormel of Austin, Minnesota.

In hundreds of such towns the labor movement flourished after 1900. Craft workers—carpenters, bricklayers, printers, molders, butchers, and others—led the way, often with the help of less-skilled but strategic employees such as teamsters and streetcar operators. Skilled factory employees followed. Apart from greater ethnic homogeneity, unionists had the advantage of personal friendships between workers in different trades. In short, a potential for an assertive workers' voice existed in smaller industrial communities. In most cases it remained latent; small-town employers also had significant advantages, including community visibility, political influence, and a vigorous open shop movement to draw upon. Beloit, Wisconsin, employers, for example, enlisted the aid of the Chicago Employers Association when their employees organized in 1903. Within six months they had virtually eradicated the local labor movement.[33]

A confrontation between Akron tire manufacturers and workers in 1913 provides a notable illustration of the delicate balance that existed in towns and small cities. Because of its links to the auto industry, Akron had become one of the fastest-growing American cities. Most of the newcomers were migrants from the upper South, selected for their brawn. Though their wages were high, they looked with envy at the power and prestige of the more than forty craft groups that had organized despite the open shop policies of the local employers association. When a dispute over piece rates at Firestone Tire & Rubber Company resulted in a walkout by skilled tire builders in February, 1913, most male employees and a substantial number of the females (who performed poorly paid, mostly non-tire jobs) joined them on the picket line. Within two days 18,000 to 20,000 workers had left their jobs. The city's small socialist party and a handful of IWW organizers created a union. The strikers retained the upper hand for nearly two weeks; some held out for six weeks. However, economic hardship, rivalry between the AFL and IWW, mounting public hostility to the strike and, above all, employer intransigence gradually undermined their enthusiasm. By late March, the union had collapsed, and its leaders had been blacklisted. Whatever their faults, the strikers had demonstrated a willingness to learn from the example of local craft groups. Ethnic differences were unimportant in the rise and fall of their union.[34]

The behavior of the Akron strikers helps explain the success of socialist parties and politicians in the small industrial cities of the Middle West. After

1900 the socialists enjoyed greater success in the Midwest than in any other region. And it was in communities like Dayton, Ohio, Flint, Michigan, and Elwood, Indiana, not Chicago, Cleveland, or Cincinnati, that they had their greatest influence; Milwaukee was the exception, not the rule. Case studies of many of these communities consistently emphasize the prominent roles of old immigrants and old-stock workers in socialist activities. In Dayton, which had one of the most vigorous local parties, socialism "attracted into its ranks older, settled, native born skilled workers."[35] In Flint it mobilized the city's "older, skilled" workers.[36] Elwood's socialists took pride in their community's ethnic and racial purity.[37] The pattern was similar in other Ohio, Indiana, Iowa, and Wisconsin towns, where the movement peaked in the early 1910s, electing dozens of mayors.[38]

The ethnic basis for midwestern socialism suggests a more fundamental association with skilled industrial work. In Dayton 63 percent of socialists were skilled industrial employees. The proportions in other cities were similar, though socialist candidates for local and party offices tended to be professionals and small-business proprietors. There was also a strong correlation between socialist voting and union membership. In many midwestern towns, socialist victories followed successful organizing campaigns. In Minneapolis, the one large city besides Milwaukee to elect a socialist mayor, the successful 1916 campaign reflected the efforts "of an aggressive (nonsocialist) trade union movement."[39] Socialists rarely did well where there was little organization or where the labor movement had collapsed. In smaller communities, as well as in Milwaukee, trade unionism and socialist voting were responses to the growth of big-business power, systematic management, anti-union zealotry, and competition from eastern-European immigrants.

Midwestern socialism was thus a protest by the old industrial working class against potentially damaging initiatives from above and below. But socialists were not simply protesters; they also advocated programs of public services that were unobtainable through collective bargaining and unappealing to broad-based parties. Socialist demands for honesty in government, regulation of big business, publicly owned utilities, and social insurance were similar to the demands of progressive Republicans; others, for public coal yards and tax relief for low-income homeowners, resembled the special-interest pleas of farm groups. Socialists, however, were too few in number and too controversial to enjoy the same degree of success. When they won municipal offices, Republicans and Democrats immediately moved to isolate them from other workers and defeat their programs. Apparently no socialist mayor (apart from Milwaukee's Hoan) ever survived a reelection campaign.

In mining towns, a final category of industrial community, the workers' voice was stronger because of the absence of competing groups and the larger role of organized labor. During the first decade of the century, the UMW became firmly established in the coal towns of southern Ohio, Indiana, Illinois, and Iowa. To succeed it had to weld together an ethnically and racially divided labor force. After several violent strikes in southern Illinois that featured the introduction of black strikebreakers, organizers made rapid progress. By 1908 the UMW represented virtually every Illinois and Indiana coal miner and 80 percent of Ohio and 70 percent of Iowa miners.[40] It also became an influential force in local politics and government, electing (among other officials) thirteen socialist mayors in Illinois towns between 1906 and 1913.[41] As the UMW grew, many employers concluded that industry-wide collective bargaining would be a hedge against competition in the labor-intensive industry. As a consequence, the midwestern coal industry entered a period of economic stability and comparative labor peace.[42] Exits declined; labor turnover was only one-half to one-third as great as in nonunion fields.[43] The UMW became the largest and most influential American union because of its success in the Central Competitive Field.

The growth of unionism in the northern copper and iron mining industries, on the other hand, led to a new era of turmoil and violence. One notable reason for this contrast was the size and the resources of the northern mining companies. Calumet & Hecla's authoritarian paternalism had long set the tone for employer-employee relations in copper country. Miners understood that the price of company houses, libraries, insurance plans, and other benefits included the open shop. The Minnesota firms were less benevolent, though U.S. Steel (which had absorbed Oliver Mining, the largest of the Minnesota companies) promised a similar trade-off. A second reason was the ethnic mix in the northern mining fields, especially the large number of Finnish immigrants. Though most Finns were former agricultural laborers, a sizable and growing minority had been urban workers, familiar with turn-of-the-century social-democratic ideas and eager to organize. The Finnish Socialist Federation, formed in 1906, soon rivaled the Lutheran Church in influence and may have attracted one-quarter of all Finnish immigrants.[44] In northern Minnesota "Finnish immigrant socialists emerged as leaders in calling for recognition of workers' rights."[45]

The turning point came in 1906–1907, as labor conflicts in Michigan and Minnesota demonstrated that unskilled recent immigrants could be as militant as old-immigrant groups. Finnish workers had sparked short, successful strikes at the Quincy Company mines in 1904 and 1905. In 1906, with the help of the Western Federation of Miners, they led a more extensive walkout for higher wages and improved working conditions. After a three-week stand-off and confrontations that resulted in two deaths and many injuries, they voted to accept a pay increase.[46] Their victory encouraged Iron Range miners, who had been organizing under WFM auspices for a year. When the union divided into Finnish, Italian, and Slavic sections, membership boomed. A

1907 walkout of 10,000 to 16,000 workers, mostly Finns, closed the mines for a month. Economic hardship and the arrival of thousands of strikebreakers ultimately doomed the union, but not before the strikers had demonstrated the potential of industrial unionism. The subsequent blacklisting of many activists embittered labor relations in Minnesota and encouraged "a rising tide of radicalism among Finnish workers on the Michigan range."[47]

These developments culminated in a ten-month Michigan strike in 1913, the most colorful and violent midwestern labor dispute of the pre–World War I years. The impetus once again came from the unskilled miners, primarily the Finns, and the WFM. In response, the companies recruited large forces of guards and strikebreakers. Conflicts between strikers and guards resulted in five deaths, numerous injuries, and the beating and kidnapping of WFM president William Moyer. They were a prelude to a December, 1913, disaster, when cries of "fire" at a WFM-sponsored Christmas party precipitated a stampede that left sixty-two children dead. By that time the strikers were desperate and disheartened. The collapse of the strike in April marked the end of unionism in the Copper Country for a quarter-century.[48]

War and the Midwestern Worker

The outbreak of war in western Europe in the summer of 1914 was a turning point in the evolution of the midwestern labor force. For five years the conflict was a powerful stimulus to the growth of industrial production and employment in the United States. As leaders in the production of steel, machinery, and vehicles, midwestern manufacturers were strategically positioned to take advantage of the boom. But the war had two other effects that also influenced their actions and policies. First, it abruptly ended the flow of workers to the United States, as combatant governments halted the departure of potential soldiers and diverted shipping to war service. Second, labor and other shortages, together with the ineptitude of the Wilson administration and the Federal Reserve in managing the boom, set off an inflationary price spiral that had a destabilizing impact on almost every aspect of American life, but particularly on industrial relations. The patterns of conflict described in the previous sections gave way to a broad-based labor rebellion.

The immediate effect of the labor shortage was to create new migration chains within the United States. By mid-1915, northern employers faced a growing labor shortage. Many hired women as machine operators, accelerating the movement of women away from clothing manufacture. Others turned to southern farmers, who did not require the special services that women (or at least their public guardians) expected. Newspaper ads and a few recruiters initiated a movement to northern cities. Once word had spread that southerners were welcome, the new pattern was virtually identical to the old.

Prospective employees bore most of the costs, followed friends and relatives, and settled in neighborhoods where they found familiar faces.[49]

Approximately one million southerners moved north between 1915 and 1920. A half-million whites, drawn disproportionately from the upper South and Appalachia, settled in midwestern cities. Between two-thirds and three-quarters of the total found jobs in Ohio and Michigan. Apart from Detroit, they favored smaller cities and towns. Despite derisive comments about "hillbillies," they quickly blended into the native population.[50] The other half-million migrants were African Americans, whose experiences were predictably different. Only half of the black migrants moved to the Midwest, and most of them settled in the largest cities or in cities such as Indianapolis and Columbus, Ohio, which had substantial black communities. Chicago became a magnet for black migrants because of its large black community, abundance of low-skill jobs, and reputation as a city of opportunity. The Chicago *Defender*, which had a large circulation in the Mississippi Valley, helped direct the movement.[51] Detroit was also attractive. By 1917 it was receiving a thousand black migrants per month. Other urban centers were less inviting. Toledo's black migrants, for example, found an environment that was as hostile as many areas in the South.[52] Table 5-4 summarizes the process.

Like the immigrants, black migrants found relatively few doors open to them. Men were welcome in the steel, meat-packing, and automobile industries. In the Chicago meat-packing plants, the black labor force rose from 6 to 32 percent between 1910 and 1920.[53] But there were few opportunities to move into skilled jobs. Outside of manufacturing black workers faced even greater obstacles. Barbers and waiters were often unable to practice their trades, and prospective entrepreneurs had difficulty borrowing money. In the 1920s there were seven times as many Italian and Polish shopkeepers in Chicago relative to their populations.[54] Black women had limited opportunities in manufacturing and were excluded from white-collar employment. Most of them became servants.

Racial bias exacerbated tensions arising from the competition for jobs. The association of black workers with strikebreaking became the focus of white antipathy, especially in East Saint Louis and Chicago, where the most notable conflicts occurred. Failed strikes at the Morris and Armour meat-packing plants in 1916 and at an aluminum foundry in early 1917 led East Saint Louis labor leaders to demand "drastic action" to rid the city of black workers. The riot that followed on July 2 killed nine whites and thirty-nine blacks and destroyed more than two hundred homes. It did not directly involve union leaders or even many union members, but AFL officials "repeatedly inflamed the whites, using racial propaganda. . . . Nowhere was the relationship between labor strife and race rioting more clearly and directly evident."[55] In Chicago blacks had played infamous roles in the defeat of the Pullman strike of 1894, the packinghouse strike of 1904, and a teamster strike in 1905. As William Tuttle writes, "the hostility of striking whites . . . had been generalized into hatred for the black race as a whole. . . ."[56] It was no accident that the great Chicago riot of July 1919, which cost fifteen white and twenty-three black lives, occurred on the eve of another period of labor conflict in the meat-packing plants.

Black workers also faced serious problems outside the factories. In most prewar midwestern cities, black residents had lived in one or more clusters in the poorest neighborhoods. But they were no more highly concentrated than many immigrant groups. As migration increased, these areas became larger and more congested. Chicago's Black Belt, an extension of the traditional red-light district on the near south side, became (after Harlem in New York) the second-largest black ghetto. By 1930 more than 90 percent of Chicago's blacks lived there, a proportion that far exceeded the concentration of any European group in the prewar years.[57] Detroit's Paradise Valley, Cleveland's near-east-side black enclave, and other ghettoes developed in similar fashion. Intense crowding and congestion were their hallmarks. Slum conditions increased the determination of white residents to exclude blacks from other areas.

In other respects, paradoxically, the war boom reduced the distinctions that had divided the industrial working class in earlier years. The labor shortage led to wage increases (Ford's five-dollar day was the going wage for unskilled labor by 1917) and inflation, which reached unprecedented, double-digit levels in 1917, creating additional pressures for increases. For the first time since the advent of modern office and store, the gains of blue-collar workers outstripped those of white-collar employees. By 1918 newspapers and magazines often ran stories about teachers and nurses who had aban-

Table 5–4
African American Population Increase, 1910–1920
(Percentage)

	Growth Rate 1910–1920	Share of Total	
		1910	1920
United States	7	10.7	9.9
Midwest	10	2.2	2.1
Chicago	148	2.0	4.1
Detroit	616	1.2	4.1
12 other cities	24	4.5	4.3

Sources: U.S. Census, *Population*, 1910, table 37; 1920, Vol. 2, table 13.

doned their professions for munitions plants. The labor shortage also created new opportunities for a formal workers' voice and new challenges for organized labor. A 1916 Mesabi Range miners' strike was illustrative. As steel production rose, the Iron Range boomed and labor became scarce. Miners sensed their advantage. As Donald Sofchalk explains:

> If . . . there was ever a possibility of drawing the miners into a conservative labor movement, it existed in the spring of 1916. The industry was preparing for a banner production year: and mining officials announced wage increases early in the spring in order to insure enough labor for the open pit mines. On the other hand . . . the sense of grievous injustice among the underground miners remained.[58]

Yet the Federation's organizers hesitated. Even after militant workers shut down some mines in early June, they refused to act. When Finnish socialists invited the IWW to fill the leadership vacuum, AFL officials cited the Wobblies' presence as an additional reason for delay.[59] The strikers finally settled for a wage increase. Their union disappeared.

The Iron Range strike underlined the institutional and psychological barriers to the organization of low-skill immigrant employees. Since the 1880s unionists had tried to insulate themselves from economic and cultural change. The war boom lessened the competition for jobs and whetted the interest of low-skill workers in unions. Would the labor movement also change? The miners' experience provided no basis for optimism. Growing public concern about political nonconformity and radicalism, evident in the Mesabi communities, suggested that organizations such as the IWW would have no greater success.[60] A perceptive observer of the 1916 strike might have predicted the fate of the labor movement in the 1920s.

The pattern of union activity in the following years largely confirmed the lessons of 1916. The AFL expanded its base in Chicago, Milwaukee, and other cities where it had a substantial membership before 1914. In some cases it encouraged organizing drives among low-skill workers. Notable examples were the Stockyards Labor Council of 1917–1921, a coalition of unions that organized packinghouse workers, especially in Chicago, and the National Committee for Organizing the Iron and Steel Workers of 1918–1920, another coalition that enjoyed its greatest success in the Chicago area. The AFL also took advantage of government operation of the railroads to organize their "shopcraft" employees. Total union membership doubled between 1915 and 1920, rising to at least 20 percent of the nonagricultural labor force. In the Midwest it probably reached 30 percent of workers in transportation, construction, mining, and manufacturing.

Yet the AFL position was highly precarious. Membership increases were highly concentrated in munitions plants and railroad shops that were engaged in war work or subject to government controls. Barring the unlikely continuation of public spending in the postwar period, some losses were inevitable. The critical issue was how union leaders would manage the transition to a peacetime economy. The dramatic but unsuccessful steel strike of 1919–1920 symbolized both the potential and the shortcomings of organized labor in the postwar era.[61] The more gradual disintegration of the packinghouse workers' organization, on the other hand, underlined the difficulties of crossing traditional skill and ethnic lines, regardless of the employers' position. In late 1919, as the steel strike was collapsing, the Stockyards Labor Council and the Amalgamated Meat Cutters, the two groups instrumental in organizing the Chicago packing industry, began to pursue separate and often antagonistic courses. Over the next year their differences widened. Together with the 1919 Chicago race riot, which alienated the industry's black workers, these conflicts undermined union power in the industry. A disastrous December 1921 strike that eradicated the union was almost an anticlimax.[62]

Two related developments provide additional measures of the importance of workers' voice in the war period. The first was the accelerated introduction of personnel management. By 1920 the largest firms, led by midwestern manufacturing companies, had taken the first tentative steps toward the private welfare systems that would emerge over the next half-century. Of their many initiatives, the most notable and innovative was probably the company union. Virtually unknown before 1914, company unions flourished in the following years. By one measure there were more than seven hundred by 1920, at least one-half of which enlisted midwestern workers. But company unions were as diverse as trade unions. The largest groups were toothless union substitutes, responses to the growth of the labor movement and government directives that forced defense contractors to bargain with employees. Most of these organizations collapsed in the postwar period, their raison d'être having disappeared. A minority, including representation plans at International Harvester and Swift, began as union substitutes and evolved into expressions of a more vigorous approach to production and personnel management. Finally, a small but important group that included Goodyear's Industrial Assembly were capstones to aggressive personnel programs designed to ensure that managers did not disregard the workers' voice.[63]

The second development was the growth and decline of worker and union-based political activism. At first the war stimulated such efforts. The Socialist party experienced its greatest successes in the municipal elections of 1917, apparently because many German Americans and other war opponents turned to the socialists to oppose to American involvement in the conflict. But the socialists' moment soon passed. The party divided over the war and lost most of its pro-war members. The indictment and trial of Eugene Debs in 1918 (nominally as a result of a speech protesting the incarceration of the Ohio party leaders) symbolized the precarious position of the anti-war socialists. Equally revealing was the break between the Milwaukee FTC and the Socialist party over Berger's unyielding anti-war stand. Whatever their personal views, Milwaukee unionists could not resist the benefits of association with the pro-war AFL. Berger, on the other hand, was indicted by the government and expelled from Congress. By 1918 Milwaukee's labor-socialist alliance was near collapse.[64]

The end of the war witnessed a brief revival of midwestern radicalism. Chicago unions, encouraged and led by the Chicago Federation of Labor and its socialist president, John Fitzpatrick, promoted local labor parties in Chicago and other industrial cities. In 1918 and 1919 they won a handful of municipal elections in Illinois industrial towns and appeared to be successors to the Socialist party. But there were major differences. The postwar labor parties drew much of their support from new immigrant groups and identified with the Russian Revolution. Their manifestos placed more emphasis on the nationalization of resources and the "democratic management" of industry than on the expansion of public services, making them highly vulnerable during the Red Scare of 1919–1920.[65] Even before they became the targets of government action, their efforts to create an alliance with Senator Robert La Follette and his backers had failed. Within a year the labor parties had collapsed along with the industrial economy.

Industrial Labor in the 1920s

The postwar recession of 1920–1921 marked the end of the boom and the beginning of a bittersweet era for industrial employees. The immediate problems were staggering: *most* workers in the fastest-growing industries, including steel, autos, and auto parts, lost their jobs over the winter of 1920–1921. Although new opportunities reduced urban unemployment in 1922, rural industrial workers faced permanent decline, as the forestry and mining industries struggled with resource depletion and interregional competition. Industrial wages rose more slowly than in the 1910s, and employers became more vigorously anti-union. Besides well-established open shop groups such as the Employers' Association of Detroit and the Minneapolis Citizens Alliance, new "American Plan" organizations flourished. The Illinois Manu-facturers Association organized more than two dozen such groups in 1921.[66]

Unions that had survived the postwar onslaught suffered huge member-ship losses. Low-skill union members were the first to go, ending speculation that the war experience had produced a new outlook among industrial workers. The collapse of the labor movement in steel, meat-packing, and other manufacturing industries (including the railroads' repair and manufac-turing facilities in the wake of the shopmen's strike of 1922) and its precipitous decline in coal mining left the comparatively small clothing industry as the only midwestern bastion of industrial unionism. Even that fortress crumbled in the late 1920s, as fashion changes and internecine conflicts within the International Ladies Garment Workers Union undermined its membership and influence in Chicago, Cleveland, and other midwestern markets.

The most graphic example of the decline of the labor movement was the near collapse of the United Mine Workers, an almost invincible force in the midwestern coal fields until the early 1920s. The war had masked the industry's mounting problems, as new fields and energy sources altered the prewar balance between supply and demand and undermined the Central Competitive Field. The emergence of John L. Lewis as the dictatorial head of the UMW was an added burden. By 1921 Lewis had concluded that his future, and the union's, required a smaller union of high-wage workers. Refusing to approve wage concessions and ruthlessly suppressing internal opposition, Lewis led the union to a Pyrrhic victory over the bituminous operators in 1922 and to a catastrophic defeat in 1927–1928. The 1922 strike was best known for the infamous Herrin, Illinois, massacre, when strikers executed twenty captive strikebreakers and mine guards, but the toll of the second conflict was also substantial. The strike decimated the UMW in southeastern Ohio, one of the older, high-cost fields, and paralyzed it in Indiana and Illinois. After more than a year of picketing and violent clashes with guards and strikebreakers, the Ohio miners and the townspeople who depended on them were impoverished. The governor used the National Guard to distribute food to starving families. By the summer of 1928 many miners had accepted substantial wage cuts and returned to nonunion jobs. The union's only remaining bastion was Illinois, and even there the evidence of decline was unmistakable.[67]

The collapse of unions in manufacturing and mining meant that construction, railroad transportation, and a handful of urban service trades were the only industries with significant representation. But the atmosphere was also different. The vigorous critiques of industrial and managerial innovation that had attracted skilled workers in the prewar years now seemed passé. The triumph of parochial business unionism in the building trades and of "gangster unionism" in the construction and service industries in Chicago and other cities supported employer charges that unionists were monopolists, bullies, or worse. The political retreat of the railroad brotherhoods after the La Follette presidential campaign of 1924 symbolized the unions' loss of organizational and intellectual vitality.[68]

Even the most successful unionists had trouble overcoming their negative image. Milwaukee unionists maintained their alliance with the Hoan administration and achieved a wide range of legislative goals, including anti-injunction, anti-yellow-dog contract, and detective-licensing laws. They also opened a cooperative store and a labor college, sponsored a municipal housing project, and promoted a summer school for women workers. Yet unorganized workers (and many who had been union members) seemed uninterested. Federated Trades Council organizing drives in 1923, 1924, and 1925 failed, and union membership in Milwaukee fell from 35,000 in 1920 to 20,000 in 1932.[69]

The decline of union activity contributed to the failure of the Socialist party to revive after the Red Scare and postwar recession. The breakup of the national party during the war left the movement in disarray. The withdrawal of much of the "left" leadership—notably the most prominent Ohioans, Charles Ruthenberg and Marguerite Prevey—into the Communist party was an additional blow. More serious was the defection of much of the "right" leadership and the socialists' failure to attract new talent. The plight of the unions in the 1920s created an apparently unfillable void. Even in Milwaukee, where the socialists retained their hold on municipal government, the leaders of the party were men who had led it since the early 1900s.[70]

This familiar account of prosperity, union decline, and political retreat may obscure as much as it reveals. Despite the collapse of the labor movement, most urban workers, including most skilled workers, enjoyed real wage gains and other improvements in working and living conditions. The urban economy grew rapidly after 1922, creating opportunities for promotions and alleviating the need for the family economy. Restrictions on immigration also eased the tensions of earlier years. Immigrant neighborhoods began "a move toward stability."[71] Thomas Jablonsky's interviews with residents of Chicago's stockyards district document a growing tolerance, as experiences in the United States began to overshadow memories of Europe and economic competition declined.[72] Immigrant children were particularly malleable, as school and neighborhood pressures to act like "American" youths mounted. Immigrant women also adopted American dietary standards.[73] Economic and cultural assimilation were not new to the 1920s, of course, but the increasing isolation of the immigrant generation and the white-collar opportunities that awaited immigrant children who finished high school accelerated it. By the 1930s English had become, again, the language of everyday life in the region's cities.

Like the immigrants, black migrants adjusted to their new circumstances. Shopkeepers and professionals soon emerged as community leaders. In Indianapolis, for example, they engineered a realignment of black voters as the Republican party became more closely identified with the Ku Klux Klan.[74] Although there is little direct evidence that black workers benefited from immigration restriction, employment conditions were sufficiently favorable to encourage additional migration in the mid-1920s.[75]

Other examples illuminate the new conditions. In Indiana auto-related manufacturing, symbolized by a group of new or expanded factories, increasingly drove the state's economy. U.S. Steel's Gary plant, the largest and most efficient in the industry, doubled its capacity in the 1920s to meet the needs of Detroit. Nearby, the Inland and Youngstown Sheet & Tube plants, almost as large, also specialized in sheet steel for the auto industry. To the south and east a less conspicuous development had even greater implications for Indiana workers. By the mid-1920s nearly every city in central and northern Indiana had one or more auto-parts producers. Drawing employees from the area's villages and towns, they provided new opportunities for many old-stock workers. By the end of the decade, Anderson had become dependent on General Motors, and Muncie and Fort Wayne were also closely tied to the auto industry. In contrast Terre Haute, long one of the state's industrial centers, experienced relative and absolute decline because of its dependence on the faltering railroad industry.[76]

In Flint, Michigan, the success of General Motors meant good times for blue-collar families and the virtual disappearance of the traditional family economy. The company's growth translated into promotions for veteran workers and jobs for younger ones. High wages raised most workers above the level necessary to provide adequate food, housing, clothing, and recreation, while the company's personnel program provided nonwage benefits and outlets for grievances. Flint families enhanced their prosperity by having fewer children and investing surplus earnings. Many wives took factory jobs and daughters dropped out of high school to work in the auto plants. Teenagers could earn as much as clerical workers and enjoy semi-independent lives based on stylish clothing, restaurant meals, and other luxuries.[77]

The management systems that had encouraged union activism in the mid-1910s now seemed benign and unthreatening. In auto-assembly plants, tire factories, and other establishments where highly repetitive activities were the rule, disputes over the work pace continued, but the pressures to increase output were no more severe than they had been a decade earlier.[78] Personnel management created additional possibilities for a nonunion workers' voice. Company unions had become fixtures in many of the largest and most influential midwestern corporations by the 1920s. David Fairris's quantitative analysis of their activities concludes that they played an "essential" role in the "peaceful reduction of labor turnover." They "provided management with workers' insights," improved morale, and increased cooperation between managers and workers. Company unions were also associated with rising labor productivity and a decline in accident rates.[79]

Among the best-known midwestern company unions were Goodyear's Industrial Assembly and International Harvester's Employee Representation Plan. Though they lacked the independence of AFL organizations, they resolved grievances, negotiated improvements in working conditions and fringe benefits, and in some cases successfully pressured managers for wage increases. In early 1926 the Assembly struck for several weeks to emphasize its demand for higher wages. By that time it had become a "union" of "the oldest and most experienced employees."[80] Assembly veterans who later became active in the CIO saw no inconsistency in their activity. Harvester's ERP had a similar history and apparently a similar impact, as did company unions at Swift and other midwestern firms.[81]

Nor were midwestern workers powerless outside the plant, though their influence is more difficult to plot after the decline of organized labor. The one example that suggests a parallel with the Non-Partisan League (though not with the fight for farm parity) was the remarkable rise of the midwestern Ku Klux Klan. The tactics of the Klan were so outrageous and its leadership so corrupt that it has often been portrayed as a symbol of postwar reaction and intolerance. That portrayal obscures as much as it illuminates, as a host of recent studies of midwestern Klan groups have demonstrated. For every D. C. Stephenson, the unscrupulous Indiana Klan chieftain, or S. Glenn Young, the psychopathic head of the Williamson County, Illinois, Klan, there was a Daisy Barr, the temperance lecturer and evangelist who headed the Indiana Women of the KKK, or an O. W. Friederich, the popular theatre owner who led the central Illinois Klan.[82] For every bigot or fanatic, a host of ordinary people came to the Klan via evangelical churches or progressive reform organizations. Only in 1925, as the abuses of Stephenson and others became known and respectable people dropped out, did the sinister side of the organization become dominant. At its peak, the Indiana Klan embraced nearly one-third of all native-born white men and a substantial minority of Protestant women. It was the "largest organization of any kind" in Indiana, overshadowing the Methodist church and the American Legion, the only other voluntary organizations that operated in nearly every community.[83]

Recent studies have demonstrated that the midwestern Klan was *sui generis*, unrelated to the Klans of the post–Civil War South and the desegregation battles of the 1950s and 1960s. It was not based on racial or ethnic hatred and was only rarely associated with violence. Working in the late 1940s, Paul Angle noted that the Klan in southern Illinois was not specifically anti-Catholic or anti-immigrant, though its enemies were disproportionately Italian because of their role in bootlegging.[84] That characterization would describe most midwestern KKK groups. With few exceptions, Klan members were no more bigoted or violent than nonmembers or many Klan enemies.

An understanding of the Klan's appeal begins with the association between occupation and Klan membership. Midwestern Klan groups included large numbers of skilled industrial workers, current or former trade unionists, farmers, professionals, small-business proprietors, and clerical workers. In

Ohio's Mahoning Valley, business and professional people dominated the Klan. In Akron and Springfield, Ohio, factory workers were the backbone of the organization. In Dayton skilled industrial workers, including most of the city's prewar socialists, played leading roles. In rural Indiana, almost everyone supported Klan objectives, though Klan tactics were another issue. In Madison, Wisconsin, the Klan drew its support from white-collar and skilled industrial workers. Leonard Moore's examination of the Indiana Klan membership records provides the most concrete evidence of this diversity.[85]

There were two exceptions. The first was low-skill industrial workers, disproportionately immigrant and Catholic even in a state like Indiana, which had a comparatively small foreign-born population. Many immigrant workers were also involved in illicit business activities, such as gambling or bootlegging, and thus became targets of Klan activity. When the offenders refused to be intimidated, the potential for violence grew. In the best-known case, Klan efforts to clean up Niles, Ohio, provoked local Italian gangsters to launch a terrorist campaign that culminated in a dramatic shoot-out on a downtown street in November, 1924. As William Jenkins writes, "The problem with the Klan was that it favored a total shutdown; it offered no living space." Klan initiatives thus elicited a "violent response from people who felt they were being backed into a corner."[86] In Herrin, Illinois, the emergence of the KKK in 1923 precipitated a series of dramatic confrontations between civic groups and criminal elements that escalated into an all-out war. Most victims of the conflict died after the Klan faded in 1925.[87]

The other exception was even more revealing. The Klan included few business executives or other notably influential citizens. Indeed, to most Klan members and sympathizers, they were the real enemy. As the business elite became more visibly isolated and more closely associated with disruptive social changes, it also became more vulnerable. Wartime mobilization, presided over by prominent executives, had raised expectations of a purified society, perhaps reminiscent of the golden age that old-stock residents recalled before the advent of modern industry and mass immigration. Postwar disillusionment and the unpleasant realities of the early 1920s, symbolized by the failure of Prohibition, created a groundswell of support for the Klan. The organization's broad appeal and faceless uniformity became counterpoints to the snobbishness and social posturing of the country club set. In virtually every community the most vigorous and determined opponents of the Klan were big-business leaders and their allies, such as ministers of elite churches. In Akron, for example, the Klan's most prominent leader was M. C. Heminger, a realtor with a working-class clientele, while the best-known anti-Klan leader was Wendell L. Willkie, a downtown lawyer with big-business clients and large ambitions. The two men, ironically, lived within a few houses of each other in a middle-income neighborhood on the city's near west side.[88] As the deficiencies of the Klan became more apparent, the elite attacks took a larger and larger toll. Elite opposition was as important as the scandals and failures of Klan-endorsed elected officials in bringing about the fall of the Klan.

In the end, the Klan's achievements were meager. It contributed to the early success of Prohibition, drew women into politics, and influenced the outcome of numerous local elections and the 1924 Indiana state campaign. But it achieved few of its legislative objectives and had no discernible influence on the behavior of immigrants. The charges that it bankrupted Jewish merchants and brought about the segregation of Indiana schools were untrue.[89] As Klan membership and influence waned, the business elite became more powerful than ever. The furor surrounding the rise and fall of the postwar KKK underlined the continuing importance of ethnic tensions in the labor force and the ability of workers to influence their environment, even in an era of reaction. These themes would be no less important in the years of economic decline that followed the collapse of agriculture and industry and the eclipse of business influence in the early 1930s.

Part III

Government and Labor in the Midwest, 1930–1953

If the defining innovations of the first third of the twentieth century were the work of executives and managers, those of the following decades came from the public sector. Except in agriculture, where a vigorous public-private partnership had emerged by the 1910s, government played a peripheral part in midwestern economic life before the 1930s. Antigovernment ideologies and interest-group conflicts had persistently and effectively limited public initiatives and services. The depression of the 1930s and World War II transformed the political environment, however, and made government initiatives more acceptable and popular. Although these events were not unique to the Midwest, government activism had important regional effects. Above all, it reaffirmed the roles of agriculture and industry in the regional economy and the importance of workers' voice in the operation of economic institutions.

The new public role evolved haphazardly in the 1930s and 1940s. It first emerged in agriculture, where politicians, government officials, and most farmers embraced a conception of "parity" that extended beyond the proposals of the 1920s. Government policy toward industry, on the other hand, was confused and inconsistent until World War II, when a government-industry alliance based on mass production and labor reform became an essential feature of mobilization. The war effort inspired renewed confidence and unprecedented acceptance of an institutionalized workers' voice in industry and society. Chapter 6 examines the midwestern response to depression while chapter 7 focuses on the war and postwar years.

6.

A New Deal for Midwestern Workers, 1930–1939

The collapse of the economy during the winter of 1929–1930 inaugurated the most severe recession of the century and a succession of traumatic experiences for midwestern workers. The onset of depression meant disastrously low prices for farmers; irregular employment for industrial employees; and doubts about the promise of scientific agriculture, systematic management, and mass production. Most efforts to address the causes or effects of the depression looked to government for greater direction and regulation. Not that there was greatly increased confidence in politicians or public administrators; government was to ameliorate the plight of individual citizens and create a new setting for private activity. This approach had many applications and wide-ranging effects. However, its most notable effect was neither novel nor exotic. Government intervention encouraged a revival of the labor movement and a sustained contest to define an institutional workers' voice.

An Agrarian Revolution

Midwestern farmers of the early 1930s had good reason to feel beleaguered. Despite their embrace of science and efficiency, they had lost ground to their urban neighbors in the preceding decades. Their numbers had continued to fall—to 17 percent of the paid labor force by 1930. Though the typical farmstead continued to have a greater array of machinery than most other workplaces, the living conditions of most farm families were deficient by the standards of city residents. Farm homes that did not have electric power, a large majority until the 1940s, resembled the poorest urban homes.[1] More serious, though less visible, was the financial legacy of the war and postwar years. Crop and livestock prices recovered sufficiently in the 1920s to alleviate the debt crisis, but many Corn Belt farmers were highly and precariously leveraged. A price decline would wipe out their profits and threaten their equity.

115

By 1930 most farmers agreed that their salvation lay in political action. Government already provided extensive research services, educational programs, and a variety of other benefits and subsidies. But farm activists demanded McNary-Haugen or some other price-fixing scheme. In 1925 farm groups with Midwest constituencies formed a Corn Belt Committee to lobby for government action. The tepid Agricultural Marketing Act of 1929 split the committee: conservatives led by the Farm Bureau supported the government program, while radicals, mostly members of the relatively small Farmers Union, held out for a more ambitious plan based on the cost of production—in effect, a guarantee against failure.

The drastic deflation of 1930–1932 greatly strengthened the radicals. By 1932, prices of the principal midwestern crops were one-half to one-tenth the farmer's cost of production, at least as farm leaders computed it.[2] Farmers everywhere suffered. A prominent Iowan, Elmer Powers, bitterly noted that unemployed city workers on work-relief projects had newer overalls than the farmers who supported them.[3] The farm bankruptcy rate in the Midwest doubled between 1931 and 1933, in line with national trends. But in Minnesota and Iowa it was much higher. In 1932 and 1933 the number of bankruptcies per thousand farms in those states was double the midwestern average. Almost 8 percent of Iowa farms changed hands due to foreclosure in 1933.[4] Not surprisingly, the lobbying programs of the 1920s gave way to a more militant approach, epitomized by the Farmers Holiday Association and its flamboyant leader, Milo Reno, the president of the Iowa Farmers Union. Formed in the spring of 1932 as the farm crisis mounted, the FHA sought to use protests and "holidays" to force government to adopt a cost-of-production subsidy plan.

The FHA was more akin to the alliance groups of the 1880s than to the farmers' associations of the twentieth century. It was decentralized and uncoordinated; Reno had no real authority, and the various state groups operated independently. Membership in the "national" organization was negligible. The FHA had only indirect contacts with the Cooperative Milk Pool, the Wisconsin organization that used FHA tactics to even greater effect. Historians of the protest movement emphasize two additional points: the FHA and the Cooperative Milk Pool drew their membership from the ranks of well-to-do farmers—corn, hog, and dairy producers in Iowa and Minnesota and dairy farmers in Wisconsin—and relatively few participants in FHA activities understood Reno's emphasis on political action. Farm militants believed that their collective acts would produce immediate, positive results. Reno proved to be a shrewder judge of the situation.

The FHA relied on two tactics: withholding actions and "penny auctions" or other efforts to disrupt the sale of farm property. Withholding actions, conducted sporadically from the summer of 1932 to the fall of 1933, attracted wide press coverage. Dairy farmers were at the forefront of the movement. Their attacks on dairy trucks came to symbolize the farm protest movement. Penny auctions, however, were far more prevalent and effective. Groups of farmers would gather at the auction site and intimidate bidders. In effect they sought to punish the individual or institution that had forced the foreclosure. By early 1933 most insurance companies had suspended foreclosure proceedings and twenty-five state legislatures (including Ohio, Illinois, Iowa, Minnesota, and Michigan) passed laws temporarily ending them. Direct action seemed to work.

The center of the farm revolt was Plymouth County, Iowa, in the northwest corner of the state. An informal band of tenants, fearful of losing their patrimony through the foreclosure of family properties, waged a campaign of intimidation and terror over the winter of 1932–1933. They battled sheriff's deputies on several occasions and were responsible for at least one fatality. But their most dramatic and offensive action occurred on April 27 at Le Mars, when they dragged a judge from his courtroom, took him to a remote area, and placed a rope around his neck. Apparently impressed with his courage in the face of death, they finally relented and freed him. Iowa's governor called out the National Guard the following day, but the Plymouth County violence continued for several months.[5]

FHA activities initially succeeded because they tapped a strong undercurrent of rural unrest and won the sympathy of many urban residents. Pictures of farmers overturning milk cans, attacking deputies, and confronting judges dramatically illustrated the farmers' plight. Midwestern governors typically expressed support for protesting farmers. Even when they had to call out the National Guard to keep order, they were restrained in their public criticism. The mounting vandalism gradually eroded public sympathy, and the Le Mars incident alienated many supporters. Yet farmer lawlessness hardly explains the rapid decline of the FHA and the Milk Pool after mid-1933. By 1935 only isolated pockets of the midwestern farm rebellion remained.

What accounted for the dramatic eclipse of the FHA and other protest groups? The response of federal government officials was unquestionably the critical factor. Reno had correctly gauged the public mood. Whereas most farm protesters hoped to influence markets and courts, he understood that the real objective was to persuade politicians to rewrite the rules of the agricultural marketplace. Although Reno and his followers never achieved their goal of guaranteed production costs, their achievements exceeded those of any other occupational interest group, including organized labor. Moreover, their successes came at the beginning of the New Deal, when public intervention had the greatest impact. By the mid-1930s a midwestern farm recovery was well underway. In addition to higher prices and incomes, it brought permanent changes in farm operations, as tractors displaced most of the remaining horses and improved seed and fertilizers increased output.[6] No less important was the change in the political climate. With their own situation secure, farmers increasingly looked askance at the demands of other groups. In 1938, for example, Wisconsin farmers abandoned the Progressives, the state's New Deal party, to vote en masse for the Republicans because of hostility to union efforts to organize employees of creameries and farm cooperatives.[7] The farmers' growing conservatism was the single most important factor in the rightward political turn of the midwestern states at the end of the decade.

The New Deal farm program of 1933–1935 reflected a variety of intellectual and political influences, including the FHA and Milk Pool campaigns. Although the details of the legislation are beyond the scope of this study, three broad efforts addressed the anxieties of midwestern farmers. First were market-oriented "recovery" programs (notably the Agricultural Adjustment Act) that curtailed production and boosted farm prices. Government intervention directly or indirectly increased farmers' incomes at the expense of consumers and taxpayers. Second were financial initiatives that consolidated and extended public lending activities. Managed by the new Farm Credit Administration, short- and long-term loan programs increased competition among lenders and drove down credit costs to farmers.[8] More than the price support programs, they removed the specter of financial disaster that haunted midwestern farmers in the early 1930s. Third was the Rural Electrification Administration, created in 1935 to extend electrical service to farm homes.

Although consistent with other New Deal farm programs, the REA was a response to the disparity between middle-class life in the city and country rather than to the economic crisis. In effect, it closed a large and embarrassing gap in the agricultural extension effort. By the late 1930s government agents eagerly promoted electricity as an essential ingredient in the modernization of farm life. Between 17 percent (Minnesota) and 62 percent (Michigan) of midwestern farms had electric power by 1940. Besides electric lights, farmers, like their urban counterparts, purchased irons, radios, and washing machines. A small but growing number of dairy and poultry farmers also purchased electrical machinery. In interviews a half-century later, farm wives recalled their excitement over their new appliances.[9]

The impact of the other major New Deal farm initiative, the rural-poverty program, is more difficult to estimate. For the nearly half-million midwestern farm families that earned no more than a semiskilled factory worker, the depression was more than a debt crisis.[10] Because their assets were so meager and their production so low, they had little to gain from the recovery or FCA programs. In earlier days they might have abandoned farming and looked for work in town, but that prospect was unattractive in the depression years. Their only immediate hope was to obtain resources that would enable them to compete more effectively. New Deal programs with that objective probably had little effect before 1937, when the Farm Security Administration consolidated the efforts of several earlier agencies. FSA activities in the Midwest featured loan programs to "rehabilitate" farmers and enable them to purchase land. In Illinois, for example, FSA helped 22,000 farmers buy seed, fertilizer, and tools and helped another 500 buy land.[11] By most measures FSA programs were well run and enthusiastically received. They were also a gauge of the shifting perspectives of rural workers in the 1930s. Well-to-do farmers who had demanded cost-of-production guarantees in 1932 and 1933 condemned FSA activities as socialistic in the late 1930s. The Illinois Agricultural Association, the largest and most powerful state farm bureau, led the attack.[12] The comparatively late arrival of the FSA and the mounting opposition of groups like the Farm Bureau meant that World War II mobilization, and not the FSA or other poverty agencies, would address the problems of farm families that had not successfully weathered the storm of depression.

The Urban Crisis

The industrial collapse of the early 1930s was particularly severe in the Midwest.[13] It included a drastic fall in raw materials prices, which decimated the mining industries; reduced consumption, which led to cuts in production and greater competition between producers; a virtual cessation of construction; and a financial contraction that resulted in bank failures and declining tax receipts. The fall in employment was one of the most dramatic measures of these problems. Table 6–1 summarizes the experiences of midwestern workers in the 1930s. It compares total nonagricultural employment and manufacturing employment in 1929 with that of 1932, the trough of the depression; 1937, the peak of the initial recovery; and 1939, the first year of the World War II boom. In general, the midwestern states experienced the greatest decline and the slowest recovery of any region.

Table 6–1 also emphasizes the diversity of the midwestern experience. Minnesota and Iowa fared relatively well, though nonagricultural employment was less important in those states than in the rest of the region. Michigan was the outlier; a severe decline, particularly in manufacturing, was followed by a strong recovery, reflecting the role of the auto industry in the state's economy and the increased market share of the Big Three. The decline or demise of the other auto manufacturers contributed to the slow recovery of manufacturing in Indiana and Ohio, though workers in these states could be thankful they did not live in Wisconsin, which experienced the deepest and most persistent industrial decline.

In the Midwest, as elsewhere, manufacturing was the heart of the problem.[14] The irony was that midwestern industrialists had done everything right:

Table 6–1
Nonagricultural Employment, 1930–1939
(1929 = 100)

	1932		1937		1939	
	Total	*Mfg.*	*Total*	*Mfg.*	*Total*	*Mfg.*
Minnesota	78	64	103	84	103	82
Iowa	82	62	96	79	100	86
Michigan	80	58	113	121	102	100
Indiana	65	53	92	94	88	86
Illinois	68	52	94	87	92	82
Ohio	67	53	96	89	91	80
Wisconsin	67	51	98	86	94	80

Source: John Joseph Wallis, "Employment in the Great Depression: New Data and Hypothesis," *Explorations in Economic History* 26 (1989): 65–70.

they had been innovative, technologically progressive, leaders in the management movement. Their efforts had transformed the regional economy, created hundreds of thousands of jobs, raised living standards, and contributed to the conviction that urban society was superior to the countryside. Even their most caustic critics conceded that they had played their economic role effectively. By the end of the decade, academic critics began to suggest that they had been too efficient, creating technological unemployment and contributing to long-term economic stagnation.[15] Like the farmers, industrialists and industrial workers of the 1930s seemed to be victims of their earlier successes.

If factory workers were the most conspicuous victims of the depression, they were not alone. In Chicago, the decline of manufacturing and construction cost the jobs of 40 percent of blue-collar men by 1931. In Williamson County, Illinois, a coal-mining center, unemployment approached 60 percent of the labor force in early 1932. Michigan copper miners shared their plight.[16] Regardless of occupation, African American workers lost the footholds they had gained in the midwestern economy. In Columbus, Ohio, formerly a city of opportunity, three-quarters of black workers were unemployed in 1930; in Milwaukee, more than 50 percent were still jobless two years later. In other communities the situation was similar. Throughout Ohio the black unemployment rate was more than twice the white rate.[17]

Nor were white-collar workers immune to distress. The plight of Chicago workers was unimaginable by earlier standards. Between 1930 and 1931 white-collar unemployment rose to 18 percent for men and 16 percent for women. Although the economic plight of industrial workers was far worse, the psychological effect on formerly secure, affluent white-collar employees was probably greater.[18]

Apart from its direct impact, the decline in service-industry opportunities meant that wives and children had little opportunity to supplement family incomes. Most contemporary surveys reported only minor differences between the employment rates of wives of unemployed men and wives of employed factory workers, clerks, and professionals. Unskilled women and children were no more attractive to employers than their husbands and fathers. One exception was domestic service: with the decline in wages and prices, more affluent families could afford maids, gardeners, and chauffeurs.[19]

Unemployment, or the prospect of unemployment, forcefully encouraged family belt-tightening. Thanks to the farm depression, most families were able to afford meat, vegetables, and fruits.[20] The automobile also remained a staple of midwestern life, though *new* cars were less common and gasoline sales fell. Home repairs, furniture, and clothing purchases were more likely to be postponed. Family-budget studies suggest that teenagers, the most conspicuous beneficiaries of the affluence of the 1920s, bore a disproportionate share of the burden of retrenchment in the less glamorous 1930s. Like their parents, they reverted to the living standards of an earlier age, albeit with access to automobiles, movie theatres, and other conveniences that had appeared in the interim.[21]

With the decline in employment opportunities, many developments of the early twentieth century suddenly became irrelevant or counterproductive. By 1931 boys had at least as much incentive to remain in high school as girls. Many firms reduced or abolished personnel departments and cut back training and apprenticeship programs. Job holders conspired to reduce competition. Reinvigorated marriage bars restricted opportunities for women; higher professional standards reduced white-collar competition; craft workers revealed "a deep streak of exclusivity"; and retirement gained new popularity.[22] An extreme example of this pattern was the fate of Mexican immigrant workers. In the early 1930s Detroit officials organized a voluntary repatriation program with the cooperation of the Mexican government. In the Calumet steel towns, more forceful measures prevailed. Inland Steel had imported Mexican laborers as strikebreakers in 1919 and employed more than twenty-five hundred by the mid-1920s. The Mexicans' association with strikebreaking and the *colonia's* reputation for vice and crime made them obvious targets. To ease relief expenses local officials began paying transportation costs for those who would voluntarily return to Mexico. In 1931 the local American Legion orchestrated a more ambitious campaign of involuntary repatriation. More than a thousand workers had left by mid-1932.[23]

The most obvious antidote for unemployment, however, was unemployment relief. Between 1930 and 1932 every midwestern state and virtually every city organized a relief program based on methods that had been used in previous recessions. Most of them relied on business leadership and private fund-raising. Had economic conditions improved, even marginally, in 1931 or 1932, these efforts might have become models of flexible and effective voluntarism. In fact, mounting unemployment made them additional symbols of failure and decline. The Chicago and Detroit programs reflected the weakness of municipal government in those cities. By 1932 systematic thievery had became a de facto substitute for relief in the region's largest cities.[24] More typical was the experience of Fort Wayne, Indiana. As unemployment increased, leaders of the Fort Wayne Chamber of Commerce, haunted by the "specter of higher taxation," organized and administered a privately financed program that provided jobs for over three thousand citizens during its first six months. Despite this impressive record, and a reputation as "one of the best local relief organizations," the Fort Wayne effort could not meet the demand for its services. Fund drives in 1931 and 1932 fell short of their targets, forcing greater reliance on local government. Mounting relief expenditures, public opposition to taxation, and tax delinquencies forced draconian reductions in public expenditures. In early 1933 county officials began to pay relief recipients in script, which recipients could use for tax payments and other purchases. Finally, the Civil Works Administration provided federal dollars for a new work-relief program.[25]

How did urban workers react to this situation? Most contemporary accounts emphasize their feelings of confusion and failure. In any case, it was difficult to do anything without money. Unemployed workers engaged in a variety of self-help enterprises, as much to keep themselves occupied as to supplement savings or relief payments. Directly or indirectly inspired by the back-to-the-land philosopher George Borsodi and his supporters in Dayton, Ohio, they emphasized barter and cooperation. In Fort Wayne, for example, the Allen County Unemployment Association, with more than five hundred members, contracted to do farm work and home repairs in return for food and the use of unoccupied buildings. It also organized social and educational programs aimed at "un-American ideologies."[26] But these expedients, alone or in combination, were rarely sufficient to maintain the living standards of jobless workers or banish the threat of foreclosure. A sense of despair grew.

Several organizations attempted to mobilize the unemployed. Unlike the self-help groups, which were loosely organized, the Unemployed Councils, Unemployed Leagues, and Workers' Committee were creatures of the Communist party, the Conference for Progressive Labor Action, and the Socialist party respectively. Communists organized Councils in many midwestern cities in late 1930 to oppose evictions and agitate for public relief. The Chicago

Council was probably the most formidable of the local unemployed groups. Its legion of "black bugs" made rent evictions virtually impossible in the south side Black Belt. The Minneapolis Council formed block committees of militant housewives. Marches and public demonstrations were common in other cities.[27] The Detroit Council's March 1932 protest at Ford's Rouge plant, which left four dead and many wounded, became one of the celebrated incidents of the early depression period. A melodramatic funeral ceremony and procession through downtown Detroit graphically symbolized the callousness of the city's employers and the restiveness of the unemployed. Ironically this incident did little for the Council, whose success encouraged other radical groups to intensify their efforts to undermine the Communists.[28]

The Unemployed Leagues and Committees had many similar features. The Leagues were concentrated in Ohio, and at their peak claimed 100,000 members, many in small towns. Guided by CPLA leader and theoretician A. J. Muste and a small coterie of associates, local Leagues encouraged self-help activities and protests against evictions and foreclosures. Facing increased competition for members and attention, Muste and his followers called a convention in mid-1933 to perfect a new, more centralized structure. Meeting in Columbus, Ohio, the delegates included Socialists, Communists, and others who "combined a radical approach to the problems of the unemployed with extreme patriotism and anti-communism." They soon realized that they had little in common except hostility to Muste and his henchmen. When a fight broke out the convention turned into "a nativist nightmare."[29] While Muste retained his influence in the Toledo area, most of the Leagues collapsed.

The Workers' Committees were concentrated in Chicago. Organized by Socialists and liberals associated with the Socialists' League for Industrial Democracy, they claimed sixty local groups and sixty thousand members by early 1932. Their popularity "overwhelmed" the LID, which shifted its focus from public education to direct action.[30] The Committees were particularly successful in pressuring the city's relief bureaucracy. Because of this record, they survived into the New Deal years, when they organized public relief workers.

Apart from their services to the unemployed, the Councils, Leagues, and Committees emphasized the possibilities of the moment. By representing the unemployed in their relations with bankers, landlords, merchants, and government officials, they demonstrated that the poor could be organized and that it was possible to improve the lives of the unemployed even if the economy did not improve. Their experiences foreshadowed the revival of the labor movement in the following years.

The flurry of governmental initiatives that followed the advent of the Roosevelt administration in March 1933 quickly overshadowed other antidepression efforts. Intended to revive the economy, their most important effect was to alter the institutional context in which workers operated. They included economic relief measures that provided assistance to the unemployed and poor, loan programs for homeowners, social insurance plans, "recovery" measures, and labor legislation that expanded the role of government in employment relationships.

Because of high levels of unemployment in the post-1933 recovery years, relief continued to be an important economic and political issue. But the scope of the relief effort and its management changed. Reflecting the popularity of work relief, New Dealers combined a federal-state system of public assistance (the FERA from 1933 to 1935 and the categorical assistance programs of the Social Security Act after 1935) for unemployable citizens with a series of work-relief programs, notably the Civil Works Administration of 1933–1934 and the Works Progress Administration of 1935–1942. Both types of relief were important in the Midwest. In late 1935, for example, 1.2 million Ohioans, nearly 20 percent of the population, were receiving some form of assistance.[31] Conservatives agonized over the costs, and employment experts worried about the lack of job training. Industrial workers, however, were more concerned about the modest stipends and inability of thousands of individuals to find places on the WPA rolls. The Social Security Act aggravated the situation by narrowing the definition of dependency and forcing the able-bodied who did not obtain work relief to rely on the mercies of local governments. The recession of 1937–1938 underlined the shortcomings of the government effort. Only later did the tendency of relief to create a semipermanent class of dependents become apparent.[32]

Apart from its economic importance, relief helped redefine the character of government and politics. The growth of Democratic majorities in industrial cities was highly correlated with work-relief expenditures. In Chicago, for example, two-party competition gave way to a one-party, machine-dominated political system in the 1930s. The political maturation of new immigrant groups, symbolized by the election of Anton Cermack in 1931, was the first step in this transformation, but New Deal programs greatly accelerated it. Unemployment relief was the critical ingredient in the wholesale shift of black voters from the Republican to the Democratic camp.[33] In Indiana, which had the most decentralized government of the pre-depression years, relief became a pretext for centralizing power in the state. In towns such as Ironton, Ohio, relief agencies became de facto courts of appeal from the decisions of local officials.[34]

Far less visible and controversial were New Deal programs to preserve the assets of urban homeowners. The Home Owners' Loan Act of 1933 protected them against foreclosure and made home ownership more attractive. The foreclosure rate dropped after 1933, and the direct costs of the program were negligible; unlike the relief effort, homeowners' subsidies produced almost no political opposition.

A complementary series of New Deal programs attempted to stimulate economic recovery by creating producers' cartels in industries that had suffered from debilitating competition. The Agricultural Adjustment and National Industrial Recovery Acts of 1933 were the best-known examples of this effort, but a number of regulatory measures adopted in the mid-1930s, after the Supreme Court had ruled the AAA and the NIRA unconstitutional, preserved the spirit and mechanism of the original initiatives in energy, transportation, and agriculture. These laws had a substantial impact on employees. By lessening price competition, government inadvertently altered the relations between employers and employees in regulated industries. This change proved to be as important as formal collective bargaining legislation in encouraging the growth of union membership.

The most controversial of New Deal initiatives, however, were labor laws that encouraged collective bargaining and regulated wages, hours, and child labor. In the 1930s their symbolism was probably as important as their substance. In effect they invited workers and union leaders to behave as if the economy were prosperous and growing.

Revival of the Labor Movement

One of the most dramatic developments of the New Deal era was the sudden, unanticipated revival of the labor movement and the rapid growth of collective bargaining. While political personalities and events influenced this development, they were not the only stimuli to union activity. Union growth began with the economic recovery dating from the spring of 1933. By the time the National Recovery Administration's codes of fair competition went into effect and a mechanism for enforcing their collective bargaining provisions had been created, half or more of the new union members of the recovery period had been enrolled. During the following years government labor policy was constantly in flux. The conflicting approaches of Congress, the Supreme Court, and the Roosevelt administration made it difficult to know at any given time what the law was or would be in the future. Unlike the farm program, the impact of New Deal labor law was highly problematic.[35]

The drama of the union revival reflected a central fact: union growth in the 1930s occurred sporadically, with losses erasing gains through most of the decade. In 1933–1935 the union experience closely paralleled the rise and fall of the NRA. The labor movement enlisted millions of new members, probably reaching its peak in early 1934. The atmosphere was buoyant; employer opposition was negligible. Militants became active outside the plant, organizing consumer cooperatives and local labor parties. Reality intruded in mid-

1934. Employer resistance stiffened and unions' weaknesses became apparent. Wholesale defections in 1935 wiped out the membership gains of the preceding eighteen months. The years from 1935 to 1938 saw only modest increases. Employers were now strongly hostile; government was impotent, at least until the Supreme Court's Jones & Laughlin decision upholding the Wagner Act in April 1937; the labor movement was torn by factionalism; and the severe recession of 1937–1938 made new organization impossible. With the economic revival of 1938–1939, the NLRB became a significant force in industrial relations. Competition between the AFL and CIO encouraged aggressive organizing, and many urban employers became more flexible. Unions grew rapidly between 1939 and 1941, matured organizationally, and became, by the eve of Pearl Harbor, semipermanent fixtures of the national and midwestern economies.

Although the revival of the economy in 1933 made the industrial recovery program obsolete, the recollections of the preceding years were too vivid not to influence public policy. Midwestern executives who should have devoted their energies to expansion and modernization spent their time on the ill-fated "codes." In the rubber industry, for example, tire manufacturers negotiated for six months to produce a code that was unsatisfactory to everyone, while the retail dealers were unable to reach any agreement until the summer of 1934.[36] Other industries experienced similar horrors. A major effect of this activity was to divert attention from Section 7A, which assured workers the right to bargain with employers and established minimum working conditions. Preoccupied with production and prices and committed to a new regime of cooperation, employers conceded measures that they would have fought and probably defeated under other circumstances.

In this circuitous fashion government encouraged the revival of the labor movement. The results included the century's greatest influx of union members and a labor movement that came closer to representing the occupational distribution of nonagricultural workers than at any prior time. During World War I public policy had permitted or encouraged union growth, but the gains were concentrated in mining, manufacturing, and transportation. In 1933 and 1934, as the newspapers of any midwestern industrial city will attest, the union impulse was broader. In Terre Haute, Indiana, for example, the revival of 1933 included the organization of workers in dairies, lumberyards, commercial greenhouses, hotels, restaurants, and public utilities as well as factories and mines.[37] In Akron, Ohio, it embraced gas station attendants, retail store clerks, movie projectionists, and waiters and bartenders as well as rubber workers.[38] The exception was the building trades, which remained depressed throughout the region.

Still, it was the factory workers' organizations that attracted the greatest attention and became emblematic of the broader phenomenon. In city after city, manufacturing workers joined existing unions or formed new organizations. The most active workers, predictably, were individuals in skilled or strategically important jobs. In the auto industry, three groups accounted for most of the new memberships: highly skilled tool and die makers, body-plant employees, and employees of small and midsized manufacturers, whose precarious economic conditions made them vulnerable to worker pressure.[39] At Studebaker, for example, organizers encountered no resistance; the near-bankrupt company could not have survived a prolonged strike.[40] In the tire industry, the tire builders took the lead in virtually every factory. They were most successful in midsized firms that depended on a single large plant.[41] Skilled workers also were disproportionately represented in the new steelworkers' locals.

The vast majority of recruits joined AFL organizations, despite the Federation's poor record in the 1920s. One reason was the AFL's new aura of respectability, a result of its association with the Roosevelt administration and the recovery program. Another was its use of "federal" (or directly affiliated) local unions to enlist industrial employees. Low initiation fees, modest dues, indefinite jurisdictions, and minimal bureaucracies, all characteristics of the federal locals, suited the limited budgets and pretensions of industrial workers. The rapid growth of the federal unions created serious tensions within the AFL, but they were only dimly visible in 1933. Non-AFL organizations, such as the extravagantly named Independent Union of All Workers, a union of packinghouse and other workers in Austin, Minnesota, probably accounted for no more than 10 percent of union recruits in 1933 and 1934.

Workers who sought to take advantage of the new political and economic climate had one other choice, the company union, which experienced a surge of popularity similar to that of 1917–1919. Large firms felt compelled to give lip service to Section 7A but not to submit to AFL opportunism. Many, including a large number that had never shown an interest in their employees' voice, embraced the company union as an answer to their dilemma. The organizations that appeared in 1933 and 1934 included a large and inconsequential group that soon collapsed and a minority that survived to become instruments of a renewed open shop campaign. The best known of the survivors was the Kohler Workers Association, formed by the Kohler Company of Sheboygan, Wisconsin, in September 1933, to compete with a new AFL federal local. The company's obvious partisanship led to a lockout and strike in July 1934 that dragged on for the rest of the decade. During the conflict, the KWA served as an auxiliary to the company's personnel department.[42]

The older company unions that represented the liberal thrust of the post–World War I personnel movement fared better. Representation plans at Goodyear, International Harvester, U.S. Rubber, Swift, and other midwestern companies were poised to take advantage of the new activism. As representatives of blue- and white-collar employees that also enjoyed close relations with employers, they seemed ideally suited to the new environment.

The rush to organize created a demand for leaders. The well-established company unions were equipped to meet this demand; the AFL, on the other hand, was extremely short-handed. The preceding decade had provided few opportunities for young activists, and the union revival of 1933 absorbed the energies of the most able men and women. When president William Green began to staff the new federal unions in the fall of 1933, he discovered that labor's cupboard was bare. There was one exception: the UMW. The continued decline of the coal industry in the 1930s and John L. Lewis's control of the UMW bureaucracy provided a centralized source of talent for organizing ventures in steel, meatpacking, and elsewhere. No other union had a comparable cadre of available leaders.

In the meantime anyone with a modicum of talent and ambition could achieve a position of responsibility. The spectrum ranged from the pugnacious James R. Hoffa, who began to organize delivery and warehouse workers in Detroit, to the soft-spoken Sherman H. Dalrymple, who became president of the large B. F. Goodrich federal local in Akron. One group, however, stood out: radicals of socialist, communist, or, less often, syndicalist, sympathies. Since the collapse of the Socialist party and the industrial union movement after World War I, leftists had been confined to a few isolated outposts. The Communists' Trade Union's Unity League, probably the most significant remnant of postwar radicalism, had organized a few clandestine locals and acquired a reputation for militancy as a result of strikes in Flint in 1930 and in Detroit in early 1933.[43] With the union upsurge of 1933, veterans of the TUUL's Auto Workers Union moved into AFL posts in Detroit and other cities. A notable example was Wyndham Mortimer, soon to be the highest-ranking Communist in the United Auto Workers. When he and several coworkers were unable to interest local AFL leaders in a campaign at the White Motor Company in Cleveland, he began to organize under AWU auspices. As his following grew, AFL officials changed their minds and urged him to accept a federal union charter.[44] Mortimer became the head of the White local and the dominant personality among the Cleveland autoworkers.

Though Communists filled a disproportionate share of leadership posts in the autoworkers and Iron Range locals that emerged in 1933 and 1934, they were only part of the radical influx. In Minneapolis, a Trotskyist group took over a struggling Teamsters local and made it the foundation of a campaign to revive the city's labor movement. In Toledo, Musteites won positions in the city's autoworkers union. In Austin, Minnesota, an IWW veteran formed the Independent Union of All Workers at the Hormel Company. The list could be extended ad infinitum.[45]

Was there a pattern to this activity? British and Irish immigrants, who dominated the tool and die makers locals in the Detroit area, and Finnish immigrants, who predominated in the miners locals in northern Michigan and Minnesota, consistently chose leftists as leaders. Southern migrants, who dominated the autoworkers locals in Cincinnati and the rubber workers locals in Akron, just as consistently rejected Socialists or Communists. But such distinctions are easily exaggerated. In the chaotic atmosphere of 1933 and 1934, political labels meant little, and any group could achieve some influence. The tactics of radical and antiradical union leaders were virtually indistinguishable. Regardless of background, ideology, or affiliation, they understood that their constituents viewed dues payments as investments in higher wages, freedom from managerial tyranny, and other benefits. Leaders were expected to produce tangible results.

By early 1934 it was apparent that Section 7A and the organizing surge of late 1933 meant less than many workers assumed. In many small towns employers fired union militants with apparent impunity. In large firms union representatives discovered that the "right" to bargain only led to fruitless discussions and that appeals to the NRA were unavailing. AFL leaders counseled patience. An unsuccessful strike by the Mechanics Educational Society of America, the powerful union of skilled autoworkers, in the fall of 1933 underlined their point.[46] Union leaders had to choose between an appearance of inaction and a likely repetition of the MESA experience.

Their answers clarified the costs of union membership. AFL representatives generally opted for delay, while local leaders often insisted on immediate gains, even if they had to be won on the picket line. Two famous midwestern conflicts of mid-1934, in Minneapolis and Toledo, led to violence, intervention by state authorities, and civic crises reminiscent of the war years. In both cases the unions won compromise settlements and survived.[47] Two lesser-known conflicts of the same period also underlined the risks and rewards of labor activism. In May 1934 agricultural workers in Hardin County, Ohio, inspired by the Toledo conflict, struck against low pay and poor working conditions. After a series of increasingly heated confrontations between the strikers, growers, and law-enforcement authorities, local residents forcibly transported the strikers to Michigan, ending the walkout and the union.[48] A few weeks later rubber workers at the General Tire Company in Akron staged a monthlong strike that featured the first sit-down and resulted in the first meaningful labor agreement in the industry's history.[49]

Clearly there was no easy or inexpensive way to achieve union goals. To some industrial workers the potential benefits of membership remained attractive. To a larger group the experiences of 1934 raised doubts. Crises in the auto and rubber industries in early 1935, which grew out of conflicts between AFL officials and frustrated rank and file leaders, confirmed those doubts. Most unions suffered substantial membership losses in 1935.

The conflicts of 1934 and 1935, together with the political and legal disintegration of the NRA, spurred Congress to adopt more comprehensive collective bargaining legislation. The new Wagner Act banned traditional anti-union activities, prohibited company unions, introduced winner-take-all employee elections and grants of "exclusive representation," and created a national regulatory agency with sweeping powers. The union collapse of 1934-1935 also provoked a wave of introspection in the AFL that had two significant results: the chartering of industrial unions for the auto and rubber industries and the emergence of the CIO under Lewis and his UMW subordinates. Tensions between old guard and industrial union leaders strongly influenced the membership revival of 1936–1937.

Industrial Relations in Transition

Although historians often identify the passage of the Wagner Act and the emergence of the CIO as the beginnings of a new era of industrial relations, their significance was less obvious at that time. To most observers, government had aggravated an already difficult situation. In contrast to agriculture, where antidepression measures had reduced discontent, industry was beset with tensions that either had not existed or had not been apparent in the 1920s and early 1930s. During the second half of the decade, these conflicts created an impression of irreconcilable antagonism. Though this situation was not unique to the Midwest, it was arguably more severe in the Midwest than in other regions. Certainly the incidents that shaped the national consciousness of labor conflict were disproportionately midwestern. The very inconclusiveness of most of the disputes emphasized the severity of the region's labor crisis.

Although favorable economic conditions continued to mid-1937, union-management relations deteriorated rapidly after mid-1935. One measure of this change was the collapse of the company union movement. Although many post-1933 organizations were moribund by 1935, even the best-established company unions faced difficulties. The dramatic end of the Goodyear Industrial Assembly, during a major strike in February and March 1936, was indicative of their plight. At the beginning of the conflict, the Assembly had the support of at least 40 percent of Goodyear workers and overshadowed its AFL rival. By the end of the strike in March, the Assembly was dead. The United Rubber Workers local (the old AFL federal union) had won the allegiance of most Goodyear employees, while a rear guard of Assembly loyalists formed a quasi-secret society to terrorize the URW. In the polarized environment of 1936, there was no room for organizations devoted to labor-management cooperation.[50] Similar but less-dramatic changes occurred in many firms. By the late 1930s most surviving company unions (recast as "independent" unions after the Jones & Laughlin decision) were closer to the Kohler Workers Association than the Industrial Assembly.

There were other revealing indicators of the new environment. In the aftermath of the Goodyear strike, Alfred Winslow Jones, a Columbia University graduate student working under Robert S. Lynd, conducted a pioneering survey of public attitudes in Akron. Published in 1941, *Life, Liberty and Property* documented the existence of class divisions based on occupation and union activity. CIO members consistently scored at one extreme on Jones's scale, but they were closer to middle-income professionals and merchants than the group at the other extreme, the big-business elite. Corporate managers were the most ideologically homogeneous, isolated group in the community.[51] In large and medium-sized cities employer attitudes had little impact outside the workplace. In small towns, however, industrialists often were able to enlist public authorities in anti-union activities. In 1933 and 1934 AFL organizers who ventured into such communities had often faced a hostile public. After 1935 they confronted paramilitary groups assisted by local police. Threats, beatings, kidnapings, and evictions became commonplace. Small midwestern industrial towns were as dangerous for union organizers of the late 1930s as they had been in the 1880s and 1890s.[52]

Deteriorating labor-management relations were a critical factor in the emergence of the era's most famous expression of worker militancy, the sit-down strike. The creation of the United Automobile Workers and the United Rubber Workers in mid-1935 may have been a turning point in the evolution of the labor movement, but initially the new unions had little influence. Both began with a handful of active members and virtually no treasury. Union leaders started to rebuild from the grass roots. Their fortunes changed in late 1935, when URW militants began to use sit-down strikes to protest anti-union policies. A series of sit-downs at Goodyear precipitated the great strike of early 1936. The union victory created a sense of cause and effect: sit-downs had caused the union's triumph. Militant workers grasped the potential of the sit-down.

Still, the sit-down movement, which created almost as many problems for union leaders as it did for employers, might have died in early 1936 except for a small group of Goodyear militants. These men, numbering fifty or fewer, were low-seniority tire builders on the night shift; they were young, rebellious, and hostile to authority. Their leader, Charles Lesley, was a bully with a checkered past. In the months after the strike, Lesley and his allies were responsible for more than a hundred incidents, including many sit-downs. Under normal conditions they would have been dismissed. But poststrike conditions in the plant were far from normal. Company managers were uncertain about their course, and union leaders were alert to any provocation. As a consequence, Lesley and his followers had de facto immunity from reprisals. As the level of conflict rose, CIO leaders became alarmed. Fearful of losing one of their most notable inroads in mass production industry, they appointed Lesley to the CIO staff and dispatched him to the Siberia of rural Indiana, where he performed capably under difficult circumstances. His removal helped calm the situation at Goodyear but did not prevent the spread of the sit-down. In late December Fisher Body workers in Cleveland refused to work, paralyzing production. Within hours Flint Fisher Body employees sat down, forcing the UAW to act. The General Motors sit-down, the greatest midwestern strike of the 1930s, had begun.[53]

The General Motors strike and its aftermath reinforced the lessons of the Akron sit-down movement. Rank-and-file militants forced the hands of union leaders, who had to abandon their gradualistic approach. To their surprise, their resources were more than adequate. With minimal preparation they created an effective strike organization, attracted new supporters, countered the company's legal and public relations maneuvers, and took advantage of the favorable political climate in Michigan.[54] The contract that John L. Lewis concluded with the leaders of the world's largest corporation on February 11, 1937, was a symbolic breakthrough for industrial unionism and a landmark in the history of auto-industry labor relations, though its substantive provisions were modest. The UAW still faced many challenges, but it was infinitely stronger and more self-confident. The conflict had been a make-or-break test that the UAW passed with high marks.

During the spring and summer of 1937, UAW leaders rode the wave of worker activism, utilizing sit-downs to win contracts at Chrysler and a host of smaller firms. The UAW grew proportionately faster in 1937 than in any other year. But union leaders also understood the costs of their tactics, especially in public and political support. By the summer they began to curb the rank-and-file movement; by the fall, as public opinion shifted decisively against sit-downs and increasingly against the labor movement, they began to work actively to stop the disruptions.[55] Like the penny auctions and other farm protests of 1932–1933, the sit-downs had initially impressed many people as a legitimate response to the inequities of the depression era. But the farmers' timing had been better. By 1937 many nonparticipants, including many industrial workers, saw the sit-downs and other forms of union militancy as a zero-sum game: the unionists' gains would come at their expense.

The other major midwestern union initiative of 1936–1937, the CIO campaign to organize the steel industry, differed in many respects. In 1936 John L. Lewis took over the moribund Amalgamated Association of Iron and Steel Workers, installed Philip Murray as the head of a Steelworkers Organizing Committee (SWOC), and launched a highly centralized campaign to organize the industry. In 1936 the SWOC effort focused on U.S. Steel, a judicious choice. Despite its reputation as an open shop bastion, U.S. Steel was more vulnerable than the major auto and auto-parts companies. Its lethargic management was probably incapable of any vigorous action. The company unions it had introduced during the NRA period had become increasingly assertive; in the Calumet region they had become essentially independent organizations before the CIO arrived. Murray's principal challenge was to enlist their leaders.[56] SWOC organizers gradually won over the company union leaders, mostly skilled workers, with promises of aggressive collective bargaining. At the same time they established ties to ethnic leaders and organizations in order to attract the less skilled. By early 1937 they had generated rank-and-file enthusiasm despite the absence of a rank-and-file movement. The March 1937 U.S. Steel agreement, which recognized SWOC without a strike, was graphic testimony to their achievement.

SWOC efforts to organize the other large steel companies ("Little Steel") in the spring of 1937 were less successful. Led by Republic Steel, the Little Steel companies were strongly anti-union. Their hostility, however, had a nineteenth-century flavor. None of the Little Steel firms had extensive personnel operations; only ARMCO among the midwestern companies had a company union. In opposing SWOC, Little Steel managers also had several old-fashioned advantages, including growing public antipathy to the labor movement and Ohio Democratic Governor Martin Davey's desire to head the conservative wing of the Democratic party. The antipathy of the Chicago police to the CIO was a bonus that they probably did not anticipate.

Clearly Murray and his organizers had their work cut out for them. Buoyed by the U.S. Steel contract, they made considerable progress in the Mahoning Valley and in the Calumet region. Since the companies had adopted the wage and hour provisions of the U.S. Steel contract, union recognition was the major issue. And since the employers would never voluntarily agree to a contract, a strike was inevitable. It began in late May 1937 and paralyzed operations in Youngstown and Indiana Harbor and greatly curtailed them in Chicago; in Cleveland, Warren, Canton, and Massillon, Ohio; and in Monroe, Michigan. More than thirty thousand steelworkers joined the strike. Most accounts of the Little Steel strike have emphasized the employers' aggressiveness in opposing the strike, especially their reliance on the "Mohawk Valley formula" to mobilize opposition to the SWOC. As James Baughman has noted, however, this interpretation greatly overstates the companies' ability to control their environment.[57]

In reality most steel towns were too large and complex for the kinds of tactics that succeeded in smaller communities. The strikers had substantial community backing at the beginning of the conflict, including the support of many public officials and newspaper editors. Only later, as the economic costs of the strike mounted, did the balance shift to the employers' side. The Memorial Day Massacre of May 30, 1937, when Chicago police killed ten demonstrators and wounded nearly a hundred others outside the Republic plant, reflected long-standing tensions between Irish and new immigrant neighborhoods in south Chicago as well as the company's ruthlessness. The Irish officers saw the pickets as a threat in and out of the plant.[58] The Chicago disaster hurt the strikers' cause because it reinforced, however illogically, the identification of the CIO with violence, but it had little impact in the Ohio towns where the struggle would be won or lost. Davey was also a serious problem, but his use of the Ohio National Guard to protect the mills after they reopened in late June was not the coup de grace. The fundamental obstacles to success were more mundane and familiar. The SWOC had too few members and too little support among the steelworkers. For most Little Steel employees, the strike raised the costs of union membership to unacceptable levels. As Baughman concludes: "The union never came close to victory."[59]

Within weeks of the collapse of the strike, the national recession emphasized the value of contracts that spelled out procedures for layoffs and reemployment. The collapse of the economy during the fall and winter of 1937 was more precipitous than the decline of the early 1930s and increased unemployment to three-quarters of the 1932 level. Even if WPA workers are excluded, the total was half that of 1932.[60] Industry was particularly hard hit and the Midwest, with its concentrations of durable goods manufacturers, bore the brunt of the decline. The UAW, at that time almost exclusively a midwestern organization, organized only 73 locals between 1937 and 1939 and lost 110 to dissolution; membership dropped at least 25 percent. The Rubber Workers losses were greater because of the simultaneous "decentralization" of the industry to nonunion communities in the South.[61] Despite these setbacks, the downturn was not comparable to the post–World War I recession. Many unions were better established, and the Wagner Act had begun to change the environment in which they operated.

The recession marked the end of the economic cycle that dated from the revival of early 1933 and the organizing cycle that paralleled it. The most notable change of the period had been the escalation of industrial conflict and the emergence of organized labor in the midwestern auto and auto-parts industries, the core of the industrial economy. The unions that appeared in those plants were necessarily innovators. Their leaders confronted unfamiliar questions: What role should organized labor play in mass production industry? How much influence could or should it exert over production and personnel management? What should it do to affect the economic and political environment in which collective bargaining took place? By 1939 they had formulated tentative answers that would serve as guidelines for union initiatives in the following years.

The Union Milieu

Unlike the unions of the World War I era, the organizations of the 1930s lasted long enough to have some impact on their members and on the communities in which they operated. They had other advantages as well: the collapse of many ethnic benefit societies in the early 1930s had created an institutional vacuum, while the repeal of Prohibition encouraged social activities based on public alcohol consumption.[62] But unions still had to win the workers' allegiance. Organizations of construction workers, printers, teachers, and other craft employees had always promoted shared ideas and values. But that function was more a result of the workers' common heritage and work environment than of union policy. The federal locals and industrial unions, on the other hand, had diverse memberships. They lacked the unifying work experiences of the craft groups and the shared sense of danger characteristic of miners. Differences in ethnicity, race, and religion compounded occupational distinctions. A common employer and a common union were often the workers' only bonds. Could industrial workers become "union-minded"?

Strikes and other conflicts influenced some workers, but a reputation for effectiveness was essential to success in the competitive environment of the late 1930s. AFL leaders had failed because they could not produce results. Were CIO leaders any better? The chaotic situation at the top of the UAW did not augur well for the most formidable midwestern union. The Steel and Packinghouse Workers Organizing Committees had the opposite problem. Their top leaders were appointed by Lewis and accountable only to him. A small group of insiders also ran the new Farm Equipment Workers, an offshoot of the SWOC. None of these organizations was comparable to the gangster-ridden Chicago Teamsters or other notorious AFL unions, but their structure and operations must have increased the wariness of many prospective members. Yet the real tests of effectiveness usually occurred at the local level. A large proportion of midwestern locals passed those tests with high marks. Regardless of other deficiencies, they attracted dedicated individuals to local leadership positions.

Judging from the available evidence, CIO local leaders were superior to the union officials of earlier days and to AFL contemporaries. A substantial proportion were idealists: employers accused them of fanaticism because they were not venal. They were also comparatively young.[63] The generation gap between AFL and CIO leaders probably accounted for other differences. CIO leaders were untainted by the defeats of the 1920s, more skeptical about the future of the economy, more distrustful of employers, and less deferential to elite society. Many of them were willing to work with Communists, Trotskyists, or other radicals. Altogether, they impressed most observers as aggressive and effective representatives of demanding constituencies.

The greatest threat to union power outside the workplace and the union hall was the poisonous relationship between the national AFL and the CIO. In the Midwest the conflict was unimportant until 1937. The Chicago Federation of Labor and the Milwaukee FTC, the region's most powerful central labor unions, encouraged industrial workers to organize, assisted federal locals and industrial unions, and worked with CIO organizations. CLUs in Cleveland, Columbus, Akron, and many other cities were equally congenial.[64] However, in May 1937, the AFL ordered central unions and state federations to expel CIO representatives. As CIO leaders moved to organize their own city and state councils, relations between the groups deteriorated.

The most critical internal issues were AFL authoritarianism and the Communist role in the industrial union councils. In 1937 national AFL leaders aggressively took control of the city and state organizations, attacking or expelling local officials who tried to maintain good relations with the CIO. Thereafter local leaders were expected to devote much of their energy to attacking the CIO. The Communist role in the CIO was an obvious target. Though numerically unimportant, Communists dominated several large UAW locals in Detroit and the Allis-Chalmers local in Milwaukee, the city's largest union. They held influential positions in the SWOC, Farm Equipment Workers, Packinghouse Workers, United Electrical Workers, and several minor CIO organizations. Their greatest influence, however, was in the industrial union councils, which were tangential to the interests of most workers and comparatively easy to manipulate. In Wisconsin and Minnesota, where the CIO was weak, Communists controlled the state IUCs and the city organizations in Milwaukee, Minneapolis, and Duluth.[65] Even in Michigan, where the CIO overshadowed the AFL, Communists held influential positions in the Michigan CIO. To AFL officials and anti-union zealots, their presence was proof of the subversive character of the CIO.

The Communist issue was especially disruptive in Wisconsin, where UAW factionalism set the stage for a broader ideological contest. Local UAW leaders associated with International president Homer Martin took the lead in attacking the state IUC and its most important base, Allis-Chalmers Local 248. Although the UAW divisions defied ideological labels, the Wisconsin conflict became a struggle between anti-Communists and Communists. Nor did the decline of the Martin faction in 1938 and 1939 end the controversy. AFL leaders, especially in Milwaukee, used it and the reputation of the state CIO to bolster their position and to dissuade many federal locals from affiliating with the CIO.[66]

Regardless of their associations, union leaders gave political activity a higher priority than in earlier years. In Minnesota and Wisconsin the state federations had long been associated with the Farmer-Labor party and the progressive wing of the Wisconsin Republican party (after 1934, the Progressive party). In other states they had worked with bipartisan groups to obtain favorable legislation. How would membership growth affect these arrangements? In each state organized labor became more active and influential, but in no state did it become the dominant interest group or even rival the farmers. Governors such as Floyd Olson and Elmer Benson in Minnesota, Philip La Follette in Wisconsin, and Frank Murphy in Michigan supported union interests and influenced the outcome of disputes. On the other hand, Paul McNutt of Indiana and Martin Davey of Ohio, both Democrats, were hostile to organized labor. McNutt broke the Terre Haute general strike of 1935, and Davey aggressively opposed the CIO, though he maintained harmonious relations with the AFL.[67] In every state union influence plummeted after 1938.

Many union activists favored a labor party. One possibility was an independent labor party based on the votes of industrial workers. Several UAW locals toyed with this idea, and the 1936 UAW convention endorsed it. Independent union candidates won local elections in Toledo and in a few other communities in 1934, though the obstacles to a more extensive effort were formidable. They included the opposition of the AFL, the CIO, and the Democrats; the divisions between workers; and the problems of mobilizing industrial employees for a party that was unlikely to win state or national elections. These impediments had not stopped workers in earlier years. Yet the commanding presence of the Roosevelt administration and the apparent importance of national legislation made control of local government seem less attractive to most union members in the late 1930s. In this setting the obstacles became insuperable barriers.

A variation on the labor party approach was a "farmer-labor" party with industrial workers playing influential roles. Wisconsin Congressman Thomas Amlie was the leading exponent of this idea and won support for it in Michigan, Indiana, and Ohio union strongholds in 1935.[68] But he and his allies had little success attracting agrarian allies. By 1935 the vast majority of midwestern farmers were deaf to Amlie's call to action. Local farmer-labor parties were in reality disguised labor parties. They were short-lived and inconsequential.

A more promising approach was to take over the Democratic party. Many union leaders favored this strategy and became enthusiastic allies of the Democrats. Rarely, however, did they have a decisive impact. Two local elections help explain their modest success. In 1937 CIO forces in Detroit and Akron ran mayoral candidates and won Democratic primaries. In both cases they mobilized union support in communities where unionists and spouses were a majority or near majority of the electorate. Yet their very strength invited opposition. AFL leaders and members feared a CIO victory, Democratic regulars felt demoted, and nonunion voters worried that unions would become parochial special interest groups, possibly hostile to them. By election day, even some CIO members had misgivings. Both campaigns failed by substantial margins.[69]

By 1939 the depression and recovery had changed the institutional context in which workers lived and worked without appreciably improving their living standards or opportunities. Government support had become more vital to farmers than ever before. It had also contributed to the revival of the labor movement, though the significance of that development for industrial relations and for the individual workers was still uncertain. One thing was clear: neither employer hostility nor a severe recession had restored the status quo ante. Beginning in 1939 a new economic environment would clarify the importance of the preceding half-decade.

7.

Change and Continuity, 1939–1953

Though political events continued to define the era, the war and postwar years introduced far-reaching changes in midwestern economic life. War mobilization revived industry and agriculture, transformed the labor force, and created unparalleled opportunities for organized labor. Postwar spending, reflecting renewed public confidence and the enhanced position of the United States in a shattered world, sustained the boom for another decade. By 1953 a new prosperity was widely proclaimed. At its core was Big Government, providing unprecedented services and mediating a novel partnership between Big Business and Big Labor. The new prosperity would be free of the obstacles to economic growth and social harmony that had beset the 1930s. Yet in retrospect the characteristic of the postwar era that stands out in bold relief was not its novelty but its similarity to the pre-depression decades. For midwesterners, the developments of the war and postwar years provided welcome reassurance that the kinds of work they knew, based on innovations they understood and respected, would again ensure prosperity and individual opportunity.

Workers and War

World War II had special importance for midwestern farmers and industrial workers because of the all-encompassing character of the mobilization effort and the way it reaffirmed their importance. The depression had devastated the careers and prospects of farmers, factory workers, and miners, but it had been at most a temporary setback for white-collar employees and professionals. War-induced spending reversed this pattern; farmers and factory workers happily found their world turned upside down. Opportunities abounded and surpluses, including labor surpluses, gave way to shortages. For midwestern workers, the new order recalled an earlier, more rewarding age.

War mobilization occurred in two phases, roughly the periods of 1939 to early 1943 and 1943 to mid-1945. During the first period industry overshadowed government. The contrast between a vigorously growing private economy and a bumbling government led to mounting criticism, devastating

Democratic losses in the midterm elections of 1942, and a tightening of the Republican hold on midwestern government. Roosevelt's subsequent moves to buttress the powers of the War Manpower Commission (WMC) in late 1942 and 1943 marked the beginning of the second and more aggressive phase of mobilization. By 1943 most new or adapted factories were running smoothly, the war agencies operated more effectively, and labor shortages replaced raw material shortages as the most serious bottlenecks to production. In every midwestern state except Illinois, the latter months of 1943 were the peak period of war production and industrial employment.

Despite the conflicts that dominated contemporary reporting, mobilization was a notable achievement. Apart from increased output, the character of American production also changed. Industrial productivity rose steadily and impressively, a unique experience among the combatants.[1] The gains were partly a reflection of the depressed state of industry on the eve of the war, but they suggested more than a return to pre-depression normality. For farmers, factory managers, and industrial workers, war production presented countless opportunities to extend and improve the techniques they had used successfully in the past.

Midwestern farmers were among the principal beneficiaries of war mobilization. Crop and livestock prices rose faster than the prices of other products, increasing farm incomes and property values. Government "action" programs of the 1930s, coupled with direct subsidies in 1944–1945, virtually guaranteed prosperity. Contemporary critics complained that farmers did not expand production as much or as fast as they could have, but that was a temporary, predictable problem, comparable to the reluctance of manufacturers to convert to war production before Pearl Harbor.[2] The combination of family labor, small production units, and private initiative augmented by publicly supported research and development, cheap credit, and price controls was ideally suited to the conditions of the 1940s. Midwestern farmers "accounted for most of the outstanding food production records turned in during the war."[3]

The most serious challenge for midwestern farmers was the labor shortage. During the 1930s the rural population had included many underemployed individuals, casualties of farm mechanization and the stagnation of the village economy. Between 1940 and 1942 apprentice farmers and "hired men" were prime candidates for both the Army and urban industry. Their departure created hardships, especially for elderly farmers. The first response of farm families was to find local substitutes. Between 1940 and 1945 the rural population of the Midwest declined by 12 percent, the rural labor force by only 5 percent. The disparity reflected the extension of the family labor system, as wives, children, retirees, and others not formerly classified as farm workers assumed duties that men had performed. By 1943, for example, nearly half of all eastern Wisconsin farm operators were "partly disabled men, single men or women, widowers, and widows."[4] Having exhausted the local labor supply, farmers cast a wider net. With the aid of compliant school officials, they recruited students for unskilled tasks such as fruit and vegetable picking. They also participated in government-sponsored programs that made prisoners of war and West Indian and Mexican migrants available for temporary work.[5]

As the shortage became more serious, farmers turned to government. In 1941–1942, as industrial production boomed and draft calls mounted, producers in areas such as western Minnesota faced potentially crippling labor shortages at harvest time. The War Manpower Commission responded by making agricultural workers eligible for draft deferments. In November 1942 the Tydings Amendment to the draft law specifically exempted agricultural workers, the only group so designated. By 1944 approximately one-third of all men with occupational deferments were farm workers. More important, about one-quarter of deferred farmers were in their late teens and early twenties, the prime draft ages, while other deferred men were almost all over twenty-five. By 1943 former farm laborers were leaving industrial positions for agriculture and safety. At the peak of the mobilization effort, 19 percent of midwestern agricultural workers held draft deferments.[6] The demands of the military, together with abuses of the deferment system (fathers who took high-paying industrial jobs while their deferred sons ran their farms, for example) led to a partial reversal of this policy in 1944. If the war had continued into the winter of 1945, most deferred farm workers would have been drafted.

Having found ways to maintain or increase production with fewer workers, many farmers were less concerned after 1945 when sons and neighbors, the traditional pool of young farm workers, returned from military service or war-industry work and decided to pursue nonagricultural careers. Mechanization and the stopgap measures of the war years, relatively simple and painless at the time, became a psychological bridge between the 1930s and the 1950s

Although industrial production was a matter of "bits and pieces" of extensive contracting between firms and factories, many of the pieces required elaborate, often new, manufacturing facilities. The best known of these were the aircraft factories and shipyards of the Pacific Coast, but the largest new facilities were midwestern: Dodge's Chicago engine plant and Ford's Willow Run airframe factory were the world's largest war plants. Nothing remotely comparable had appeared since the completion of the River Rouge plant in the early 1920s. Like the Rouge, the Chicago and Willow Run factories were examples of what could be done when volume production took precedence over other objectives. Chrysler's Detroit tank plant; Buick's Melrose Park, Illinois, engine factory; Goodyear's Akron aircraft plant; and Chicago Bridge and Iron's Seneca, Illinois, landing-craft assembly plant—the "prairie shipyard"—were nearly as impressive.

Unlike conventional mass production, which had depended on technological and organizational innovation to increase volume and reduce unit costs, World War II production relied more heavily on additional labor and a more elaborate division of labor. The demand for immediate results, reliance on cost-plus contracts, and shortage of skilled workers dictated this approach. Since the Office of Production Management and the War Production Board provided little direct assistance, private engineers and managers, aided by a new figure, the "expediter," filled the gap. Given virtually unlimited demand and a commitment to standardization, most assignments could be broken down to the point that prior industry or product-specific experience was unimportant. Aware that ordnance blueprints intimidated potential subcontractors, the head of Link-Belt's Chicago operation made a point of not showing them to contractors. Instead he "loaned Link-Belt engineers to plan production and breakdown jobs into several operations, . . . bought materials for all subcontractors, conducted time and motion studies, . . . and sent instructors to train new workers."[7] Though less important, technological change also contributed to the results. A 1942 survey cited specialized tools, welding techniques, improved heat-treating, metal spraying, prefabrication, and new materials as results of the war effort.[8] A host of other product and process innovations appeared before 1945. Many of them, including improvements in electronics and pharmaceuticals, were products of midwestern laboratories and universities.

Who was to do this work, much of it esoteric and difficult to master? Until 1943 the answer was simple: the more than seven million people who had been unemployed at the beginning of the decade. By 1942 nearly all of them had found jobs, no small achievement considering the record of the 1930s. The experiences of Detroit and Muskegon, Michigan, were probably representative. In 1940 the unemployment rate for Detroit and its suburbs was 14 percent, or 150,000 men and women, one-quarter of whom were on work-relief rolls. In Muskegon the unemployment rate was 17 percent for men and 12 percent for women. Forty-five percent of the Muskegon men and 50 percent of the women were on WPA rolls. By 1944 the WMC listed both cities as areas of severe labor shortages. In general, unemployed workers filled about 44 percent of the jobs created by 1942. In Detroit and Muskegon, the comparable proportions were 48 percent and 46 percent.[9]

There were inevitable disparities between the locations of workers and jobs. Between the spring of 1940 and the fall of 1943, before government controls (apart from the draft) had a marked effect, Michigan, Ohio, Indiana, and Illinois had a net gain of 600,000 interstate migrants, while Iowa, Minnesota, and Wisconsin had a net deficit of 487,000.[10] Thousands of individuals also moved within states. Of newcomers to the Detroit area, for example, one-quarter came from other Michigan locations.[11] The social costs of this mobility included congested city neighborhoods and trailer camps and shantytowns that appeared in the wake of the migrants.

A more serious obstacle to increasing production was the mismatch of skills and work requirements. Military production required the redesign of machinery; the production of jibs, fixtures, dies, and tools; and other skilled tasks. Yet the depression had sharply depleted the stock of skilled industrial workers. Intermittent employment had taken its toll, while cutbacks in formal and informal apprenticeship programs had reduced the number of young craft workers. A 1941 study of unemployed workers in Indianapolis concluded that only 15 percent of them had useful skills. Most of the others had never worked, had not worked steadily for five years or more, or had been laborers or unskilled service workers.[12] Virtually none of them were prepared for the jobs most critical to the war effort. Recognizing this problem, OMB, WPB, and WMC officials launched ambitious remedial efforts that became highlights of the early mobilization experience and models of public-private partnership. The need was well defined, and the resources—primarily public school facilities and manufacturing plants—were readily available. Given labor-market opportunities, the retraining of workers proved to be comparatively easy.

As mobilization accelerated, the demand for labor grew rapidly. The U.S. Labor Department estimated that besides the formerly unemployed workers who filled more than 40 percent of new wartime positions, young people eighteen and over entering the labor force filled approximately 20 percent, and nontraditional workers (the elderly, housewives, students, and racial minorities) filled the remainder. Students and high school dropouts overshadowed other nontraditional employees. In Detroit they accounted for nearly a third of the nontraditional group; in Muskegon, almost two-thirds. Experts bemoaned the student exodus, probably unnecessarily. A 1944 Michigan survey discovered that boys who worked part-time received better grades than those who did not work and were less likely to be truants. Most of the dropouts came from low-income families and probably would have left school before graduation under any circumstances.[13]

Approximately half of all nontraditional workers added to the labor force during World War II were female. For many women the war afforded opportunities to move to new, higher-paying positions. In Minneapolis-Saint Paul, for example, female employment rose by sixty thousand (or 54 percent) between 1940 and 1945. The services and professions lost workers, while manufacturing and trade boomed. Women filled men's positions in stores, banks, and government offices and took new jobs in factories. Manufacturing accounted for more than half of all job changes and nearly one-third of all women workers in the Twin Cities by 1945.[14] In Kenosha, Wisconsin, retail employees moved en masse into manufacturing; together with housewives who entered the paid labor force, they made up more than half of all manufacturing workers by 1944. Kenosha's store owners turned to high school dropouts and part-time employees to fill their vacancies.[15]

In the beginning at least, women workers understood that their new jobs would be temporary. As the years passed, many of them, including many who had married, began to view their positions differently. Studies of women workers at the Willow Run complex in 1944 reported that they seemed shocked at the prospect of losing their jobs, though they had always known that the plant would close.[16] Others became sensitive to wage discrimination and gender-based seniority lists that threatened to eliminate them in favor of returning soldiers. The length of the war period, the high pay and status of war workers, and the accumulating evidence that women could perform as well as men had a substantial impact on the perceptions of female employees.

A related issue attracted more attention and concern. The influx of women workers included large numbers of wives as employers relaxed marriage bars and women responded to patriotic appeals. As the labor shortage became severe, employers, WMC officials, and local politicians often organized campaigns to persuade housewives to enter war industries.[17] In Chicago, for example, a shortage of electronics workers in 1944 prompted a massive torchlight parade, the selection of a "radar queen," and door-to-door recruiting. In Joliet, Illinois, shortages in munitions factories produced a similar effort:

> With the assistance of the mayor, a committee, and Joliet industrialists, the WMC area director and local USES office launched a "Work for Victory" campaign. Employers pooled advertising to sponsor full-page newspaper appeals for workers, retail stores removed lingerie and hats from windows, [replacing] them with instruments of war. A parade featuring war plant displays and military units brought 20,000 persons to the curbstones. Floats carried workers operating machines. Climaxing the campaign, 50 women war plant employees canvassed the town, [urging] women to "sign up." The drive brought 2,500 recruits, most of them women.[18]

In many cases the results were less satisfactory. Wives who had not worked before the war and mothers of young children rarely took jobs outside the home.[19] Of 18,700 Akron housewives who indicated a willingness to consider outside employment, a mere 630 actually took jobs.[20] The pattern of wartime female employment thus had two peaks: one in the teenage years, representing single dropouts, and one in the middle years, thirty-five to fifty-five, representing wives whose children were in school or away from home. Table

Table 7–1

Female Employment, Detroit–Willow Run Region, June 1944

(Percentage)

	Total	Single	*Husband Present*		*Husband Absent*		*Widowed, Divorced*	
			no children under 10	children under 10	no children under 10	children under 10	no children under 10	children under 10
White	39	86	30	12	72	39	52	49
(ages)								
18–24	63	83	46	11	73	37	—	—
25–29	41	91	21	11	67	41	—	—
30–34	36	90	44	12	65	—	—	—
35–44	38	83	38	14	69	—	74	—
45–64	26	70	18	9	33	—	41	—
Non-white								
All ages	49	91	40	18	65	—	52	—

Source: U.S. Dept. of Commerce, Bureau of the Census, *Population*, Series CA–3, No. 10, table 9, pp. 14–15.

7-1 provides a detailed portrait of Detroit's women workers in June 1944, organized by age, race, and marital status.

In wartime Detroit, nearly 40 percent of white women were in the paid labor force. Almost all single women and a large majority of married women whose husbands were in the armed forces or otherwise absent, together with divorcees and widows, worked outside the home unless they had young children. Women whose husbands were present were much less likely to have paid jobs, and wives whose husbands were present *and* who had children under ten years of age were rarely employed outside the home. Nonwhite women were more likely to have paid jobs than white women, but in other respects they behaved similarly. Nonwhite mothers of young children were only marginally more likely to be in the paid labor force than white women. The number of Detroit women who listed their occupations as housewives actually increased in the 1940s, despite the area's important and highly publicized role in war production.[21] Lukewarm public support for day-care services and scandals involving "door-key kids" probably explain their preferences.[22]

The most sensitive gauge of the labor shortage was the growth in African American employment in war industries. On the eve of the war, blacks held low-skill jobs in meat-packing plants, steel mills and foundries, and firms with conspicuously liberal or anti-union employment policies. (International Harvester, a leader in employing African Americans, qualified on both counts.)[23] Foundries at Ford and other Detroit-area auto companies were becoming known as "black" departments.[24] In most cases integration dated from the World War I boom. During the 1920s and 1930s African Americans had continued to find positions in those companies but not in others. As a result they gained little from the economic revival of 1939–1941. In Illinois one-third of black workers were unemployed or on relief rolls in 1940. Blacks accounted for nearly one-half of all relief cases in Chicago and 60 percent in East Saint Louis.[25] Many had been laborers or domestic servants. Yet a "surprising" number had worked in skilled jobs.[26] By 1942 market pressures began to erode discriminatory hiring practices.

Two other forces accelerated the movement of African Americans into industry. One was government policy, symbolized by Roosevelt's executive order 8802 of June 1941 and the work of the Fair Employment Practices Committee. Although the FEPC had little actual power, as a well-known confrontation with the Olin Company and its white munitions employees in East Alton, Illinois, strikingly emphasized, it had an effect similar to the NRA labor boards in 1933–1935.[27] Powerless in the face of resolute resistance, it was able to influence the pace of change where employers were sensitive to economic forces. In Milwaukee, for example, economic and government pressures opened skilled industrial occupations to black applicants. In Cincinnati, the FEPC successfully encouraged small, vulnerable businesses to revise their hiring practices.[28] The second, complementary force was the CIO, which was most influential in the fastest-growing industries. For practical and idealistic reasons, CIO leaders favored an inclusive approach. In contrast most AFL unions continued to exclude or segregate black workers and resist outside pressures.

Several Illinois studies before and during the war document the decline of formal discriminatory practices. A 1941 poll of 146 firms with defense contracts found that two-thirds had no black employees. Most of the others hired blacks only for janitorial positions. Employers cited custom, doubts about the abilities of minority employees, union opposition, and public opinion to justify their policies. The most significant exceptions were Chicago-area corporations such as Western Electric, International Harvester, and Swift. Three years later a study of ninety-four Chicago firms reported that most companies considered all applicants, did not segregate jobs or employee facilities, and encountered little opposition from white employees and supervisors. Most employers expressed satisfaction with the results.[29] Though such studies reflected employers' views and values, they provide a rough benchmark of war-induced policy changes.

Table 7–2, drawn from the Detroit-Willow Run population data, compares the experiences of white and black Detroit-area residents. Migrants accounted for more than 50 percent of the black population increase and were almost twice as prevalent in the black community as elsewhere. Nearly all of the black migrants were adults. Most came from the South, but relatively few—14 percent of the migrant group, or 3 percent of the black population— had been farmers. White migrants were more likely to have come from the Midwest, but they, too, had been predominantly village or small-city residents. Less than 2 percent of Detroit-area resident had been farmers in 1940.

The employment of African Americans in Detroit industry rapidly undermined the racial status quo. Most notably it accelerated the decline of living conditions in the squalid ghetto known as Paradise Valley, where most black Detroiters lived. It also encouraged the local chapter of the National Association for the Advancement of Colored People (NAACP) to become more assertive and to develop links to the UAW. However, it had little effect on Detroit's public officials, who made no effort to ease racial tensions or modify the prevailing pattern of racially segregated housing.

Two developments of 1942 underlined the explosive potential of this situation. First were "hate" strikes by white workers against the promotion of blacks to production jobs. Beginning at Packard in the fall of 1941, the protests spread to Hudson, Dodge, and Timken Axle in 1942, posing the first critical test of the UAW's fair-employment policy. Union leaders strongly opposed the strikes and refused to defend the instigators. Their reactions, together with government pressures on the companies, soon halted the strike wave. They also set the UAW apart from other Detroit unions, such as the Teamsters, and pushed it toward an informal partnership with the NAACP.[30] The second development of 1942 was the controversy over federal government plans to locate an all-black public-housing project in a white neighborhood.[31] Protests against the plan culminated in a February riot that led to twenty injuries and more than two hundreds arrests. Together the hate strikes

Table 7–2
Detroit–Willow Run Population Changes, By Race, 1940–1944
(Percentage)

| | *Population Growth* *1940–1944* | *Migrant* *1944* | *Migrant* | | |
			from South	*from Midwest*	*Farming 1940*
White	5	9	45	51	17
Nonwhite	46	16	64	19	14

Source: U.S. Department of Commerce, Bureau of the Census, *Population*, ca. 1944, Series CA–3, No. 10.

and the riot provided indisputable evidence of the seriousness of racial conflict in Detroit. Yet city officials did nothing. As one historian notes, "No city expected racial trouble more than Detroit, and none did less to prevent it."[32]

Tensions rose in 1943 as the flow of black job-seekers swelled and living conditions in Paradise Valley declined. A second series of hate strikes culminated in a walkout of Packard employees in early June. Amid predictions of more serious conflicts, a black-white brawl at a city park on June 20 ignited the most serious riot of the war period. For nearly a day mobs assaulted motorists and pedestrians and police struggled to keep the two sides apart. Nine whites and eight blacks died in the initial assaults, and police killed another seventeen blacks, mostly in looting incidents. At least 419 other individuals, evenly divided by race, were hospitalized.[33] Most businesses in Paradise Valley were ransacked. Only the belated arrival of federal troops prevented more extensive bloodshed and damage.

The severity of the violence was due largely to the slow response of public officials. The mayor, governor, and federal civil and military officials took almost a day to dispatch nearby soldiers to the riot scene. Mayor Edward Jeffries' only initiative during that period, a meeting with black community leaders at the height of the violence, may have made the situation worse.[34] Most serious of all was the breakdown of police discipline. White officers often acted like rioters and fired wantonly when confronted. In some instances they shot in self-defense; in others they killed individuals fleeing crimes; and in still others they fired with little apparent provocation.[35] But two points were indisputable: only one of the victims was armed, and all were black. The mayor and his associates may have been unable to prevent violent racial incidents, which occurred in many cities in 1943, but their dilatory response on June 20–21 transformed an ugly situation into a bloodbath.[36]

Though the Detroit riots of 1942 and 1943 marked the beginning of a new era of ethnic conflict, as profound in its implications as the conflicts of earlier decades, the wartime violence quickly subsided. Mayors of most large cities appointed biracial civic committees that addressed the most obvious problems. The gradual decline of war production in 1944–1945 also lessened tensions associated with housing congestion, although Detroit, south Chicago, and other former war production centers remained racial tinderboxes. But the most significant factor in diffusing the situation was economic: racial conflict was an outgrowth of the wartime labor shortage. By 1944 the shortage had ended, and by 1945, as the end of the war became imminent, the prospect of a surplus grew. The employment situation not only slowed the flow of job-seekers to war production centers but diverted attention from social to economic issues.

To contemporaries the most surprising feature of the adjustment to peacetime conditions was the absence of an employment crisis like that of

1920–1921 or the early 1930s. Public policies that eased the adjustment of veterans to civilian life, the voluntary or involuntary withdrawal of married women from the industrial labor force, and the continued growth of the economy explain the relatively painless transition of 1945–1947. Wartime savings, pent-up consumer demand, and high levels of defense spending, particularly during the Korean conflict of 1950–1953, sustained the demand for midwestern products and industrial workers at levels below those of 1943 but far above those of the 1930s. In this environment a new equilibrium emerged. It included black employees in industrial positions and simmering antagonisms outside the factory, but its most notable feature was the enhanced role of organized labor in industry and society.

The Rise of Big Labor

The events of the 1940s transformed the labor movement of the 1930s into a substantial, seemingly permanent force in midwestern society. The change was quantitative and qualitative. By 1939 union leaders had enlisted nearly one-quarter of midwestern nonagricultural workers except in Iowa and Minnesota. Unions were stronger than in any other region.[37] Yet their future was far from certain. Some of the region's largest corporations, such as Ford and Republic Steel, had defeated well-led union initiatives. Others had revived their personnel departments and were vigorously contesting union demands at the bargaining table and in the courts. Still others, such as Firestone Tire & Rubber, began to shift work to new plants in nonunion communities. In 1940 the UAW had only a foothold in General Motors (14 percent of production workers) and no presence at Ford.[38] The SWOC had lost two-thirds of its members in the Calumet region, despite its contract with U.S. Steel. The meat-packing and farm-implement industries, concentrated in Illinois, Iowa, Wisconsin, and Minnesota, were largely unorganized.

Anti-union employers had reason for optimism. By 1940 Republicans controlled the governorships of all the midwestern states except Illinois and Indiana. (They would capture Illinois in 1940.) Their triumphs reflected public disillusionment with the New Deal and the success of the farm program in defusing rural unrest. Their success also meant that organized labor could not count on official support despite its large membership. The AFL-CIO split greatly aggravated the situation. Many employers found the AFL a willing and useful foil against the CIO. In one particularly bitter incident, the Chicago Federation of Labor and the AFL printing trades joined the anti-union Hearst Company in destroying the CIO's American Newspaper Guild at the Hearst papers in Chicago.[39] Conflicts between rival city and state central bodies underlined organized labor's political impotence.

The more conservative atmosphere of the late 1930s also made leftist union officials a liability. CIO officials purged Communists from the SWOC in 1937 and from the Packinghouse Workers Organizing Committee in 1939. They also helped restrict the UAW's substantial contingent of Communist leaders to local union and staff positions. AFL leaders were less subtle. Teamsters president Dan Tobin simply declared war on the Trotskyist leadership of the powerful Minneapolis Teamsters. He made comparatively little progress until the antisubversive Smith Act of 1939 enabled him to enlist the Roosevelt administration on his side. In 1941 eighteen of the Minneapolis radicals were convicted of Smith Act violations and imprisoned.[40] Among other effects, Tobin's victory created a leadership vacuum in the growing Central States Drivers Council that James R. Hoffa, the dominating figure in the Detroit Teamsters, quickly filled. In the meantime the Roosevelt administration helped orchestrate opposition to the Communist leadership of UAW Local 248 at Allis-Chalmers in Milwaukee. The Allis-Chalmers radicals barely survived a bitter strike in the spring of 1941.[41]

Yet the most acute indicator of the new environment was the fate of Wisconsin's venerable socialists. Beginning in 1939 the leaders of the Milwaukee building trades and Teamsters challenged the long-time officers of the Wisconsin State Federation of Labor. Their opposition was generational and ideological; they were younger, "more conservative," and "less politically oriented."[42] In 1940 and 1941 they waged a successful campaign for the top positions in the State Federation, defeating Jacob Friedrich, the last of the old-guard socialists. The contest was a harbinger of the eclipse of socialist influence in the labor movement and Milwaukee politics in the following years.

In spite of the new conservatism, the midwestern labor movement grew rapidly in the months prior to Pearl Harbor. What had changed? The most significant difference was the role of government in the economic recovery. Unlike the NRA years, which featured indirect government controls, the pre–Pearl Harbor boom was based on public sector spending and government direction of the economy. Despite the widespread perception of bungling and inefficiency, nearly everyone conceded the need for a more forceful industrial relations policy. Given the developments of the 1930s, collective bargaining became an acceptable, conservative way to ensure labor peace in a period of rising demand and skilled worker shortages. The outcome was not preordained. Public policy was permissive rather than prescriptive, and employers were as hostile as ever. But unions had an opening, emphasized by the influential presence of Sidney Hillman and other union officials in the mobilization bureaucracy.[43]

There were many examples of the new atmosphere, such as the capitulation of Ford, Republic Steel, and Goodyear within a few months in 1940–1941, and the mounting unpopularity of John L. Lewis and other uncooperative union leaders. Equally notable was the transformation of industrial relations in the farm-implement industry, concentrated in large plants in northern Illinois and adjoining states. In 1937 Chicago SWOC officials had exiled leftist organizers to a campaign against International Harvester. They became the nucleus of the CIO Farm Equipment Workers, a small Communist-dominated union. The FE made little progress until 1941, when the NLRB ruled that International Harvester's "independent" unions were company dominated. With the AFL poised to take over the independents, the FE struck and won representation elections at four Harvester plants, including the company's major Chicago operations. The International Harvester breakthrough sparked a series of competitive campaigns pitting the UAW and AFL against the FE. By 1943, 70 percent of farm-machinery employees were union members. The FE, with 55 percent of the total, was dominant at International Harvester, Oliver, and some John Deere plants. The UAW, with 20 percent, represented J. I. Case, Deere, Allis-Chalmers, and a minority of IH employees. AFL affiliates and federal locals represented the remainder.[44]

These events, almost unimaginable in 1939, underlined several features of union growth during World War II. First and foremost was the influence of government. As a purchaser of industrial products, government had greater leverage than it had had as a promoter and regulator in the 1930s. It could reward or punish individual firms and guarantee that the financial costs of labor agreements, and labor peace, were passed on to the consumer, ultimately the taxpayer. In effect mobilization made manufacturing a regulated sector of the economy, like transportation and energy. Union contracts became a badge of cooperation and social responsibility.

Second, mobilization gave leftists a new but precarious lease on life. The organizing campaigns of 1940–1941 created a renewed demand for experienced organizers; in the farm-machinery industry, for example, men who had been discarded in 1937 reemerged in 1941 as influential union officials. The shift in Communist policy to support for the war in mid-1941, after the German attack on the Soviet Union, was also helpful. Communist unionists thus temporarily avoided the unpopularity of former allies such as Lewis.

Third, the experiences of 1940–1941 emphasized the renewed popularity of unions among industrial workers. Some new members had had prior union experiences and had become "union minded"; others, including a large percentage of female and black workers, had been indifferent or hostile. What accounted for their new perspective? It seems unlikely that they became more hostile to their employers. Most of them probably viewed union membership as a way to enhance their positions in a rapidly changing bureaucratic environment.

The rise of the UAW to preeminence in the American labor movement was a gauge of the larger process. By 1939 the UAW was the largest and most visible of the new unions. It had matched—at 170,000—the membership of the Teamsters and Amalgamated Clothing Workers. Yet like the URW, it had succeeded mostly among the industry's vulnerable medium-sized firms. Despite many well-established locals, able secondary leaders, and a formidable base in the Detroit area, its prospects were uncertain. The UAW foothold at GM was precarious, and its seemingly endless leadership conflicts threatened to discredit it among workers and employers. By the time of Pearl Harbor, however, UAW membership had doubled to more than 400,000, mostly because of employment growth; its leadership had stabilized with the secession of the divisive Homer Martin faction; and it had concluded a landmark contract with Ford. For the next three years the parameters of UAW expansion did not change. The union added half a million members as existing locals grew. It became more closely wedded to the Big Three firms, which accounted for 31 percent of UAW members in 1941 but 48 percent in 1943, and it began to diversify by organizing war workers in aircraft and farm-machinery plants. UAW membership peaked at more than a million in 1944.[45]

Growth lessened the tensions that had kept the UAW in turmoil. Martin's removal eliminated a major irritant, while the burgeoning membership lessened the influence of Detroit-area activists, who continued to fight the battles of the 1930s. By 1942 the UAW had two broad-based factions, "power-seeking and patronage-hungry machines," similar to political parties.[46] They competed vigorously but mostly over details such as the desirability of incentive pay systems. For five years the union's leadership was divided and balanced, a situation that apparently did not displease many members. Even though Walter Reuther had become the most visible UAW official by the early 1940s, he was unable to win the presidency until 1946 or to consolidate his hold on the union bureaucracy until 1947, when his opponents' tactical errors and associations with Communists tipped the balance in his favor. The story of UAW politics during those years is a fascinating chapter in the history of union democracy, but it should not obscure the fact that the union grew and flourished under leaders from both factions.[47]

The wartime challenges the UAW faced were markedly different from the problems unions had faced in the 1930s. The least formidable of these was the adjustment to a racially mixed membership. During the Ford campaign of 1941, UAW leaders won over black community leaders and defused racial tensions.[48] By the end of the conflict, most black Ford employees were pro-union. In 1942 and 1943 UAW leaders courageously opposed "hate" strikes and segregated housing. UAW president R. J. Thomas was a leading critic of police tactics during the 1943 riot. In 1944 the union created a Fair Practices Committee to investigate charges of discrimination. Racial tensions remained at the local level, but the position of the union was clear, and few white members publicly challenged it.[49]

UAW leaders were less vigorous in defending their female members during and after World War II. Like most union officials, they viewed the influx of women as a temporary and potentially destabilizing phenomenon. Assuming that their primary duty was to safeguard the jobs of permanent union members, including members serving in the armed forces, they tried to preserve the status quo through separate seniority lists and related measures.[50] However, as the number of female war workers grew and women began to agitate for better treatment, UAW leaders became more accommodating. They demanded equal pay for equal work, maternity leaves, publicly subsidized day-care centers, and counselors for women workers. In 1944 they created a Women's Bureau in the International Union.[51] Yet a government investigator reported in 1944 that employers and union officials alike anticipated "wholesale lay-offs of female workers in the postwar period." Those who remained would "face the prospect of reverting to their prewar positions."[52]

The most pressing problem for UAW leaders was rank-and-file opposition to wage controls. Government policy made it easy to recruit members but difficult to improve living or working conditions. While unions were supposed to discourage strikes, the National War Labor Board was slow and parsimonious in responding to wage demands. Intra-union tensions were inevitable. The intense public backlash against John L. Lewis and the UMW in 1943 and 1944 emphasized the pitfalls of any action that appeared unpatriotic. On the other hand, rank-and-file hostility toward URW president Sherman Dalrymple, an outspoken defender of the no-strike policy, underlined the dangers of adhering too closely to government directives. Given this situation, UAW leaders, and most other union officials, waffled, opposing strikes but not too vigorously. NWLB officials tried to help by approving disguised wage increases. But short of a government decision to abandon wage and price controls, there was no satisfactory solution.

The results of this impasse included an escalating wildcat strike movement, an erosion of union discipline, and a mounting public relations crisis for organized labor. Some strikes, such as the conflict that shut down the Akron rubber industry for four days in July 1943, involved thousands of workers; most, however, were "quickies" reminiscent of the sit-downs of 1936–1937. A majority of UAW members in the Detroit area were involved in one or more incidents that violated the union's no-strike pledge.[53] Employees at the Timken Detroit Axle company, for example, struck six times in 1942 and early 1943. They struck forty more times between May 1943 and November 1944. The auto industry as a whole experienced 132 strikes, 102 of them in Detroit, between December 1, 1944, and February 28, 1945. Wage demands accounted for only a handful of strikes.[54] The remainder were the results of minor disputes, disciplinary actions by supervisors, or misunderstandings.

A closer examination of the wildcat movement in the Detroit area under-lines the powerlessness of union leaders. During the critical months of December 1944 and January and February 1945, for example, General Motors plants had six strikes, while Ford had thirty-one. The River Rouge and Willow Run factories, with fourteen strikes each, accounted for most of Ford's problems. Two features of the Ford situation were notable: its workers had virtually no prewar union background, and the strikes, while numerous, were also inconsequential. Only eight of the thirty-one involved more than a hundred workers. Only two, at the Lincoln plant in December and at the Rouge in February, involved more than a thousand employees.[55] Moreover, there was no apparent difference between the causes or duration of the wildcats at the Rouge and Willow Run plants, despite vast differences in the character of the work and the labor force. The Rouge's veteran, all-male, one-third black labor force behaved much like Willow Run's transient, white, largely female labor force.

Apart from Ford, the other strike leaders were Packard, with eight; Dodge Main, with seven; and Briggs's Mack Avenue factory, with seven. No other plant had more than four, and only three factories (Hudson with four and two other Briggs plants with three each) had more than two strikes. The Packard, Dodge, and Briggs plants also had the most serious strikes. Briggs's record was especially dismal.[56]

Clearly management, not labor, was the critical variable in the strike wave. Five plants of the hundreds in the area accounted for half of all the strikes and virtually all of the important ones. Ford management was in disarray even before it embarked on its ill-considered Willow Run enterprise.[57] Chrysler's archaic industrial relations policies had given the union a powerful voice at Dodge Main and other plants in the 1930s, though Chrysler executives remained implacably hostile. Plant managers improvised as best they could.[58] The turmoil at the company's giant Chicago aircraft-engine plant, whose strike total exceeded even that of River Rouge and Willow Run, was another indication of these failings. At Packard and Briggs, the wildcats were the beginning of a death rattle that would grow unmistakably with the return of competition.

By late 1944 midwestern unions confronted an additional challenge, the long-anticipated reconversion to civilian production. Industrial employment declined gradually in 1944 and precipitously in 1945; by late 1945 the great Willow Run and Dodge Chicago plants, and dozens of smaller facilities, were shuttered. Between 1944 and 1946 the UAW had lost nearly 200,000 mem-bers, including a disproportionate share of its women members. Other unions suffered similar setbacks. Labor leaders who remembered the post–World War I years were especially anxious. Yet their fears did not materialize. Indeed, the postwar period came close to fulfilling the expectations of union leaders in 1919. The demand for industrial labor remained high, enabling most laid-off war workers and soldiers to find positions in industry or elsewhere. The strike wave of 1945–1947 paralleled that of 1919–1922, but it focused on wage and other material gains, not union recognition; losing a strike meant settling for the employer's offer, not extinction. By the early 1950s unions were stronger than ever and seemingly poised for even greater gains.

Midwestern Unions in Operation

Wartime conditions permitted union officials to think more seriously about the goals of large and reasonably secure movement. For the next decade they had unprecedented opportunities to explore the meaning of Big Labor. Two options received the greatest attention. They could build on past achievements, ensuring that organized workers, regardless of skill or status, benefited from the growth of the economy and the prosperity of individual firms, or they could focus on government, adopting a course similar to that of many European unions in the postwar years. At the national level, the choice was simple, given the growing conservatism of the electorate. In the Midwest union prospects were better because of the high concentration of members. But did a political strategy make sense? The farmers' experiences suggested that it did, and many activists agreed. The result was a hybrid approach, dependent on the political climate of a particular state. Unions successfully blunted employer counterattacks, created private employer-financed welfare systems, and became a force in the Democratic party. In Michigan and Minnesota they also inaugurated a labor service state that paralleled the agricultural service state of earlier decades.

There was good reason to believe that postwar industrial relations would duplicate the pattern of the early 1920s. Demobilization promised to create a buyer's market for labor, while an increasingly conservative Congress attacked the Wagner Act and communism in the labor movement. But the economy did not collapse, and industrial relations were not deregulated. After a brief downturn at the end of the war, union membership and influence continued to grow. Yet the analogy with the earlier postwar period was not wholly misleading. It correctly anticipated important elements of the environment of the late 1940s: the persistent anti-unionism of employers, the antipathy of the public to strikes and other coercive tactics, and the vulnerability of individuals or organizations associated with communism. What it missed was the continuation of the wartime consensus that unions and collective bargaining were consistent with prosperity and economic growth. A description of postwar Peoria, Illinois, captures this view: "the basic conservatism" of the city "led to a concern primarily with jobs and income" and acceptance of organized labor as long as it did not "restrict the postwar return to normalcy" or exhibit "communist sympathies."[59]

Midwestern unions often walked a narrow line between acceptance and disaster. While employers demanded the "right to manage," members insisted on exploiting their market power. The strike wave that began in 1945 continued with gradually diminishing potency until at least 1952. In this atmosphere poor leadership or a competitive disadvantage could be fatal. The Packinghouse Workers disastrous 1948 strike erased the gains of a decade. Although UPWA leaders managed to rebuild the union and keep the opportunistic AFL at bay, some losses were permanent. In Ottumwa, Iowa, for example, UPWA Local 1 leaders had assumed an influential public role during the war and mistakenly counted on community support during the strike. They discovered that Ottumwa residents equated the company's position with the city's future well-being. When strikers resorted to "directed" violence against supervisors,   the estrangement was complete. Though Local 1 survived, it would never again enjoy the position it had had during World War II.[60]

The farm-machinery industry was at the center of the postwar upheavals. International Harvester, Allis-Chalmers, and J. I. Case executives were consistently and vigorously anti-union. Their provocative policies on union security and other labor issues encouraged union resistance. Rivalries between the Farm Equipment Workers, UAW, Electrical Workers, Machinists, and others unions that had footholds in the industry also exacerbated the conflict.[61] The Quad Cities of Illinois and Iowa, where all the major companies had plants, were the scene of nearly continuous strife.[62] Southeastern Wisconsin was another battleground. In 1946 J. I. Case managers precipitated a strike over union security, defied the NLRB and the Wisconsin Supreme Court, held out for fourteen months, and ultimately prevailed. UAW Local 180 barely survived.[63] A bitter yearlong strike at Allis-Chalmers in 1946–1947 was an even better indicator of the postwar industrial relation climate. UAW Local 248, long identified with Communist elements in the UAW and the Wisconsin CIO, faced the combined forces of Allis-Chalmers, the Reuther faction of the union, and an increasingly hostile public. The company's victory symbolized the beginning of a new era that would feature more narrowly focused confrontations and limited victories.[64]

Theodore Purcell's comparative study of Swift & Company plants in Chicago and East Saint Louis, represented respectively by the CIO Packinghouse Workers and the AFL Amalgamated Meat Cutters, provides additional perspective on the new environment. The Chicago plant had long been a center of radical unionism. UPWA Local 28's aggressive corps of stewards led numerous slowdowns and departmental strikes; grievances per employee in Chicago were twice as high as in East Saint Louis. Yet the local was "insecure" and divided. Dissidents attacked the officers' disruptive tactics and Communist affiliations. Local 78 in East Saint Louis, on the other hand, was less militant and more united. The Amalgamated emphasized wage and benefit improvement and opposed strikes. Local 78 had fewer stewards, filed fewer grievances, and discouraged shop-floor activism. Morale, however, was high. Local 78 members rejected the UPWA approach because it was "too radical" and "mean[t] strikes." Even black employees, who favored the CIO's commitment to racial equality, did not "like the radicalism and aggressiveness of the UPWA."[65] Purcell concluded that most workers had a "dual allegiance" to company and union and resisted efforts to force them to choose sides.

Most unions survived and flourished because they were adaptable and realistic. The organizing campaigns of the late 1930s and early 1940s had been training grounds for a new generation of labor leaders who were comfortable in the postwar setting. Tested in war and in union politics, they were ready to take advantage of the favorable economic conditions of the late 1940s. Three midwestern union leaders symbolized this group.

In the 1930s Walter Reuther had been indistinguishable from the other radicals who flocked to the UAW. His management of the 1939 General Motors tool and die makers' strike made his reputation, and his direction of the union's GM department, which included nearly a quarter of all UAW members by 1946, ensured his prominence within the union. During the war he became known for proposals to enlarge the role of government and labor in war planning. Almost single-handedly, he created the impression that the labor movement would compromise the "right to manage." Reuther's election as UAW president in 1946 was almost an anticlimax to his rapid rise. As union president he demonstrated impressive talents as an administrator and union strategist, but he was most successful as a politician. Quickly consolidating his position in the UAW, he created a formidable internal organization that outmaneuvered or intimidated rivals. The UAW soon resembled other large unions.[66] At the same time Reuther became a prominent figure in liberal political organizations, finding there a larger constituency and a more expansive role.

Joseph Germano, the head of USWA District 31, embracing the Calumet area, rose to prominence on the eve of World War II as a SWOC organizer. Appointed district director in 1940, he consolidated his position during the war, eliminating Communists and factional rivals from positions of influence by 1946. In the following years he devoted much of his attention to state and local politics. Although Germano gave lip service to liberal causes, his own interests were more parochial. To Adlai Stevenson, running for governor of Illinois in 1948, he was a typical labor boss, eager to trade union votes for representation in the new administration.[67] In later years he became particularly close to Mayor Richard Daley of Chicago. For thirty years he remained a behind-the-scenes power in the industry, the USWA, and the Calumet communities.[68]

Like Reuther, James R. Hoffa was a product of the turmoil that engulfed Detroit in the 1930s. Shrewd and opportunistic, he and his associates built the local Teamsters organization with "utter disregard for those in their path."[69] By 1945 Hoffa dominated the Michigan Teamsters and the Central States Drivers Council. In the late 1940s he used the Council to extend and centralize collective bargaining in the industry. His success was based on an understanding of the importance of long-distance trucking to the postwar economy, together with a ruthlessness that impressed the most hard-bitten employers. In 1941 he obtained the assistance of Detroit's organized-crime leaders in combating CIO incursions into the local trucking industry. "From then on," his biographer reports, "his relationship with the underworld was to be an ongoing one."[70] Hoffa maintained rank-and-file support with wage and benefit increases. By the early 1950s he was poised for an even larger, national role.

These men and other postwar leaders understood the possibilities and limitations of the postwar environment, avoiding the Scylla of unpopular political entanglements and the Charybdis of industry co-option. They created multi-plant and multi-employer bargaining units that enhanced union power and permitted "connective" bargaining. They emphasized "job control" issues, creating unprecedented rights for low-skill workers and lowering barriers between skilled and unskilled workers. And, building on the war experience, they devised new employee benefits that reduced the distinctions between blue- and white-collar employees.

Even wage agreements took innovative forms. Collective bargaining encouraged job analysis and rate rationalization with or without incentive payments. The most notable example was the union-management assault on base-rate inequities in the steel industry. This effort, aimed at the principal cause of grievances and work stoppages, began in 1942 and culminated in a 1947 wage-standardization agreement. Besides eliminating the hodgepodge of rates that had grown up over the years, the agreement forced the union to become involved in an intercompany industrial-engineering program.[71] In other industries negotiators devised wage formulas, such as the Annual Improvement Factor, introduced by General Motors and the UAW in 1948, and cost-of-living adjustments adopted in auto and other major contracts in the late 1940s. Many unions won paid vacations and elaborate provisions for overtime pay. Together with grievance systems and seniority-based promotions and layoffs, postwar wage innovations eliminated the last of the traditional foreman's arbitrary powers.

If one pillar of job-control unionism was the negotiated contract, the other was the grievance system, which gave union stewards and committeemen and ultimately rank-and-file workers a potentially larger voice in day-to-day operations than ever before. By the 1940s most collective bargaining agreements restricted the employer's power to discipline and discharge blue-collar employees, creating a new realm of negotiation. "Fractional bargaining," the day-to-day give and take between supervisors and now-secure union stewards and committeemen, gradually produced a "common law" of the shop floor that transcended the formal contract. Aggressive stewards were the key. They could become de facto managers, with powers rivaling those of the foremen. In the tire industry, fractional bargaining was heir to the sit-down tradition and probably had as much impact as formal union-management relations.[72] At International Harvester's Melrose Park, Illinois, plant, informal negotiations, together with the appeals permitted under the contract, fostered a sense of control, an élan rarely found among semiskilled employees.[73] But few stewards had the interest or commitment to play this role effectively. One study reported that only 25 to 50 percent of them were notably active.[74]

The most significant breakthroughs of the postwar years involved the creation of extensive, employer-financed benefit plans. The War Labor Board's emphasis on benefits as wage substitutes accentuated a trend that dated from the mid-1930s, when the Wagner Act revived interest in peaceful union-avoidance techniques and the Social Security Act made employees more conscious of economic security issues.[75] The coal-industry contract of 1946 publicized pensions for blue-collar employees, still a novelty. Many unions embraced pensions in the following years, and the 1949 Ford-UAW contract, together with a steel-industry agreement shortly thereafter, were landmarks. The Steelworkers led a parallel movement for health insurance. By the early 1950s most members of the USW, the UAW, and other powerful unions enjoyed some nonwage benefits.[76]

The immediate impact was modest. Only the largest and richest corporations extended their welfare programs in the postwar years, regardless of union pressures. A 1953 study of UAW contracts found that most plants with a thousand or more employees had pension plans but that only about 15 percent of smaller plants had them.[77] Benefits (and costs) were low, though rising. In the auto industry, for example, benefit expenditures including Social Security and unemployment compensation, amounted to 13 percent of wages in 1947.[78] However important these initiatives were as precedents, their effects on workers' living standards and expectations must have been slight.

What impact would the newly expanded labor movement have outside the workplace? With a greatly augmented membership and a new generation of aggressive, confident leaders, it was certain to be larger and more assertive.[79] Executives agonized over the prospect of "creeping socialism." Conversely, union activists continued to dream of a third party and an independent union presence in American politics. In reality the postwar union role in midwestern politics, and in other areas of community life, did not conform to either vision. The labor movement became more involved in partisan politics, but it was successful only when it operated as a partner in a coalition of Democratic party constituencies.

The opportunities for union initiatives varied within the region depending on the state of the Democratic party. In Minnesota, Iowa, Wisconsin, and Michigan, where the party had been weak to nonexistent before the war, either because farm-based, insurgent third parties had overshadowed it (Minnesota and Wisconsin) or because of the state's Republican heritage (Iowa and Michigan), unions became the dominant element in a new Democratic coalition. In Ohio, Indiana, and Illinois, where rural activism had been more subdued and Democrats better organized, union officials had less room for maneuver. They could work with established Democratic groups or operate outside the political mainstream, as a third party or a nonpartisan interest group. Some AFL leaders opted for nonpartisanship, but the majority, and almost all CIO officials, preferred the Democratic orbit. Other parochial factors, such as the progressive legacy of nonpartisan elections in Michigan and the lack of such legacy in Illinois, were also influential.[80]

In every midwestern state, however, the Democrats were on the defensive in the mid-1940s. The Republican resurgence of the late 1930s had been in part a backlash against union power and Republican officeholders were generally unsympathetic to the labor movement. In Michigan, an extreme case, the Republican party was an adjunct of the automobile manufacturers' trade association.[81] The passage of anti-union statutes, such as the Wisconsin Employment Peace Act of 1939 and the Taft-Hartley Act of 1947, made union leaders aware of their failure to translate workplace power into political influence. Finally, the Cold War, by eliminating Communists and their allies from positions of influence, smoothed and probably accelerated the alliance of unionists and Democrats. The role of Popular Front elements in the Minnesota Farmer-Labor and Wisconsin Progressive parties had kept those organizations in turmoil, alienated AFL leaders, and contributed to Republican successes. The new Democratic coalitions of the mid-1940s were explicitly pro-union, liberal, and anti-Communist.

Michigan was instructive. Democratic fortunes had plummeted during World War II. By 1945 the issue was not whether organized labor would take over the party, but whether the UAW or the Teamsters would play the leading role. Reuther's consolidation of power led to a vigorous contest with Hoffa that extended into the 1950s. The UAW prevailed because of its enormous Michigan membership, though Teamster and AFL opposition continued. In the process the UAW and the Democratic party came to be closely identified with each other. In no other state was the relationship between party and union so close.

The results, however, were comparatively modest. Union candidates running as Democrats became lightning rods for anti-UAW groups. The

1943 and 1945 Detroit mayoral races, in which UAW candidates lost to more conventional Democrats, provided a surefire formula for opponents: combine class and interest-group appeals to nonunion voters with racial appeals to white UAW members. Outside the Detroit area it was even easier to turn elections into referenda on the UAW. UAW leaders had little choice but to throw their support to nonunion liberals. G. Mennen Williams, elected governor in 1948 and for five terms thereafter, became the epitome of the new Democratic officeholder. Yet Williams and his UAW backers faced a legislature dominated by rural politicians whose opposition to urban interests and values was intense. The result was a stalemate that slowed the extension of unemployment compensation, public assistance, and other services that aided working-class voters and union members.[82]

Labor-Democratic alliances reshaped the politics of other states. The closest parallel to Michigan was Minnesota, where Democratic liberals, led by Hubert Humphrey and Orville Freeman, and AFL leaders took over the Democratic Farmer Labor party (a 1944 merger of the Farmer-Labor and Democratic organizations) and elected prolabor liberals to municipal and state offices. Humphrey and Freeman, however, were never union candidates. Their other base, the farm cooperatives and agri-business corporations, probably had a greater influence on their behavior.[83] In Wisconsin the labor movement became the mainstay of the Democratic party after 1944, though it had little success in attracting farmers who had voted Progressive in the 1930s. Perhaps because there were no liberal candidates comparable to Williams or Humphrey, the union-Democratic coalition remained a pale facsimile of the La Follette machine of earlier years. It could mount a vigorous effort against Senator Joseph R. McCarthy's 1952 reelection campaign, but it could not consistently challenge the dominant Republicans.[84] In Illinois the liberal Stevenson won the governorship in 1948 despite AFL opposition and grudging CIO support. In Ohio AFL-CIO rivalry and entrenched Democratic conservatives severely restricted union influence. In Indiana and Iowa organized labor had a negligible impact. Both states passed right-to-work laws.

Epilogue: White-Collar and Service Workers

Compared to the growth of manufacturing, the changes that occurred in offices and stores attracted little attention. The contributions of service industries to the war effort were less obvious, and white-collar workers played almost no role in the labor movement. In general they resisted identification with blue-collar workers. In the few cases (Chrysler, B. F. Goodrich) where office workers joined industrial unions, they were not particularly influential and received little assistance from fellow unionists.[85] Yet it is misleading to view the experiences of farmers, industrial workers, and white-collar workers through the same lens. War mobilization and the return of prosperity introduced or accelerated changes in service industries that were ultimately as important as the spread of collective bargaining or the revival of the Democratic party.

The wartime emphasis on goods production and the concomitant view of services as unnecessary luxuries created a different type of labor shortage in offices and stores. As young male workers disappeared and many women moved into industrial positions, employers had few choices and little official assistance. They could recruit older women or other employees they would not have considered under normal circumstances or leave the positions unfilled. A substantial number of small-town professional and service workers moved to urban areas after 1942 to take advantage of such opportunities. The loss of rural teachers was particularly heavy. In addition retail clerks, hotel and restaurant workers, and office employees worked overtime with little of the acclaim that industrial workers received. Standards of service declined. While the severity of the shortage was a function of the unusual demand for industrial labor, the persistence of professional and service opportunities anticipated the growth of white-collar occupations in the postwar years.

In the meantime the most notable result of the white-collar shortage was the decline or disappearance of marriage bars in women's employment. At Sears, where female employment rose from 45 to 75 percent of total employment, "women were repeatedly hired to replace men in jobs which had previously 'demanded' male incumbents."[86] The influx of older, married women undermined popular assumptions about married women in the workplace at the same time the booming economy eroded prejudice against multiple-wage-earner families. When war production declined most young married women left the paid labor force, creating an impression of a return to an earlier normality. But older married women were much more likely to find new jobs, particularly in the booming service sector. Employers welcomed them because of their high educational levels, experiences during the war years, and willingness to work for low wages. By the early 1950s the marriage bar had virtually disappeared in women's professions such as teaching and nursing and was under attack in other occupations.[87]

These observations reflect the experiences of later years more than the situation in 1945 or 1953. The dominating feature of the midwestern economy in the postwar years was the extraordinary health of farm and factory, the industries and jobs that had shaped midwestern society since the turn of the century. For farmers, industrial workers, and young people facing career choices in the early 1950s, the past appeared to be a reliable and productive guide to the future.

Part IV

The Decline and Rebirth of the Midwest

For twenty years government had been the single most important stimulus to change in the midwestern economy. Policies and programs designed to combat the ravages of depression and the threat of foreign aggression had had profound and often unanticipated effects. By the 1950s they had also become the basis of a broad consensus. Most midwestern workers conceded the essentials of farm policy, the desirability of a substantial military establishment, the value of social insurance, and the compatibility of adversarial collective bargaining and rising living standards. Regardless of political perspective, they sensed that government had contributed to a new era of prosperity and stability. They also realized that it had preserved as much as it had changed; amid the upheavals, a vital center based on agriculture and manufacturing remained. To most of them, the future looked inviting and secure.

The postwar order proved to be surprisingly vulnerable. In the 1960s and 1970s new threats emerged and in the early 1980s midwestern workers faced the most serious economic crisis since the 1930s. The problem was twofold: the decline of opportunity in agriculture and large-scale manufacturing and the absence of comparable, compensatory opportunities in other industries. Though service employment grew rapidly in the Midwest, as in other regions, it was not associated with the kinds of innovations that had made agriculture and industry engines of growth and mobility in earlier decades. And it provided few opportunities for former farmers and factory workers. By the 1980s the gulf between goods and service production would be as wide as the earlier gulf between farm and factory. Chapter 8 examines the mounting problems of midwestern agriculture and industry and the impact of the economic collapse of the early 1980s. Chapter 9 adds a brief overview of the 1980s.

8.

End of an Era, 1953–1983

The patterns we have followed since the late nineteenth century culminated in the years after 1953. With the end of the Korean War, government became less intrusive, Big Labor encountered more difficulties, and city and country remained as far apart as ever; in short, the Midwest and its workers returned to a normality reminiscent of the pre-depression years. Yet in one important sense the similarity was deceptive. Scientific agriculture and mass production were no longer novel, and nothing of comparable importance appeared in the post–World War II years to sustain the region's association with organizational innovation. The consequences were apparent by the 1960s. Though healthy by most economic measures, agriculture and industry ceased to provide opportunities for young workers or to attract outsiders to the Midwest. In the 1970s the problems of both sectors became more serious, endangering current employees as well. During the late 1970s and early 1980s, agriculture and industry faced separate, equally severe crises, and the comparative absence of alternative opportunities attracted attention for the first time.

Troubled Prosperity, 1953–1960s

For midwestern workers, the decade following the Korean War was a period of prosperity and contentment, of seemingly frictionless growth. Though this theme is easily exaggerated (as citizens of Sheboygan, Wisconsin, and South Bend, Indiana, sites of bitter labor struggles, would have attested), it suggests both the improved material conditions of most workers and their mood.[1] That the two were linked seems indisputable. The rise in incomes, employment, wages, and other indicators of economic health gradually but decisively erased the memory of the 1930s and the suspicion that prosperity depended on government regimentation. Two legacies of that unhappy era, moreover, made the future even more promising. New Deal programs now offered guarantees against hardship, and a devastated world provided new opportunities for American farmers and manufacturers. The future looked bright indeed.

165

A more careful examination of the postwar economy (which may be possible only in retrospect) suggests a less sanguine analysis. The destruction of the European and Japanese economies was an immediate boon but a long-term threat to American industry, as midwestern steelmakers could testify by the late 1950s. The postwar baby boom had similar implications. The extraordinary opportunities of the 1940s and 1950s reflected the low birth-rates of the depression era as well as the vitality of the postwar economy. The burgeoning school population of the 1950s foreshadowed a more competi-tive labor market in the 1960s and after. The most serious problem, however, was what did not happen. Midwestern life in the 1950s was comfortable partly

Table 8–1

Midwestern Employment Changes, 1950–1970, by Industry

	Percentage change 1950–1970	Percentage male employment 1970
Above Average		
Education	186	39
Hospitals	174	20
Finance	86	48
Public Administration	57	68
Wholesale trade	50	76
Utilities	45	86
Retail trade	44	48
Trucking	39	90
Motor vehicle manufacturing	30	87
Construction	29	94
Relative Decline (0–28%)		
Communications	28	52
All manufacturing	26	76
All transportation	16	86
Metal manufacturing	4	90
Absolute Decline		
Food manufacturing	-14	75
Railroads	-53	92
Agriculture	-56	90
Mining	-67	92

Sources: U.S. Census, *Population*, 1950, table 30 for seven states; 1970, table 55 for seven states.

because there were fewer disruptive changes than in earlier periods. The workplace in particular declined as an arena of innovation.

Table 8–1 summarizes the employment experiences of midwestern workers in the 1950s and 1960s. It distinguishes three groups of industries: those whose employment grew more than 28 percent, the average for the region; those whose employment grew at a slower rate than the regional labor force; and those whose employment declined. The many entries in the top two categories reflect the generally robust economy of those years, the opportunities available to prospective job-seekers, and the growth of the female labor force. Altogether, 3 million new white-collar positions appeared in the 1950s and 1960s, at least 1.8 million of which were due to structural changes in the economy rather than population growth. In effect the region exchanged 900,000 farmers for 900,000 teachers and other school employees. Two hundred thousand railroad workers and nearly as many miners disappeared, while 400,000 additional hospital employees were added to the labor force. The largest single gains were in manufacturing (1.2 million) and retail trade (934,000), though the growth rates of those industries were only marginally above the average. In 1970 manufacturing had the same share of the regional labor force (32 percent) that it had had in 1950.

The remarkable disparities documented in table 8-1 reflected the continuing technological revolution in goods-producing industries as well as the growing demand for services. Although automation (usually equated with the advent of the "automatic factory") was a popular concern of the 1950s and early 1960s, the most important labor-saving technologies were comparatively simple extensions of machines that had long been used in non-manufacturing activities. Large excavating machines, for example, revolutionized road building and ended most underground mining. The last underground mines in Minnesota's Iron Range closed in the 1960s, despite the presence of rich ores. Even with improved machinery and a skilled labor force, underground operations were more costly than open-pit operations. Coal miners faced a similar fate. New coal cutting and transporting machinery increased their productivity but did not make them competitive with open-pit workers. Most displaced coal miners had no choice but to abandon the industry. By the late 1960s there were fewer midwestern miners than firefighters or garbage collectors. The near-ghost towns that dotted the mining regions were grim testimony to the social costs of technological change. The simultaneous political and moral decline of the United Mine Workers was an additional reminder of the vulnerability of seemingly powerful institutions.[2]

In transportation the pattern was more complex. Technological change and the competition of autos, trucks, and airplanes devastated the railroads. The advent of the diesel locomotive, delayed by World War II, reduced opportunities for operating and repair workers as well as employees of suppliers that did not adapt. The collapse of the Lima, Ohio, Locomotive Works in 1956 was a critical blow to a formerly prosperous industrial city.[3] On the other hand, the decline in railroad passenger traffic had comparatively little effect on employment and was accompanied by substantial increases in bus and airline jobs. The most important transportation development of the postwar decade, the rapid growth of long-distance trucking, was also a boon to midwestern workers. A result of improvements in roads and highways, notably state-owned turnpikes in Ohio and Indiana and the beginnings of the interstate highway system, trucking created opportunities for thousands of drivers and mechanics and reoriented the labor movement in the regulated sector of the economy.

Construction workers faced two challenges: the introduction of improved bulldozers, cranes, and other labor-saving machinery and the substitution of metals and plastics for traditional materials. Survival required flexibility. The Chicago Carpenters, for example, relaxed their already permissive attitude toward the introduction of new, factory-made materials. This policy accelerated the "deterioration of traditional wood craftsmanship" and "multiplied the number of specialty crafts," but it enabled the carpenters to work steadily and preserve their standing in the local labor movement.[4] Plumbers confronted similar challenges with the introduction of welding, air conditioning, plastic pipe, and other innovations. Failure to adapt could spell disaster, as the Plasterers discovered.

Declining employment in agriculture also reflected postwar technological changes. Tractors and power implements had been significant innovations of the 1920s and 1930s, but the technical frontier in agriculture gradually shifted from the factory to the laboratory. Improved seeds, fertilizers, pesticides, herbicides, and medicines enabled midwestern farmers to increase output and efficiency and utilize machinery more effectively. They also reinforced the farmer's dependence on the agricultural service state. Their most important effect, however, was to accentuate a trend toward factory-like operations, specialization, and involvement in urban business institutions. Reacting to these external developments, farmers increasingly concentrated on one or a few cash crops. Advances in poultry science, for example, led to large, specialized, "industrial" chicken and egg farms. In Iowa, and probably in other states, scientists and extension employees encouraged this trend, seemingly oblivious to the fact that traditional, decentralized production had provided thousands of farm families with a steady cash income and a buffer against the vicissitudes of the marketplace.[5]

Other innovations compounded this trend. The extension of electrical power and the paving of country roads in the immediate postwar years encouraged farmers to adopt urban fashions and consumption patterns, further increasing their reliance on cash incomes. By the 1960s the image of the farmer as "hick" or "hayseed," out of touch with more fashionable urban society, was as obsolete as the draft horse. The price of this achievement was a further decline in rural self-sufficiency. The prospects of farm families in the late twentieth century increasingly resembled those of the village manufacturers they turned to when their fortunes soured.

Yet new production methods were only one factor in the closing of the agricultural labor frontier. Though most of the new postwar technologies (unlike those in many industries) could be used profitably on farms of all sizes, the decline in agricultural employment was almost exclusively among small and medium-sized operations.[6] Most losses were not consequences of technological innovations per se, but of technological advances coupled with public policies introduced, paradoxically, to preserve the family farm.

During the 1950s and 1960s, years when agricultural prices drifted downward, government price and credit policies protected farmers against a crisis similar to that of the post–World War I years. Judging from the number of farm bankruptcies, they succeeded. But making an income comparable to that of a middle-class city worker remained a challenge. Falling prices forced farmers (especially those who were highly specialized) to expand in order to maintain their incomes; expansion in turn required them to borrow. Government policies "increased the capacity of individual farmers to leverage their operations."[7] Midwestern farming became increasingly speculative. Successful farmers depended on government subsidies, while others became disheartened and sold out. As land prices rose and incomes stagnated, young farmers found it virtually impossible to buy land. Ohio, known for its diversified agriculture, lost 30 percent of its farms and 40 percent of its farm population in the 1950s. Many other Ohio farmers combined city jobs with agriculture.[8]

For those who remained the character of farm work changed as radically as the economics of farming. John Johnson, a hypothetical Iowa farmer of the 1950s, is a useful example.[9] With a hired man and a variety of expensive machines, Johnson raised corn, soybeans, and hogs on twelve hundred acres, earning $30,000 to $50,000 annually on an investment of $1,600,000 and a gross income of $390,000. Johnson's day began at dawn, just as his father's had, but instead of milking the cows (he had none), he drove to town to have breakfast and discuss farm conditions with neighbors and friends. During the planting and harvesting seasons, Johnson worked twelve or more hours per day, mostly as the operator of an air-conditioned tractor or combine. The hogs required additional attention but little actual labor, since machines supplied them with food and water. Like a merchant or industrialist, Johnson recognized the importance of good management. "He had become a skilled businessman. . . . Failure and bankruptcy were the grim alternatives to good management."[10] In the meantime Mrs. Johnson washed clothes in her automatic machine, watched television, worked in her flower garden, and attended club meetings. She rarely became involved in farm work and purchased the family's food at a supermarket. Most of her social contacts occurred in town. The Johnsons vacationed in Florida and sent their children to college. Their work was not particularly laborious or time-consuming and rarely involved contacts with neighbors or other family members. Visitors were no more common than in a suburban neighborhood.

Not all midwestern farm families lived like the Johnsons. Dairy farmers, for example, continued to work sixty-hour, seven-day weeks. Machinery and electrical power enabled them to enlarge their herds but not to alter the routine of cattle raising and milking or reduce the time they devoted to their work. Even more striking was the contrast between Mrs. Johnson and the dairy farm wife (and many less affluent farm wives), who managed the home and devoted twenty or more hours per week to the fields and barn. Much of this labor replaced work that had formerly been done in the home. Rather than caring for children and laborers who performed outdoor chores, they did the outdoor work themselves. Most of them had little time for television or social activities and cherished their infrequent vacations.[11]

Many farm wives also became business managers. They did the family bookkeeping, prepared tax returns and reports to government agencies, and participated in investment decisions. As the farm became enmeshed in complex financial systems, they bore greater responsibility for its economic success. In earlier years the wife's butter and egg sales had helped stabilize the family's income. In the 1950s and 1960s the wife's business acumen contributed more directly to the success or failure of the farm enterprise.[12]

Many farm families found the new environment threatening. Confronted with growing competitive pressures, accelerating costs, and declining prices, they looked for villains and found them in the marketplace. In 1955 a group of western Iowa farmers revived the idea of collective bargaining with processors to raise commodity prices. Their organization, the National Farmers Organization, grew rapidly to more than 100,000 members in the midwestern states, awakening memories of the alliances, the Farmers' Union, the Non-Partisan League, and the Farmers Holiday Association. "Farmers can solve their own problems within a few days' time," asserted an NFL pamphlet, "when they make up their minds to use their bargaining power."[13] But most farmers were skeptical or hostile. Unable to reach agreements with processors, NFO leaders sponsored a series of holding actions between 1959 and 1969. NFO "strikes" attracted wide newspaper and television coverage (particularly when they resulted in violence) but had little impact on agricultural prices. Too few farmers participated, and activists gradually became discouraged as they saw their nonstriking neighbors benefit from temporary price increases. Most of the John Johnsons disregarded or actively opposed the NFO.[14]

The decline in farm employment reverberated through the countryside, curtailing opportunities for current and prospective farmers and reversing the traditional relationship between farm and village. As the number of farm families declined and highways freed the rest from dependence on local retailers, villages withered or changed. A surprising number of them evolved into industrial communities. In 1950 the rural nonfarm population exceeded the farm population in Ohio, Indiana, Illinois, and Michigan; by 1960 it exceeded the farm population in every midwestern state and in the aggregate was twice as large. The greatest percentage increases were in medicine, education, and finance, but the largest absolute gains were in manufacturing.[15] By the 1960s midwestern villages ceased to be refuges for notably labor-intensive or anti-union employers. Their growing popularity as industrial centers reflected their proximity to a reasonably well-educated, mechanically sophisticated but comparatively poor rural population. To hard-pressed farmers they offered tempting prospects: taking a factory job without moving to a city and preserving at least part of the world they had known.

Table 8-2 summarizes these changes and compares them to the experiences of the remaining farm labor force. Part-time farmers and other family members who worked off the farm account for the seemingly contradictory "rural farm" labor force engaged in manufacturing and other nonagricultural activities. Apart from the precipitous decline in farm employment, the rural farm data suggest that farm families with one or more family members

Table 8–2
Rural Labor Force Changes
(Percentage)

	1950–1960			1950–1970		
	Total	*Men*	*Women*	*Total*	*Men*	*Women*
Rural Nonfarm	26	18	52	56	26	128
Manufacturing	43	40	57	86	71	156
Rural Farm	-28	-34	6	-46	-54	2
Agriculture	-39	-39	-30	-64	-36	-63
Manufacturing	-8	-12	-14	-7	-15	33

Sources: U.S. Census, *Population*, 1950, table 30; 1960, table 61; 1970, table 55 for seven states.

employed in manufacturing were more likely to remain in agriculture than families devoted exclusively to farming. To many postwar farmers, the presence of a nearby factory was as vital to survival as the price of corn or hogs.

The decline of traditional agriculture occurred with remarkably little fanfare. The success of the John Johnsons and the movement of their less fortunate neighbors into nonagricultural occupations made the experience difficult to interpret and easy to disregard. The NFO was a pale replica of the protest organizations of the 1890s or 1930s, and few visitors to the rural Midwest would have confused it with Appalachia. The losses were more subtle. Within a generation the largest single group of skilled, manual occupations, occupations that had offered unusual opportunities for personal autonomy and individual creativity, had almost disappeared. The horizons of midwestern workers narrowed.

In contrast service-sector work changed little as it became more prominent. The increase in hospital and other health-related occupations reflected postwar technological innovations in medicine and the spread of private health insurance plans. Still, neither development substantially changed the work of caring for the injured and sick, which remained labor-intensive and included skilled specialties (nurses, laboratory technicians) as well as many semiskilled and unskilled activities. Discounting and franchising began to change the character of retailing, but they made faster headway in other regions. Electronic computers transformed data processing in banks, insurance companies, and other information-intensive businesses, but had almost no impact on other workplaces. Except in medicine, the most important changes were quantitative, not qualitative. Indeed, the most notable change of the postwar era was the growing number of women, especially married women, in the paid labor force.

Like the immigrants of the late nineteenth and early twentieth centuries, women filled new jobs, worked for low wages, and rarely moved into managerial positions. But the postwar growth of the female labor force was overwhelmingly a local phenomenon that attracted little attention or concern, probably because it was consistent with prewar patterns, involved familiar faces, and did not result in visible differences in decision making. Wartime experiences undoubtedly had some impact, but the critical development was not the war but the earlier expansion of public secondary education that prepared women to take advantage of the growing demand for services.[16]

By the 1960s two additional developments influenced the behavior of married women. A now declining birthrate shortened the most demanding homemaking tasks by one-third or more, and labor-saving machinery reduced other household duties by comparable proportions. Studies of homemaking between the 1920s and 1960s suggest that women who were not employed outside the home devoted as much time (fifty-five hours per week in the

1960s) to household tasks as their mothers and grandmothers had, while employed women devoted only half as much time (twenty-six hours) to the same activities. This disparity may be partly a statistical aberration, but it also reflects new options in household management. Remote shopping centers, larger wardrobes, and more exacting hygienic standards accounted for the relatively long work week of full-time homemakers, while frozen and packaged foods, synthetic fabrics, proliferating restaurants and dry cleaning shops, and a modest revival of domestic service probably explain the abbreviated working hours of the others. Differences in work pace, performance standards, and attitudes toward housework also contributed to the differential.[17] But the essential factor was the increasingly indeterminate character of household work. Scientific and technological advances could be labor-saving, depending on other considerations, including the attractions of the labor market. Household labor had always depended on a small number of variables: family size and wealth, social class, and the cost of domestic labor. By the 1950s and 1960s, a longer list of variables resulted in more varied behavior.

The postwar expansion of white-collar occupations preserved and perhaps reinforced the image of white-collar workers as docile, cooperative employees. Their apparent lack of activism at a time when the labor movement had greater influence and visibility than ever before reflected the pleasant realities of white-collar work: generally safe and comfortable surroundings, a varied pace, and little direct supervision. But it also underlined the importance of the exit option. Low wages, meager opportunities for advancement, and offensive behavior by male supervisors kept turnover rates high but rarely spurred union activity. The major exception was government, where civil service regulations and other forms of employment security encouraged long tenures and low turnover. Union activity began to appear outside the largest cities in the mid-1960s; of particular importance were stirrings in the traditionally somnolent and management-oriented National Education Association. Competition with the American Federation of Teachers, which had organized the Chicago, Detroit, and Cleveland public school systems by the 1950s, spurred NEA to embrace collective bargaining. The Michigan and Wisconsin state associations were particularly active. After 1962 NEA made rapid gains in suburban school systems and became the most formidable new force in the midwestern labor movement.[18]

Industry, 1953–1960s

Compared to mining, construction, or agriculture, midwestern manufacturing hardly changed at all. The automation scare notwithstanding, technological innovation was gradual and undramatic. It did not threaten many workers, but it did not create many opportunities either. Though some industries and states such as Wisconsin showed signs of decline, midwestern manufacturing in general flourished. The foundations of that growth were familiar: metals, food processing, machinery, and automobiles in particular. The techniques of Henry Ford, Richard Feiss, and other pioneers were well established by midcentury. As in the burgeoning service industries, economic progress depended on people and on piecemeal improvements in machines and methods. The single most important cost-cutting technique, the employment of women, occasioned little comment.

Although employment opportunities in manufacturing paled in comparison to the pre-depression years and to opportunities in contemporary service industries, they did sustain the wartime movement from South to North. More than two million southern-born migrants lived in midwestern cities by the 1960s. The largest proportion were whites from the mountainous areas of the upper South. Kentuckians settled in Cincinnati, West Virginians in Cleveland; many former miners went to Chicago and Detroit. Regardless of destination, they moved to cities where jobs were available, re-creating the immigrant "chains" of earlier years. A study of Cincinnati migrants found that whites from Appalachia were most likely to settle in the city because of specific employment opportunities. (Black migrants, on the other had, were more likely to follow family members or friends, without a specific occupational objective.)[19] In most cases, migrants became semiskilled factory workers. Together with a substantial minority of black southerners, they took low-skill jobs in steel mills, meat-packing plants, and auto factories.[20] As a result of this influx, the Midwest of the 1950s and 1960s became comparatively unattractive to immigrants, now largely Hispanics and Asians. By 1970 immigrants and their children would constitute only 17 percent of the midwestern population, highly concentrated in the Chicago area. Indeed, Chicago had more immigrants than all of the midwestern *states* together except for Michigan. An influx of invited railroad and steelworkers during World War II revived Chicago's south-side Mexican community, and it continued to attract immigrants in the postwar period.

The outlook for these and other industrial workers was less hopeful than in the 1940s. In autos, rubber, and meatpacking, decentralization and plant closings became a serious threat. Notable casualties included thirty thousand Chicago packinghouse employees who lost their jobs as the industry moved closer to livestock suppliers.[21] However, Chicago's loss was Iowa's and Minnesota's gain, and most new plants were quickly organized. In the auto industry decentralization reduced opportunities in Detroit and Milwaukee and contributed to the collapse of the "independents" after the lifting of wartime production controls in 1953. As GM, Ford, and Chrysler resumed their expansion programs, mostly outside the Midwest, the independents, largely single-plant operations, fell further behind. The decline of Studebaker was especially difficult because of its role in the South Bend economy. Heralded in the 1940s for its cooperative relationship with UAW Local 5, the company became a textbook example of corporate mismanagement.[22] As it declined the workers came under growing pressure. Concessionary agreements tore apart the union but did not save the South Bend operation, which closed in the early 1960s. Yet the failure of Studebaker (as well as the collapse of the other independents) was analogous to the closing of the Chicago packing plants. It had little meaning for the industry or its midwestern base.[23]

The steel industry probably best exemplified postwar "stability." Recollections of the 1930s haunted steel makers, causing them to resist expansion and innovation.[24] The USW became a willing partner in a conspiracy against change. When David J. McDonald succeeded Philip Murray as USW president in 1952, he hoped to inherit Murray's mantle. To buttress his position, McDonald set out to raise steelworkers' wages above auto-industry levels. The manufacturers reluctantly cooperated, fearing the consequences of his failure. Generous wage increases became a pretext for substantial price increases. Because of the visibility of the industry and the impact of steel price changes on the economy, this "rite of spring" provoked intense political conflict. By the end of the decade, the manufacturers were worried about excessive labor costs and foreign competition; McDonald remained unpopular within the USW; and inflation had become a sensitive political issue. The stage was set for a disastrous 116-day steel strike in 1959, a turning point in the industry's history.[25]

Stability was also a notable theme of day-to-day industrial relations. In no other area of business activity had events of the 1930s and 1940s brought greater changes. Although most executives remained hostile to unions and collective bargaining, they adopted a pragmatic or "realistic" approach, at least in the short term.[26] Government regulation, a resourceful labor movement, and an expanding economy made the price of resistance prohibitive, as the Kohler Company, the most famous midwestern holdout, demonstrated. When the company's independent union, the Kohler Workers Association, voted to become a UAW local in 1952, Kohler managers provoked a strike that led to another decade of turmoil and staggering costs to both sides. The Kohler strike became a political cause célèbre. In the end the company had to rehire the strikers and bargain with the UAW.[27]

Having implemented the new strategy, most large and medium-sized midwestern corporations introduced an appropriate structure, typically an industrial relations department and staff. By the 1950s the head of industrial relations was often a vice-president who reported to the chief executive and whose position was comparable to that of other top executives, a remarkable achievement for a new specialty. Industrial relations managers bargained with union officials much as purchasing managers bargained with suppliers. At the plant level they saw themselves as impartial experts who mediated the divergent interests of production managers and union officials. Confounding the stereotypes of labor-management relations, they often took the sides of aggrieved workers and hard-pressed union officials.

Corporate realism in turn encouraged union "maturity."[28] As unions became more secure, union leaders devoted less attention to organizing and more to wages, job-control issues, and the bargaining relationship. Strikes increasingly became part of the bargaining process, a calculated way to influence negotiations. Contracts became longer and more detailed, spelling out contingencies in the assignment, supervision, promotion, and demotion of union members. Working rules reminiscent of the unionized construction and printing industries became common. Decisions were subject to multiple appeals, including a final appeal to a neutral outsider. The handling of grievances became a delicate issue, since every decision became a precedent. In the early 1950s International Harvester executives resolved to improve the company's poor industrial relations climate by eliminating a vast backlog of unresolved grievances. They quickly settled eight thousand complaints by conceding most of the workers' demands. The result was even more tortured relations as business pressures mounted.[29]

Postwar collective bargaining attracted many critics. Hostile executives pointed to the growing disparity between the treatment of unorganized and organized workers and the mounting costs of contract administration. Union critics charged that union officers were more interested in maintaining stable relationships with employers than in defending workers' interests. Investigations of the Teamsters, the UMW, and other unions revealed numerous examples of "sweetheart" contracts. Even in the auto industry, long contacts led to "civilized" relationships between union leaders and executives that ill-served union members, or so it was charged.[30]

Postwar union leaders consistently opposed fractional bargaining. In the early 1950s URW leaders cooperated with production managers in a major crackdown on stewards in the Akron tire plants. After numerous discharges and suspensions, the brief walkouts that had characterized shop-floor relations since World War II declined. The long-term effects of the crackdown were more problematic. Workers resorted to slowdowns rather than work stoppages, and managers began to recognize informal "mutual agreements."[31] In other industries, a similar sequence was common; the suppression of informal shop-floor agreements in the auto and steel industries probably contributed to the grievance "explosion" that occurred in the mid-1960s.[32]

Despite opposition to fractional bargaining, industrial relations managers and union leaders could point to major changes in shop-floor relations. The end of the foreman's unilateral authority to assign, discipline, and fire workers addressed the single most important source of friction. Veteran workers typically cited it as the most notable union achievement.[33] Similarly, the substitution of hourly or daily rates (often "measured day work," or time rates with a minimum output requirement) for incentive plans reduced another source of conflict. During World War II many incentive plans had become "demoralized" as manufacturers searched for ways to raise wages without violating government regulations. After the war workers resisted adjustments. Rather than cut rates and invite strikes, managers replaced the incentives with time rates. The effect was often salutary. Workers became less sensitive to minor changes in production methods and supervisors were freed from the paperwork burden that the incentive systems imposed on them. As Slichter, Healy, and Livernash reported in 1960, "good labor relations are easier to attain under daywork than under incentive."[34]

One other feature of postwar collective bargaining substantially affected worker attitudes and expectations. The emphasis on "fringe" benefits that dated from the 1930s and 1940s increased during the 1950s and 1960s. Aware of the significance of nonwage benefits and the niggardliness of the welfare state, workers and unions insisted on more and more generous benefits. Managers generally were more receptive to these pressures than to wage demands. Pension and insurance plans spread rapidly in the 1950s. An additional innovation, supplementary unemployment benefits (SUB), introduced in the 1955 Ford-UAW contract, was a direct response to the inadequacy of the state systems. Yet private welfare plans also had unintentional effects. In particular they reduced the attractiveness of the exit option for disgruntled employees. Surveys of employees revealed many cases of unhappy workers who kept their jobs because of insurance or pension rights.[35] Private plans also defused pressures that might have led to the extension of state plans.[36] Finally, they inflated production costs at a time when manufacturers faced growing regional and international competition.

The most compelling examples of union maturity, however, were outside the workplace. By the early 1950s the unions' alliance with the Democratic party was firm and flourishing. Nonpartisanship and independent labor activity, the strategies of earlier generations, were now passé. A survey of Chicago plumbers, Chicago-area farm-machinery workers, Wisconsin clothing workers, and southern Illinois miners reported virtually no support for independent labor action. Indeed, most workers were wary of any union effort to influence elections.[37] Other surveys echoed these findings. Since most industrial workers were also members of ethnic and racial groups that traditionally voted Democratic, the alliance with the Democrats was not controversial; but it was not especially influential either. The refusal of rank-and-file members to accept the decisions of their leaders helped explain the limited influence of the labor movement in the Democratic coalition and the frequent success of conservative Democratic and Republican candidates.

Still, union voters could and did elect approved Democratic candidates. Freed of most legal restraints on expenditures by favorable judicial decisions, unions played aggressive roles in primary and general elections.[38] The most impressive union victory came in Ohio, where the AFL and CIO traditionally wielded little power. In 1958 the virulently anti-union state chamber of commerce, inspired by the passage of right-to-work legislation in Indiana and initiatives in other states, placed a right-to-work constitutional amendment on the ballot. This "incredibly stupid decision" galvanized labor and Democratic voters. An ambitious, expensive campaign portraying the amendment as an attack on union membership and blue-collar living standards brought hundreds of thousands of union members and sympathizers to the polls. Their overwhelming rejection of right-to-work contributed to the defeat of the incumbent Republican governor and Senator John W. Bricker, the state's best-known politician.[39]

In general, however, the union role was more circumscribed. Activists faced two major obstacles: the resiliency of nonunion political groups and the unwillingness of union members to follow union dictates on issues unrelated to collective bargaining and union security. In Chicago, for example, unions were an essential component of the Democratic coalition and were rewarded with jobs, lucrative wage agreements, and prestigious appointments. Yet they had little influence on other government policies. No one, least of all the leaders of the Chicago Federation of Labor, suggested the Chicago had a "labor" government.[40] In nearby East Chicago, USW members outnumbered the rest of the population and could have controlled the municipal government. But union leaders and members took little interest in local affairs and rarely opposed the corrupt Democratic machine that controlled the city. During strikes, union leaders could count on favorable treatment from municipal officials, especially the police. Otherwise, the steel manufacturers were able to "get whatever [they] desired."[41]

In Detroit the UAW had remarkably little influence, despite its huge membership and activist leadership. The pattern of the 1943 and 1945 mayoral campaigns persisted through the 1950s. Voters, including UAW and other union members, divided along racial lines, undermining UAW efforts to create ideological and class alignments. As a result the city had a succession of conservative mayors, committed to maintaining the racial status quo. By the end of the decade, UAW officials had largely abandoned efforts to influence Detroit elections.[42] The postwar history of municipal politics in Cleveland, Minneapolis, and Milwaukee differed only in detail. Unions may have overshadowed other groups, but their influence was decisive only when work-related issues were paramount.

Origins of Upheaval, 1960s to 1975

The years from the early 1960s to the energy crisis and the severe recession of 1973–1975 were, by most measures, a period of opportunity for midwestern workers. Stimulated by large increases in government spending, aggregate employment rose steadily and wages and earnings continued to grow. Many of the trends of the postwar years continued to reshape the midwestern labor force, but there were also disturbing changes. By the 1960s the decline of farm employment had created a social and institutional vacuum in some areas. Rising racial tensions revived memories of earlier ethnic conflicts. The failure of organized labor to keep pace with the evolution of the labor force raised new questions about the efficacy of unions as mechanisms for expressing the workers' voice. Most ominous of all, the poor performance of the economy in the 1970s together with the maturation of the baby boom generation threatened the prospects of all workers.

Employment patterns reemphasized the contrasting fortunes of rural and urban workers. Mining employment continued to decline, although the energy crisis of 1973–1974 temporarily halted the flow of unemployed coal miners to midwestern cities. At the same time, the increased availability of foreign ores devastated the Minnesota mining industry. By the mid-1970s only the most efficient mines remained open and the Mesabi had become a depressed area. Farm employment continued to decline as rising land prices and government support programs effectively eliminated most full-time farm families of modest means, leaving a substantial number of well-to-do but urban-oriented farmers; a larger number of part-timers and rural residents who rented land to full-time farmers; and a small, transient group of harvest workers. These developments also spurred an extensive but little noticed enclosure movement. An aerial study of three rural Indiana counties concluded that the "principal change" of the 1960s was "the enlargement of fields by the removal of fences and the joining of . . . small fields." In remote and comparatively poor Jay County, farmers who could not afford to buy out their neighbors farmed more intensively by concentrating on dairy or hog production. However, this strategy forced them "to buy most of their feed, since they can produce only a fraction of what they need."[43] Rising grain prices in the 1970s hurt these farmers and did not increase farm employment. Inflated land values set the stage for the most severe farm crisis since the 1930s.

The most visible measure of the changing character of midwestern agriculture was the growing role of migrant laborers. Although wage workers were familiar figures in midwestern agriculture, they were typically apprentice farmers and were perceived (and usually perceived themselves) as occupying a rung on the agricultural ladder. The migrants were different. After World

War II Mexican workers increasingly took the places of local harvest employees. By the 1960s twenty-five thousand of them worked in Ohio and Michigan fields, moving from area to area as fruits and vegetables ripened. They received little encouragement to remain. Most residents, including most farmers, looked upon them as outsiders whose sole virtues were their willingness to work for low wages and live in hovels that made the meanest tenant dwellings seem appealing.

The growth of migrant-labor activism in California in the mid-1960s dramatized the plight of farm laborers there and elsewhere. Ohio and Michigan migrants reacted by attempting to bargain with growers. In northwestern Ohio, Baldemar Velasquez and other migrant leaders formed a Farm Labor Organizing Committee in 1967 and negotiated contracts with more than twenty growers in 1968. They won recognition but were unable to obtain higher wages or benefits because of the growers' fixed-price contracts with canneries. FLOC activism also provoked ominous countermeasures. The Farm Bureau mobilized to oppose collective bargaining, and many growers bought mechanical tomato pickers. Faced with devastating job losses, the FLOC abandoned its collective bargaining campaign in 1969.[44] It reemerged in 1978 claiming two thousand members and tried to reopen negotiations with Ohio farmers. When that tactic failed it struck some Ohio and Indiana growers and tried to mount a boycott against the canneries. The boycott led to violence, numerous arrests, and substantial losses for many workers and farmers. Most farmers around Leipsic, Ohio, the boycott center, shifted to grain crops, and the UAW, which had provided financial assistance to FLOC, abandoned it. By 1979 the organization appeared moribund.[45]

Velasquez and other activists persisted, however, and eventually recruited new allies, including the United Farm Workers; Ray Rodgers, a labor consultant who specialized in attacking anti-union companies; and the National Council of Churches. Rodgers's campaign against Campbell Soup, including a 1983 march from Toledo to the company's Camden, New Jersey, headquarters and a threatened boycott of Campbell products by church groups, ultimately produced results. In 1985 Campbell agreed to a contract that provided wage increases, health insurance, and other benefits. Other processors agreed to similar terms.[46] Temporarily, at least, the efforts of Velasquez and his allies paid off.

Urban workers fared better by most measures. Defense-related industries expanded during the Vietnam War and manufacturers generally did well. Trucking grew rapidly and construction expanded, especially in the largest cities and in suburban areas. White-collar occupations grew fastest of all. Most of the new service-sector jobs were semiskilled positions in health services, retailing, and government and paid low wages relative to farm ownership or mass production manufacturing. While many industries grew, none of them seemed to have the potential to create large numbers of highly paid jobs or to transform the regional economy.

The most significant developments of the 1960s and 1970s occurred in manufacturing and underlined—like the rapidly diminishing farm population—the fraying of the postwar order. The postwar industrial relations system and the high level of organization in midwestern manufacturing were, ironically, the destabilizing forces. Despite the unions' acknowledged successes in improving shop-floor management, providing an outlet for grievances, and defending the interests of the inarticulate, the industrial relations climate was hardly more favorable than it had been a decade before. The adversarial nature of collective bargaining was a source of continuing friction. The cumulative effects of contract bargaining and grievance decisions raised production costs and made shop-floor innovations difficult. Most of all, the disparity between membership levels in the Midwest and the South and Southwest, together with the increasing attractiveness of those regions, tempted manufacturers to move rather than confront their problems.

The mass production industries provide the best examples. Three features of their experiences stand out. First was the residual hostility of executives to organized labor. As surveys of executive opinion emphasized, the accommodation of the 1940s and 1950s was a truce rather than a partnership. Acceptance of unions was confined to industrial relations managers, who had a personal stake in collective bargaining. Second was the growth of personnel activities outside the sphere of collective bargaining. The expansion of technical and clerical employment created large groups of independent but nonunion workers who required as much attention as organized production workers. Together with the public regulation of employment and working conditions, which increased substantially in the 1960s and 1970s, their presence rapidly overshadowed more traditional concerns. Symptomatic of this trend was the rise of "human resources" management, which increasingly superseded conventional personnel management and its emphasis on production workers.[47] The third factor was the rising number of applicants, especially for unskilled and semiskilled jobs, as the baby boom generation began to enter the labor force. Labor-market competition reduced union power and lowered the profits of organized firms.[48]

These developments led to the rise of nonunion industrial relations systems in many manufacturing firms. The new systems differed from the open shop plans of the pre-depression years.[49] Most corporations made no effort to eliminate unions from their existing plants. However, they undercut the unions' appeal in new plants by paying comparable wages, providing similar benefits, and introducing grievance procedures. They also built plants in small towns and rural areas, especially in the South. Nonunion industrial relations systems were thus a threat to the midwestern industrial economy as well as to organized labor.

The fate of the tire industry illustrated the growing vulnerability of midwestern industrial workers. In the 1950s tire production was still highly concentrated in Ohio and the Midwest. Virtually every plant was organized, and pattern settlements created uniform wages and working conditions. The industry's sensitivity to strikes and strike threats enabled tire workers to enjoy the highest hourly rates of any factory workers, though the archaic six-hour day and thirty-six-hour week (which the union defended, supposedly at the insistence of workers who held second jobs) lowered earnings. These conditions gradually changed the character of the industry. In the 1910s and 1920s it had attracted a physical elite of muscular young men; by the 1950s it employed only high school graduates who excelled on vocational aptitude tests. But tire-industry industrial relations also had an ominous side. High wages, elaborate work rules, and the accumulated wounds of twenty years of collective bargaining hardened managerial hostility to the United Rubber Workers. After a study of the industry's employment policies, Herbert Northrup reported that union policies were the "dynamic factor" in the evolution of "production methods and labor requirements."[50] To curtail union power, manufacturers emphasized mechanization and automation and shifted as much production as possible to new southern plants.[51] Employment in the Akron plants gradually declined.

The industry's preoccupation with industrial relations, labor costs, and production methods had other effects. Until the late 1960s, most accounts of the industry described it as technologically dynamic and linked that dynamism to labor issues. Yet as Northrup noted, these references were to process innovations, designed to reduce production costs. In retrospect it appears that this focus on production, coupled with the "civilized" competition of a mature oligopolistic industry, diverted attention and resources from other pressing concerns. In the 1970s and 1980s new challenges related to product innovations would devastate the industry.

The danger first became apparent in the early 1970s. American firms were slow to embrace the superior radial tire, creating a vacuum that Michelin, the European leader in radial production, quickly filled. By the early 1970s Michelin had three nonunion plants in South Carolina. The energy crisis of 1973–1974 increased the appeal of fuel-efficient radial tires and encouraged other foreign radial makers to enter the American market. By the mid-1970s the American manufacturers faced their most serious business challenges since the 1930s. The industry's handful of small firms negotiated concessionary contracts with their workers and gradually shifted to radial production. The large firms had another choice: they could close their existing factories and open new plants in more hospitable settings. URW leaders, pressed by veteran workers to maintain wage parity with the auto industry, inadvertently helped make the choice. In 1976 the URW struck the major firms for a cost-of-living formula and substantial wage increases. The conflict lasted more than three months. Union success "contributed to a continued dispersion of production away from organized facilities." It also reinforced the manufacturers' determination to end master agreements and pattern bargaining.[52] In the following years, the Akron locals agreed to various of work-rule changes but were unable to stop the exodus to southern, nonunion plants. An innovative agreement between General Tire and URW Local 9 in 1979, providing for a new Akron plant, collapsed during the subsequent recession. By 1981 automobile and truck tire production had ended in Akron, and rubber-industry employment was only 15 percent of its postwar peak.[53]

Several features of this story distinguish it from earlier union-management conflicts. The major disruptive forces originated outside the domestic industry. In the 1980s competitive pressures led not only to plant closings, job losses, and union decline, but also to the merger of the Uniroyal and the Goodrich tire operations (and eventual takeover by Michelin) and the foreign takeover of Firestone and General Tire. Despite these challenges, the manufacturers did not advocate a return to the open shop, at least in the northern centers. Similarly, union leaders struggled to balance their members' long- and short-term interests once a significant nonunion producer had emerged. Worker demands for wage increases made any deviation from established practices politically difficult, perhaps impossible. As a result, union policy contributed to the industry's mounting crisis.

Even in industries that did not face similar competitive challenges, union leaders had to confront the effects of three decades of job-control bargaining. In the auto industry, the most prominent example, the level of shop-floor turmoil markedly increased in the 1960s. Employee turnover rose, grievances mounted, and wildcat strikes became more frequent. Given UAW successes in winning wage and benefit improvements, most analyses attributed the turmoil to changes in worker values, a growing generational gulf between union officers and members, and the suppression of shop-floor activism.[54] An erosion in employee quality, associated with the increasingly negative image of auto work, was also a factor. The Big Three hired one and a half million workers between 1960 and 1966 to increase employment by 250,000, a record that recalled the turnover of the pre–World War I years. After the disastrous 1967 Detroit race riot, the auto companies hired inner-city residents "on the spot." In other cities the pool of applicants was so small that virtually no one was turned away. A Detroit personnel official acknowledged that "if we discharged for days off and tardiness like we should, we would not have a labor force."[55]

A three-week wildcat strike by General Motors employees at Lordstown, Ohio, in early 1972 emphasized the severity of the problem. When GM managers increased assembly line speeds, leaders of the Lordstown local union urged restraint and negotiation. Restive workers struck against the union as well as the company, precipitating a crisis in the plant and attracting nationwide publicity. "Once prototypes of efficiency," proclaimed one observer, "the Lordstown factories had now become the prototypes of revolt."[56] At the same time a widely read government study, *Work in America* (1972), reported pervasive discontent and "blue-collar blues."

Though this concern soon gave way to more concrete worries about the future of mass production industry, it generated widespread interest in work reform and numerous experiments. Though most of the activity was "piecemeal" and "eclectic," reminiscent of the early days of systematic management, it had two major emphases: the redesign of semiskilled jobs and the participation of production workers in shop-floor decision making.[57] At General Motors, "Quality of Work Life" activities aimed at alleviating unrest in some plants and at improving productivity in other, notably southern, nonunion plants. In many factories they elicited suspicion as well as cooperation. Many efforts floundered after a year or two. Where they proved more durable, worker-participation schemes (increasingly modeled after Japanese "quality circles") often became an addition to, rather than a substitute for, plant-level job-control unionism.[58] Their most important function may have been to serve as a preliminary step toward more comprehensive reforms.

During the same period a rebellion within the Steelworkers provided additional evidence of a mounting crisis in the labor movement. Critics in and out of the union charged national and District 31 USW leaders with complacency, accommodating relations with employers, and unsavory political alliances. Hostility to the regime of president David J. McDonald led to his defeat in 1965 and to the end of the Human Relations Committee, a cooperative effort to improve working conditions.[59] Joseph Germano's retirement as District 31 president eight years later began a new and more dramatic phase of the contest between stalwarts and insurgents. Germano's designated heir faced a challenge from Edward Sadlowski, past president of U.S. Steel's South Works local and an advocate of more aggressive bargaining and political independence. After a bitter and controversial campaign, Sadlowski won by a two-to-one margin. His electoral base was the steel mill locals of south Chicago and northern Indiana.[60] Sadlowski's calls for greater responsiveness to rank-and-file concerns also reflected his sensitivity to the changing ethnic character of the mills. Germano and his allies had symbolized the rise of the new immigrants. Sadlowski championed black and Hispanic workers who filled many low-skill positions by the 1960s.

In retrospect it appears that Sadlowski's ethnic alliances rather than his well-publicized militancy accounted for his success. Two years later, when he ran for the USW presidency on a similar platform, he lost badly, though he carried the Calumet area. His District 31 allies also encountered problems. Their independence cost the union much of its local political influence, and their promises of greater militancy worried members who had become anxious about the industry's mounting troubles. In 1981 the reformers lost control of the district.[61]

Complicating the problems of midwestern factories and unions in the 1960s and 1970s was an escalation of racial conflict. Two factors ensured that the tensions of the postwar years did not disappear. The first was the continuing migration of southern blacks, displaced by the mechanization of southern agriculture and the decline of industries that had traditionally hired unskilled African Americans. Black men continued to find jobs in foundries, steel mills, packinghouses, auto-assembly plants, and other manufacturing plants in the largest cities. In many cases they became members of CIO unions that promoted racial equality. Yet numerous obstacles remained. The decline of meatpacking in Chicago and East Saint Louis in the 1950s and early 1960s underlined the precariousness of life in northern cities, even for those with high-paying jobs and union protection. Black unemployment rates in the 1960s and 1970s were typically three to four times white rates.

The second factor was the hostility of white ethnics, who continued to view blacks as a threat to jobs and neighborhoods. Polish Americans were the core of the conservative alliance that dominated Detroit politics between the 1940s and 1960s.[62] They and other eastern-European groups also pressured the Daley machine to preserve the racial status quo in Chicago. When those tactics failed, they forcibly resisted the movement of blacks into all-white neighborhoods.[63] After living in a steel mill neighborhood, sociologist William Kornblum concluded that opposition to blacks was "a general phenomenon throughout the South Chicago area. Only the numerical importance of the Poles and their location in the direct path of racial invasion have caused them to be singled out for their racism."[64]

By the 1960s racial animosities overshadowed other ethnic rivalries in the region's cities. Besides the overtly discriminatory policies of many craft groups, inadvertent distinctions became racial issues. The UAW, for example, had had a Fair Employment Practices Committee since 1944, but it was "more educational than action-oriented" and antagonized many blacks who saw it as a meaningless gesture.[65] Other liberal unions confronted similar problems. De facto social segregation was the rule in the Packinghouse Workers and Amalgamated Meat Cutters and probably in other unions.[66] Regardless of their occupations or unions, African Americans lived in racially homogeneous neighborhoods that were often geographically removed from their jobs. In the minority of cases where black neighborhoods were near centers of black employment, like the stockyards area of Chicago, the association was a reflection of the industry's precarious state and bleak future.

Public-policy initiatives, civil rights legislation, and the war on poverty directly or indirectly addressed many of these problems in the 1960s and early 1970s. Although they helped lower employment barriers, especially for minority women, their immediate effect was often counterproductive. Tensions and inflated expectations associated with the war on poverty contributed to disastrous riots in Detroit (1967), Cleveland (1968), and other cities. Violence in turn accelerated white flight to the suburbs and left riot areas permanently blighted.[67] Public support for government programs soon declined. The most significant legacy of the war on poverty, ironically, was the expansion of the welfare state, as support for antipoverty measures evolved into backing for Social Security and other conventional benefit programs.

The turmoil associated with civil rights and antipoverty legislation also highlighted divisions in the labor movement. Although no hard-and-fast line existed, many craft unions preserved racial restrictions in their constitutions and bylaws and maintained the color line in practice. Their policies reflected their character as family or ethnic monopolies. Plumbers organizations, for example, often had an informal, fraternal quality and resisted external challenges.[68] The high pay of craft groups added to their cohesion and to the resentment of those who were excluded.

Title VII of the 1964 Civil Rights Act, banning employment discrimination, and other related measures were challenges to the status quo and invitations to contest union policies.[69] In Chicago, which had the highest-paid construction workers and the most influential building-trades locals in the region, conflict over exclusionary hiring and promotion practices continued for more than a decade. Civil rights groups focused on Washburne High School, which prepared workers for the building trades. Protests eventually resulted in increased black enrollment at Washburne and greater minority employment in the Chicago construction industry.[70] Similar conflicts occurred in virtually every midwestern city, though the objective gradually shifted from black employment to female employment. The opening of crafts to women proved to be less contentious and emotional. By 1980 there were more women than black men in the midwestern construction trades.

Yet craft unions were not the only centers of resistance to racial integration. Civil rights agitation increasingly divided industrial unions, which had long championed integration and had large black minorities. Conflicts over assignments, promotions, and union representation often galvanized white majorities against minority workers. Other threats to union influence occurred outside the plant. In 1964 Milwaukee's Polish Americans and other blue-collar workers embarrassed the Wisconsin AFL-CIO and the Johnson administration by giving George Wallace 34 percent of the Democratic vote in the state's presidential primary. Civil rights was the central issue of the campaign.[71] By 1966 a mounting white backlash substantially compromised labor's political efforts, as union members refused to vote or voted for Republican protest candidates. Their reaction "shifted from apathy to retribution" as the threat became more local and personal.[72] Two years later many union members again supported Wallace or Richard Nixon, exposing the unions' inability to mobilize union households for liberal Democratic candidates. Race, more than any other issue, undermined the unions' carefully nurtured influence outside the workplace.

Climacteric, 1977–1983

By the mid-1970s the bases of midwestern prosperity were less secure than they had been since the 1930s. Farming had ceased to be a source of opportunity, though production and productivity continued to rise. Village life was more likely to revolve around a factory than the agricultural hinterland. Urban industry sustained a large and comparatively affluent industrial labor force, though opportunities had diminished and unrest was widespread. White-collar occupations continued to increase, but the number of high-wage jobs grew more slowly than in other regions. Less-skilled positions were either traditional women's jobs or low-wage occupations that paid a fraction of the typical construction or steelworker's wage. But were these signs of trouble in the region or simply reflections of a national economy growing too slowly to provide opportunities for many workers? Until the late 1970s, it was possible to argue that the basic problem had little to do with the Midwest or its workers.

A series of disasters in the late 1970s and early 1980s demonstrated that the problems of the preceding decade were more serious and fundamental than most midwesterners had imagined. The worst recession since the 1930s ended opportunities for workers in farming and manufacturing—and for many in offices and stores as well. Hardest hit were the industries most intimately associated with midwestern economic growth. Well-known firms like International Harvester and Republic Steel collapsed and disappeared. Many powerful industrial managers lost their influence and often their positions, leaving a social and civic vacuum. Scholars debated whether these changes reflected a cyclical downturn or a more disturbing process of "deindustrialization."[73] Regardless of the answer, the immediate results of the crisis of the early 1980s were profound. Abandoned factories, permanently displaced workers, and distressed communities transformed the region into the nation's "rust belt."

The farm crisis of the early 1980s resulted from a disastrous misuse of farm political power. That danger had existed since the early twentieth century, when country lifers and aggressive political organizations in Wisconsin and Minnesota created mutually supporting links between government and agriculture. It grew substantially in the 1930s, when the federal government became committed to agricultural "parity" and to providing low-interest loans to farmers. But the threat was obscure as long as interest rates remained low. The inflationary years of the mid-1970s raised land prices and borrowing costs to unprecedented levels. As interest rates rose, indebted farmers became increasingly vocal about the perils of exorbitant credit costs. Congress responded with a series of measures that vastly expanded the volume of low-interest loans offered through the Farm Credit system and the Farmers Home Administration. Subsidized credit fueled greater speculative activity and even higher land prices. When Federal Reserve policy finally brought the inflationary boom to an end in the early 1980s, land prices plummeted and thousands of seemingly prosperous farmers lost everything.[74]

The agricultural crisis was nationwide in scope and most severe in the Plains states, where vast areas were threatened with depopulation.[75] Many Iowa and Minnesota farmers shared the fate of their western neighbors, and many other midwestern farmers suffered to some degree. Additional government subsidies alleviated the effects of the collapse, but only for farmers per se. Workers in towns that depended on agricultural spending had no comparable buffer, and some of the subsidy programs actually accentuated their problems. Among those hardest hit were farm-implement dealers. Their plight in turn spelled disaster for companies that made farm machinery, accelerating the simultaneous decline of midwestern manufacturing.

In retrospect there had been many warnings of trouble in manufacturing. The region's emphasis on products that were familiar and even old-fashioned by the 1970s, the appearance of new competitors in and out of the region, the increasing rigidity of production management and industrial relations, and the apparent complacency of industrial managers and workers were often cited in later years. The gradual disintegration of the midwestern tire, meatpacking, and steel industries in the late 1970s might have been foreseen by anyone who had taken a close and critical look at at their operations.

Meatpacking had become more geographically dispersed in the postwar years, as manufacturers moved closer to raw materials sources. The initial beneficiaries included Hormel, Oscar Mayer, Rath, and Dubuque Packing, all unionized, high-wage firms. But the changes continued. In the 1960s a new firm, Iowa Beef Processors, adopted an aggressive growth strategy based on improved manufacturing methods and union avoidance that kept the industry in turmoil. IBP built specialized one-story plants, equipped with the most modern labor-saving machinery. It paid low wages and vigorously fought efforts to organize its employees. By the 1970s IBP dominated beef packing. Other firms adopted the IBP strategy, leading to plant closings and more contentious labor relations. Iowa lost more than two thousand jobs in beef packing between 1975 and 1979, and another thousand jobs in pork packing.[76] The most notable casualty was Rath.[77] Even Hormel, one of the industry's most profitable firms, known for high wages and good labor relations, insisted on major wage concessions before building a new, single-story plant next to its old factory in Austin, Minnesota.[78]

The collapse of the farm-machinery industry was equally notable because of its concentration in large plants in Illinois and Wisconsin. By the mid-1970s secondary producers such as Allis-Chalmers and J. I. Case had begun to resemble the "independent" auto firms of the 1950s. More surprising was the decline of the industry leader, International Harvester. As the farm market weakened and profits fell, Harvester executives blamed excessive wages and restrictive work rules. A new president demanded major concessions from the UAW in early 1979, precipitating a 172-day strike that further weakened the company. The final blow was the economic collapse of 1980. By 1981 the company had been dismembered, many plants had been closed, and most employees had been laid off for varying periods. The demise of Allis-Chalmers was only slightly more prolonged. John Deere emerged as the dominant manufacturer in a shrunken market.[79]

By the 1970s steelworkers faced similar problems. Japanese imports had become a threat in the 1960s, and nonunion minimills, which reduced costs by recycling scrap steel and paying lower wages than unionized firms, became an additional challenge in the 1970s. In the new, more competitive environment, the old, integrated companies were vulnerable, and the mills of the Pittsburgh district and Ohio's Mahoning Valley, which lacked water transportation, were most vulnerable of all. By the early 1970s the Mahoning mills had twenty thousand fewer workers than in the 1940s.[80] The 1969 takeover of Youngstown Sheet and Tube, the area's largest employer, by the Lykes Company, a diversified firm with no background in steel, added to the uncertainty. Yet the decision by Lykes in 1977 to close the giant Youngstown plant and dismiss more than four thousand workers shocked nearly everyone.

The Youngstown debacle stimulated a series of community efforts to reopen the plant. The first and most vocal of these was spearheaded by an Ecumenical Coalition of religious leaders, local union officials, and radical activists that sought federal subsidies to purchase and operate the plant. The Coalition's activities generated controversy and opposition, particularly from steel manufacturers, who did not want a subsidized competitor, and USW leaders, who viewed the Coalition as a rival force.[81] Although USW opposition was probably sufficient to sabotage the plan, the most surprising feature of the campaign was the Coalition's meager success in enlisting Youngstown residents, including laid-off steelworkers. Most residents and workers were convinced that the plant would reopen or that other jobs in related industries would materialize.

There was some basis for this conviction in 1978 and 1979. Terry Buss and F. Stevens Redburn, who interviewed several hundred laid-off Sheet and

Tube employees, concluded that the shutdown had a surprisingly modest effect. Laid-off employees received unemployment compensation, supplemental unemployment benefits, and other assistance that minimized their losses. Most of them found new jobs in other mills, construction firms, or auto plants. A large number were recalled to Sheet and Tube for limited periods; some even left new jobs to take temporary positions at the mill, confident that it would resume operations. The most critical factor in the adjustment, however, was the rapid expansion of the nearby GM Lordstown plant, which added more than four thousand additional workers in late 1977 and early 1978. In the meantime the close-knit Youngstown community helped blunt the effects of the closing. "Looking over the whole pattern of community change before and after 1978," Buss and Redburn reported, "the short-run impact of the massive layoffs appears slight."[82]

No one suggested that the other impending disaster of the late 1970s, the imminent collapse of the Chrysler Corporation, would have a similar outcome. Chrysler was much larger and more geographically concentrated, with more than sixty thousand employees in Detroit. Nor were Chrysler employees, and particularly the company's twenty-five thousand black employees, likely to find new jobs as readily as the Sheet and Tube employees had. The 1967 Detroit riot had devastated the city's economy; other firms were leaving, not expanding. For many workers Chrysler was the only high-wage employer, perhaps the only employer. The implications of a Chrysler collapse were only slightly less ominous in Kokomo, Indiana, and in other cities with Chrysler plants.[83]

Because the anticipated results of Chrysler's bankruptcy were so catastrophic and because the company's problems were results of poor strategic and financial management, the community response was more effective. State and local politicians mounted an aggressive campaign for federal funds. New executives promised immediate improvements. Most notable was the reaction of UAW leaders, especially Douglas Fraser, the new international president. In 1978 Fraser had organized the Progressive Alliance to promote labor-oriented causes and oppose business interests. Although the Alliance sponsored some of the early deindustrialization studies, it became an obstacle and potentially an embarrassment as the Chrysler crisis became more severe. Fraser, who had headed the union's Chrysler department and was well-acquainted with the company's problems, had to choose between an antibusiness, political agenda and the bailout. He chose the latter, becoming a champion of the kinds of protectionist and anticonsumer measures that the Alliance had been created to oppose.[84] Government subsidies, together with restrictions on Japanese imports and a series of labor contracts that included the most significant wage concessions since the 1930s, saved Chrysler.

These experiences were a prelude to the more serious and widespread problems that accompanied the downturn of the economy in early 1980 and the more severe recession of 1981–1982. As demand declined, competition became intense, especially in newly deregulated industries such as airlines and trucking. Manufacturing, however, bore the brunt of the recession. Of particular importance for midwestern workers was a precipitous decline in automobile sales, a result of high interest rates, foreign competition, poor workmanship, and the recession itself. The fall in auto sales, which began in 1979, led to massive layoffs and plant closings in the auto, auto-parts, steel, rubber, and other related industries. More than one-third of all auto and steelworkers experienced layoffs between 1979 and 1983. By early 1981 nine of the ten cities with the highest unemployment rates were in the Midwest; seven were in Michigan. By early 1982 unemployment rates exceeded 20 percent in many of those cities. More alarming was the wave of plant closings that accompanied the layoffs. Despite the Chrysler bailout, more than fifteen thousand Detroit-area Chrysler workers lost their jobs in a series of closings. The Calumet steel towns were another disaster area.[85] In Youngstown the recession led to three additional steel mill closings in 1980, permanently displacing an additional five thousand workers and prompting a series of related layoffs and closings in local businesses. Total job losses may have exceeded fifty thousand.[86]

Victims of plant closings faced a situation more like the 1930s than the 1970s. In Barberton, Ohio, for example, five large plants with more than five thousand employees closed between 1980 and 1983. The first was Seiberling Rubber, a Firestone subsidiary, with one thousand well-paid production workers. Many Seiberling employees were unconcerned at first; temporary layoffs had been common in the past, and the city's other factories had been alternative sources of jobs. Some displaced workers went hunting or devoted their time to home improvements. But other factories closed, and the national recovery had only a modest impact on Barberton's economy. Two years after the Seiberling closing, only 20 percent of laid-off workers had comparable positions. Forty percent had less-desirable jobs, and 40 percent were still jobless. By 1983, 10 percent of the city's homes were for sale, and many commercial buildings were empty. Ill health and crime also had increased.[87]

The fate of Barberton workers was typical of many auto and steel employees in the early 1980s. One study reported that 40 percent of the steelworkers who lost their jobs in the early 1980s were still unemployed in 1984. Most of the others had accepted large pay cuts. Nearly half of the former employees of U.S. Steel's South Works had been unable to find new jobs; others had become discouraged and stopped looking. Long-term unemployment was associated with increased alcoholism, family violence, and crime.[88]

The labor movement was another casualty of the recession. The decline in union density that resulted from the growth of industry in the South and West and the expansion of professional and service occupations was barely apparent in the Midwest until the late 1970s. By 1984, however, the union share of the labor force had fallen in every midwestern state; on average it was five percentage points less than in 1953. Only in Michigan and Indiana did it remain at more than a quarter of the labor force.[89] Although unions in virtually every industry registered declines, the membership losses of the UAW and USW, numbering in the hundreds of thousands, had no precedent except in the immediate post–World War II years.

The character of union activity also changed. Faced with the prospect of greater job losses, many unions agreed to lower wages or longer hours. Many employers also demanded more fundamental changes, including an end to pattern agreements, uniform wages and benefits for employees in different plants, and the job-control focus of labor-management relations. Innovations included reductions in job titles, broader work assignments, and team systems of production. Many contracts also continued the move away from wage incentive plans. In exchange union leaders often won profit-sharing plans and guarantees of continued employment. Auto-industry agreements of the early 1980s, for example, traded immediate labor-cost reductions for longer-term financial security and labor-management cooperation.

The contracts of the recession era were symptomatic of a broader movement for work reform that grew out of critiques of the status quo and increasing familiarity with the techniques of Japanese corporations. Rejecting conventional production management as well as job-control unionism, the reforms blurred distinctions between management and labor and enlarged the roles of production workers. Introduced by new firms such as Honda, Nucor, and Cyprus Minerals and older, troubled companies such as General Motors and Ford, they won a large and attentive following by the mid–1980s. Gauging the effects of this interest is more difficult; as in other cases of managerial innovation, a large and often deceptive gap separated theory from practice.[90]

No innovation, however, could obscure the most painful lesson of the recession years: neither farm nor factory was likely to be as important as in the past or to provide the same kinds of opportunities for midwestern workers. Table 8–3 provides a rough measure of the changing character of the midwestern labor force in the 1970s. It lists the service industries that experienced above-average employment gains and the role of women workers in them. Agriculture and manufacturing, at the bottom of the table, provide comparative perspective. At a time of modest economic expansion, service industries were adding over 400,000 employees. There were subtle changes from earlier years: education grew less rapidly, health-related occupations continued to expand, and business and social services became major employers.

Table 8–3
Employment Growth Rates, by Industry, 1970–1980
(Percentage)

	Total	Female Employment
Service Industries	26	36
Business services	88	104
Health services	84	98
Social services	75	113
Food and drink	71	70
Banking	59	81
Hospitals	50	49
Entertainment	45	59
Insurance	41	61
Wholesale trade	28	43
Education	27	31
Agriculture	-2	85
Manufacturing	1	15

Sources: U.S. Census, *Population*, 1970, table 55 for seven states; 1980, table 69 for seven states.

The pattern of union activity between the 1960s and 1980s was also a gauge of the changing character of the labor force. While traditional unions languished, white-collar organizations grew rapidly. A critical factor was the passage of public-employee collective bargaining laws. Wisconsin was a pioneer, adopting a collective bargaining statute in 1949. Illinois unions struggled unsuccessfully through the 1950s and 1960s before succeeding in 1973.[91] Other states followed, though Ohio did not adopt a public-employee collective bargaining statute until 1983, and Indiana had no law as late as 1990. Nevertheless, by the 1980s the American Federation of State, County, and Municipal Employees (AFSCME), the principal union of state and local government workers, was among the largest and most influential midwestern labor organizations.

Although all of these developments had roots in the years before 1953, the surprising, often devastating pace of change after the mid–1960s distinguished this period from earlier ones. The supposed golden age of midwestern industry and Big Labor, inaugurated by World War II, had benefited a single generation of industrial workers. In terms of individual opportunity, the region had evolved from one based on agriculture and industry to one based on neither in less than three decades. In terms of work experiences, the pattern was less clear, as the roles of technology, organization, and skill fluctuated in diverse and unpredictable ways. In 1950, as in 1900, workers had some notion of what lay ahead and how they might take advantage of it. By the 1980s they had little sense of what to expect.

9.

Afterword:
Work and Workers in the 1980s

For midwestern workers, the significance of the events of the early 1980s was an issue of the utmost importance. Had the downturn accelerated the trends of the preceding twenty years or simply distorted them? Would the return of prosperity lead to a revival of the comfortable world of farm and factory, or had that world disappeared? If it had disappeared, what would take its place? The events of the 1980s provided no reliable answers to these questions and only the most general outline of a new configuration of opportunity and work. Farm and factory remained important, more important than in other regions, but most workers were found in offices, stores, laboratories, public institutions, and other white-collar settings. They were organized in small units, worked more independently than factory workers, and relied on informal methods to influence their environments.

Midwestern Workers, 1983–1990

Table 9–1, which summarizes employment changes by industry in the 1980s, emphasizes the divergent fates of workers in goods and services production. Agriculture and mining provided even fewer opportunities than in earlier years, while midwestern factories were the most important contributors to the region's "rust belt" image. Alone among goods-producing industries, construction provided opportunities for midwestern workers. In contrast trade, finance, and services of all types continued to add employees. The gain in retailing alone offset the decline in manufacturing. Workers with appropriate qualifications, which increasingly meant academic rather than mechanical skills, could look forward to fully employed futures, though often at lower real wages than their parents had enjoyed. The more important question was whether any of these activities would distinguish the Midwest from other regions or provide a foundation for long-term employment growth.

The highly aggregated data in table 9–1 provide at best a partial guide to the fate of midwestern workers in the 1980s. Agriculture is a prime example. Though farm employment continued to fall, small farms (apart from "contrary" farms that embraced the diversified approach of the early twentieth century) faced the greatest challenges because of the rising optimum scale of corn and soybean production. By the end of the decade, the average-sized farm of 1950 was a part-time enterprise. Many farmers looked for market niches, specialties such as nursery stock or organic vegetables. But if part-time farming and specialty crops could slow the erosion of the rural population and the disintegration of rural institutions, they were unlikely to have a substantial impact on the climate of opportunity or on rural employment.[1]

Midwestern miners would have been delighted to have had the farmers' problems. Except in Ohio, where captive mines of electric utility companies added workers, the decline in mining employment continued through the decade. Reduced demand for midwestern coal, new steel-making technolo-

Table 9–1
Employment Changes, 1980–1990
(*Percentage*)

	1980–1990
All Industries	10
Goods	-7
Agriculture	-5
Mining	-31
Construction	21
Manufacturing	-12
Services	21
Transportation–communication	7
Wholesale trade	16
Retail trade	15
Finance	27
Business services	35
Personal services	10
Professional services	26
Health	22
Education	7
Public administration	0

Sources: U.S. Census, *Population*, 1980, table 69 for seven states; *Population and Housing*, 1990, Summary Tape 3C.

gies, and strip mining lessened the demand for workers. The success of Cypress Minerals' innovative, nonunion operation near Silver Bay, Minnesota, formerly a bastion of organized labor, was emblematic of the miners' plight.

It was the Midwest's factories, however, that accounted for most of the job losses. The Midwest's share of U.S. manufacturing had gradually declined in the 1960s and 1970s; it fell much more rapidly in the 1980s as manufacturers accelerated their search for lower-wage, nonunion settings.[2] Plant closings slowed after 1983, but there were few signs of recovery. Indeed, the largest firms and factories, former symbols of the region's industrial prowess, accounted for most of the job losses. Auto, steel, and machinery firms faced intense competition from more efficient and better-managed producers, mostly in other states and countries. To survive they had to become more like their competitors, which meant reducing costs and employment.

The other notable change was geographical. Since the mid-nineteenth century, large-scale manufacturing had been associated with large cities. The gradual erosion of that relationship attracted little attention until the 1970s. In the 1980s the growth of rural manufacturing accelerated, largely because of the attractiveness of the rural labor force. By the end of the decade, hundreds more midwestern towns had become industrial centers. They provided the most hopeful exception to the rust belt image of midwestern industry.[3]

Among the most prominent examples of this change were the new Nucor "minimill" at Crawfordsville, Indiana, and the Honda complex near Marysville, Ohio. The Crawfordsville facility, like other minimills, successfully competed against large, vertically integrated steel mills by using scrap steel and the latest technology and adopting a minimalist approach to industrial organization. Nucor gave employees substantial responsibilities and paid generous bonuses. But it had no use for experienced steelworkers or union organizers, paid virtually no benefits, and had only a small personnel staff.[4] The Crawfordsville facility made sheet steel, the last stronghold of the old-line producers. By the late 1980s, it had proven a formidable challenger. Labor costs per hour at Crawfordsville and at U.S. Steel's Gary works were comparable, but Nucor employees produced twice as much steel per hour as U.S. Steel workers.[5]

The Honda complex was also a revealing example of the flight of manufacturers from established industrial centers. Part of a concerted effort by Japanese manufacturers to circumvent American import barriers, the Marysville complex grew rapidly in the 1980s. Honda executives picked the site because of its proximity to Interstate 75, which was becoming the new geographical axis of the auto industry, and its large German American rural population, which Honda officials perceived as disciplined and hard-working.

Whether this perception was accurate mattered less than the fact that Honda recognized prospective employees as more than interchangeable parts of the manufacturing process. The company initially defined its hiring area to exclude Columbus and other central Ohio cities and sought workers with no automobile manufacturing experience.[6] In reaction to complaints that this approach excluded virtually all black applicants, Honda officials expanded the area but continued to screen potential employees and exclude anyone who did not seem adaptable and cooperative. By 1985 Honda had more than two thousand hand-picked employees.

The Marysville complex became a high priority for the UAW. The union stationed an organizer there in 1981 and won a profession of neutrality from the company in 1982. By the summer of 1985 UAW officials believed they had a substantial following in the plant and launched a public campaign for members. They discovered that "neutrality" did not exclude unofficial support for anti-UAW workers groups or pointed commentaries on the fates of organized autoworkers in Michigan and Ohio. Their effort soon stalled. After conducting a telephone survey of Honda workers in December 1985, the UAW abandoned its campaign.[7] As much as any development, this failure was a measure of the changed climate of the 1980s.

The decline of manufacturing, coupled with the shift from cities to villages, had other repercussions. No longer did the region's cities attract the poor and unskilled or provide opportunities for those who were already there. At a time when Hispanic and Asian immigrants were transforming unskilled (and some skilled) labor markets in many parts of the United States, the Midwest was largely undisturbed. By the 1980s it was more ethnically homogeneous than at any time in the twentieth century. The region's industrial decline also meant that earlier generations of industrial workers faced new insecurities. For example, the number of black employees in manufacturing fell by one-third in the 1980s; among young workers, the decline was considerably higher. Despite a variety of retraining programs, most displaced employees were never able to find comparable positions.[8] One legacy of the 1980s would be a large group of unemployed and underemployed workers in the largest cities.

The decline of midwestern manufacturing was also a devastating blow to the labor movement. Membership continued to fall and union influence declined in the 1980s. Employment losses in organized industries were the most obvious problem, but union organizers made little progress in attracting new members. Fear of reprisals, a tight job market, and a growing tendency to look to government for enforcement of labor standards all contributed to the unpopularity of organized labor. Managerial innovations and improved internal communications were also factors in a minority of workplaces. Whether these developments signaled the emergence of a "representation gap" or a proliferation of informal channels for expressions of the workers' voice was less clear.[9]

A bitter strike at the Hormel Company in 1985 and 1986 symbolized the unions' dilemmas. The Hormel conflict grew out of the upheavals that were transforming meatpacking into a rural, low-wage, nonunion industry. In the late 1970s Hormel abandoned the incentive plan that had long made its employees the industry's highest-paid workers and in 1983 demanded additional concessions, citing competition from low-wage firms like IBP. The ensuing negotiations brought other tensions to the surface. A militant anticoncession group won control of the Austin local and hired Ray Rodgers to attack Hormel. By 1985 the local leadership and the Rodgers campaign had antagonized a substantial minority of the local's members, as well as the leaders of the United Food and Commercial Workers, the local's parent. When the local struck in August 1985, it faced a hostile employer, an angry international union, a dissident movement within the local, and an increasingly anxious community.[10]

The Hormel strike nevertheless attracted wide attention and sympathy, in part because of Rodgers's skills and in part because of its symbolism. To frustrated union activists and political radicals, the strikers' determination to resist the company's demands was a welcome departure from the conservatism and submissiveness that seemed to characterize the contemporary labor movement. Austin became "a pilgrimage site" for labor militants.[11] Money from outside groups sustained the strike through the winter of 1985–1986, and strike leaders became celebrities. Yet this activity only served to prolong the strike and increase its costs. Hormel reopened the plant in early 1986 and began hiring new workers. Five hundred of the fifteen hundred strikers crossed the picket line; the others, together with several hundred union members at the Hormel plant in Ottumwa, Iowa, who had struck in sympathy, lost their jobs. Because of its notoriety, the Hormel disaster was also a psychological blow to the many groups that had organized to fight plant closings, layoffs, and compliant union officials. If the Hormel militants, with ample funds and wide exposure, could not achieve their objectives, who could?

The midwestern workers who produced services, two-thirds of the total by 1990, faced very different challenges. The growth in service employment during the 1980s left little doubt about their importance in midwestern economic life. But service employment embraced a host of dissimilar jobs, technologies, and organizations, including thousands of positions in government and nonprofit institutions. The experiences of the 1980s provide only limited insights into their role in the economy.

Three characteristics of service work in earlier decades became more evident in the 1980s. First, it provided limited opportunities for former farmers, miners, and factory workers. Low entry-level wages discouraged many industrial employees, as did the association with "women's work." The exodus from midwestern industry presumably should have weakened traditional conceptions of men's and women's jobs, but the effect was slight. Women took advantage of equal-employment legislation to move into men's jobs, but the movement in the other direction was negligible. Most boys from low-income families continued to choose careers in manufacturing or construction, despite the uncertain prospects of those occupations. Most significant was the emphasis on communication skills in service-sector employment. Promotions often depended on the ability to speak and write with facility. Retraining programs could provide entry-level qualifications but not the more general background that prepared workers for high-wage positions.

Second, the relationship between academic training and success in the workplace became stronger and more evident as white-collar opportunities grew. A high school diploma had been irrelevant to farmers and factory workers during the first half of the century. As the economy evolved, secondary school attendance rose, and manufacturers began to require high school experience or even diplomas. By the 1980s individuals who failed to graduate had little hope of success in the workplace, a fact that created insidious downward pressures on academic standards.

Third, the Midwest continued to lag in the creation or attraction of the highest-level white-collar jobs. The region's share of scientists and engineers, to cite one convenient measure, trailed the Northeast and Pacific Coast by a wide margin. A substantial outmigration of skilled professional and technical workers, including a large share of the Midwest's science and engineering graduates, widened the disparity.[12]

In other respects the 1980s brought significant changes. The expansion of state and local government employment, which had spearheaded the growth of the service sector between the 1950s and 1970s, came to an end. Public education was a barometer of this change. By the 1980s school and university systems in most states faced recurring financial crises and cutbacks. Declining opportunities in turn accelerated pressures for organization, as government workers faced growing deflationary pressures. In education, where teachers took the lead, financial exigencies were only part of the problem. Political interference and weak management created a noneconomic role for unions that often overshadowed their economic role. The combination of economic and noneconomic challenges, coupled with permissive state legislation, created a healthy public-sector labor movement that contrasted strikingly with private-sector organizations.

A more immediate issue was the future of the expanding private service sector. Many economists expressed concern over the comparatively slow growth of service-sector productivity in the 1970s and 1980s. Many workers, especially low-wage employees, may have owed their jobs to the absence or misuse of machines. The apparent failure of electronic computers to increase office productivity became a symbol of these shortcomings. The recession of 1990–1992 introduced a more ominous development: the type of cost pressures that had provoked cutbacks and layoffs in manufacturing. Far more than automation, these pressures foreshadowed harder work and declining working conditions for many service-sector employees.[13]

Health care, the most rapidly growing service industry, underlined these challenges and opportunities. Based on rapid scientific and technological advances, and the spread of private health insurance plans, hospitals and other health-care facilities became major employers in most midwestern communities by the 1970s. They also created a new and visible elite, as physicians superseded industrialists as conspicuous consumers in many communities. But two additional trends also became more apparent. Technological change encouraged specialization and mechanization, while employer-financed health insurance encouraged cost-plus pricing and weak management. As a result costs grew as rapidly as employment, provoking demands for reform and government regulation. By the early 1990s financial pressures and government-encouraged competition threatened to restrict employment opportunities for health workers at all skill levels.

There were signs of similar developments in other service fields. Professional workers were subject to increasing competition and insecurity; mechanization and managerial reform, reminiscent of the process that had transformed factory and industrial work in the early decades of the twentieth century, also became more common. The effects of these developments remained unclear and probably unpredictable, though it is likely that the patterns of work in offices and stores, which had changed far less since the turn of the century than the patterns of work in farm and factory, will evolve more rapidly in the future. They will, in any event, take center stage in the subsequent history of the midwestern labor force.

Midwestern Workers in Retrospect

This study has argued that the experiences of the midwestern states since the late nineteenth century have been characterized by common themes that make it possible to think of the region as a meaningful entity and to distinguish it from other regions. The end of the distinctive combination of occupations and workers that characterized the area for more than a century does not obviate its historical significance; indeed, it may well enhance it. Without attempting to summarize the substance of the foregoing account or extract arbitrary conclusions from the endless variety of human activity, the following observations seem especially pertinent to an understanding of what has happened and the legacy of that experience.

For nearly a century the midwestern worlds of farm and factory were separate and, from the worker's perspective, unrelated. In the most obvious sense, workers seldom moved from one sphere to the other. Although industry grew rapidly during the nineteenth century and first two-thirds of the twentieth century, it attracted relatively few workers from the midwestern countryside. Industry thus came to depend on outsiders, immigrants and, later, migrants from the American South, who reinforced the rural worker's aversion to the factory and sustained the social and cultural chasm that separated country and city. Only in the latter years of the era, as *manufacturers* began to seek out rural and small-town workers, did the worlds of farm and factory overlap. The distinction between city and country remained substantial but was no longer based on the respective appeals of farm and factory.

The difference between farm and factory had another, more intriguing and possibly more significant manifestation. Although farmers and factory workers shared many common grievances and endorsed many of the same antidotes, they seldom worked together or (as far as historians can ascertain) even thought of each other as potential partners. Farm and labor organizations were more often antagonists than allies. The occasional cases of farm-labor cooperation, mostly in the political arena, stand out because they were exceptional. The La Follettes' remarkable alliance of Wisconsin farmers and urban workers lasted only as long as they did and gave way to a farmer-business alliance that proved equally formidable. The Minnesota Farmer-Labor party had little success against the farm-based Republican establishment until economic hardship and the charismatic leadership of Floyd B. Olson created a larger constituency. In the Midwest, as elsewhere, differences within the farm community and within the labor movement contributed to this fragmentation. Yet the separate spheres of farm and factory, and the long-standing suspicions that reinforced the operation of the labor market, were probably more important. The point can be exaggerated: farmer-labor ties in other states were usually not very productive either. But there was a critical qualitative difference. Unlike other regions with large groups of agricultural workers, the Midwest had a formidable labor movement and thus the possibility of a genuine farmer-labor partnership. Yet it was during the years of union ascendancy, the middle third of the century, that farmer-labor ties practically ended and midwestern farmers overwhelmingly chose exit over voice when confronted with economic adversity.

The health of farm and factory was originally simply a reflection of the region's natural resources, which gave the Midwest a comparative advantage over less well endowed areas such as New England. That advantage explained the sustained prosperity of the countryside, the simultaneous growth of cities and industry, and the labor shortages that spurred large-scale immigration and the appearance of cultural fault lines between city and country. But the region's resource endowments became less important over time; the forests were destroyed, the mines were exhausted, and the factories faced growing competition. The Midwest continued to flourish, however, because it became a center of economic and technological innovation that translated into new ways of organizing workers and work. This creativity, apparent by the last decades of the nineteenth century, became the dominant stimulus to economic and employment growth in the early twentieth century. It also made the Midwest a beacon for other regions and countries in the decades between the turn of the century and the depression of the 1930s.

Although these innovations involved a variety of technologies and institutions, their common theme was superior organization. Improved organization tempered the hazards of the marketplace, enabled large aggregations of people and machines to operate with unprecedented efficiency, and permitted individuals to rise to unaccustomed wealth and responsibility. Above all, it allowed producers who had lost or were losing their earlier advantages to remain competitive in a rapidly expanding capitalistic environment.

Innovation created problems as well as opportunities. It favored some individuals over others and spawned inequities and resentments. Groups that stood out included the poorest farmers, who found the first step up the agricultural ladder increasingly difficult to negotiate; the least-skilled industrial workers, who were able to move into semiskilled jobs that paid high wages; and the manufacturing elite, whose wealth, community standing, and social isolation all increased substantially. The depression of the 1930s reinforced the association between innovation and instability and spurred a variety of institutional constraints on potentially disruptive activities. These measures dampened the positive as well as the negative effects of innovation, a point that most midwestern workers did not appreciate until the 1970s. Together with several postwar developments, including the heightened sense of self-confidence and even complacency that grew out of the experiences of the war years, they inhibited the process of renewal that had been essential to midwestern prosperity. By the 1970s midwestern workers faced the worst of both worlds: some producers had become obsolete, while others continued to innovate in traditional ways (mechanizing operations, for example) that limited employment opportunities. What was missing was the creative activity that had characterized the Midwest in the early twentieth century and now apparently characterized the New England and Pacific Coast economies.

Though elites were responsible for the innovations that sustained the pattern of midwestern economic life, they did not operate in isolation. Probably more than that of any other region, the labor history of the Midwest reflected the influence of inconspicuous individuals and organizations that articulated their collective voice. Farm organizations were notably active in the years before World War II, setting standards for interest-group performance. Unions were the most visible and influential of the industrial workers' organizations, particularly in the years between 1900 and 1920, when larger, more impersonal business enterprises and policies designed to reduce exits increased the utility of a formal voice, and between 1933 and 1953, when government constraints on the economy and employer behavior strongly favored independent unions and adversarial collective bargaining. The decline of agriculture and organized labor, the rise of labor-management cooperation, and the shift to service-sector employment in recent decades has complicated the task of assessing the workers' influence. The role of workers' voice in white-collar occupations, for example, is still largely unexplored.

What did the workers achieve? The farmers' list is particularly long, though apparently no longer than in other regions. Union successes, mostly the result of private contracts, were also impressive. They included formal and informal means for resolving shop-floor issues; high wages, especially for low-skill employees; and a role in extending and shaping the growth of welfare capitalism. In the 1940s and 1950s the most successful unions, such as the UAW, greatly reduced the traditional disparities between white- and blue-collar work and between skilled and unskilled workers. Whether those disparities will reappear as the labor movement declines is less clear.

The union record outside the plant was less impressive. In periods of booming membership, labor activists attempted to introduce novel institutions such as consumer cooperatives and independent political parties. Yet they had trouble enlisting the support of rank-and-file members and often antagonized nonmembers. Though no more outspoken or extreme than farmers, they somehow appeared more provocative. In any case they were more successful when they joined forces with other groups. By the 1960s a nascent labor service state had appeared in the upper Midwest despite the substantial power of anti-union forces in those states.

Organized or not, farmers and factory workers overshadowed the region's service producers. They were more numerous and, except for elite professionals, more influential. Industrialists and industrial managers were wealthier and more prominent than merchants, doctors, and lawyers, and the comparatively high wages of the region's industrial wage earners gave them a parallel advantage over most employees in retailing and personal services. Another fundamental distinction was hardly apparent until the 1950s. Except in the relatively unimportant textile and clothing industries, most industrial workers were men, while a growing proportion of service-sector workers were women. The advent of the typewriter and high school, the persistently labor-intensive character of retailing before midcentury, and the low wages of service employees account for this disparity and probably explain its failure to attract more attention and comment.

The rapid increase in the number of women, especially married women, in the paid labor force during the second half of the twentieth century reflected forces that were operating almost everywhere. On the one hand technological innovations reduced the minimum time required to raise children, cook, clean, and otherwise maintain a home, while changes in the institutional environment, especially the expansion of public education, had complementary effects. On the other hand the growth of the service sector provided abundant opportunities for employment in jobs that had long been considered part of the women's sphere, including many part-time positions. Between the 1960s and 1990s the number of married women who provided one-third or more of their family's income doubled, to nearly half of the total.[14]

The most important and durable distinction between goods and services production, however, was the dynamism of industry and the relatively unchanging character of most service industries. The region's achievements in agriculture and manufacturing were apparently all-absorbing and precluded breakthroughs in other areas. As opportunities declined in agriculture and industry, the relatively undeveloped character of the midwestern service sector—apart from medicine—and the contrast between the Midwest and other, better-situated regions, became more evident.

How will this pattern affect the character of work and innovation in the future? Will the Midwest remain a distinctive region of the United States? These questions are not likely to be answered in the 1990s. What can be suggested is that the legacy of the past century, a century that featured the incongruous dominance of farm and factory, will continue to have a marked influence, regardless of the kinds of jobs, machines, and organizations that prevail.

Notes

Preface

1. See Richard B. Freeman and James L. Medoff, *What Do Unions Do?* (New York: Basic Books, 1984), chaps. 1, 6.

1. Midwestern Farmers, 1880–1900

1. See Donald Marti, "Answering the Agrarian Question: Socialists, Farmers, and Algie Martin Simons," *Agricultural History* 65 (Summer 1991): 53–69.

2. Hubert G. H. Wilhelm, "Settlement and Selected Landscape Imprints in the Ohio Valley," in Robert L. Reid, ed., *Always a River: The Ohio River and the American Experience* (Bloomington: Indiana University Press, 1991), pp. 85, 92, 97.

3. See Gregory S. Rose, "Hoosier Origins: The Nativity of Indiana's United States-Born Population in 1850," *Indiana Magazine of History* 81 (September 1985): 201–32, and Rose, "Upland Southerners: The County Origins of Southern Migrants to Indiana by 1850," *Indiana Magazine of History* 82 (September 1986): 243–66.

4. James M. Berquist, "Tracing the Origins of a Midwestern Culture: The Case of Central Indiana," *Indiana Magazine of History* 77 (March 1981): 1–32.

5. Allan G. Bogue, *From Prairie to Cornbelt: Farming on the Illinois and Iowa Prairies in the Nineteenth Century* (Chicago: University of Chicago Press, 1963), p. 15.

6. Robert A. Wheeler, "Land and Community in Rural Nineteenth Century America: Claridon Township, 1810–1870," *Ohio History* 97 (Summer-Autumn 1988): 101–21.

7. Michael P. Conzen, *Frontier Farming in an Urban Shadow: The Influence of Madison's Proximity on the Agricultural Development of Blooming Grove, Wisconsin* (Madison: State Historical Society of Wisconsin, 1971), p. 59.

8. Kathleen Neils Conzen, "Peasant Pioneers: Generational Succession among German Farmers in Frontier Minnesota," in Steven Hahn and Jonathan Prude, eds., *The Countryside in the Age of Capitalist Transformation: Essays in the Social History of Rural America* (Chapel Hill: University of North Carolina Press, 1985), pp. 78–79. For the Dutch experience, see Richard L. Doyle, "Wealth Mobility in Pella, Iowa, 1847–1925," in Robert Swierenga, ed., *The Dutch in America: Immigration, Settlement, and Cultural Change* (New Brunswick: Rutgers University Press, 1985), pp. 162–67.

9. Jon Gjerde, *From Peasants to Farmers: The Migration from Balestrand, Norway to the Upper Middle West* (Cambridge: Cambridge University Press, 1985), p. 8.

10. Robert C. Ostergren, *A Community Transplanted: The Trans-Atlantic Experience of a Swedish Immigrant Settlement in the Upper Middle West, 1835–1915* (Madison: University of Wisconsin Press, 1988), p. 158.

11. Robert D. Swierenga, "Ethnicity and American Agriculture," *Ohio History* 89 (Summer 1980): 323–44.

12. Ostergren, *A Community Transplanted*, p. 15. Also see Yda Saueressig-Schreuder, "Dutch Catholic Immigrant Settlement in Wisconsin," in Swierenga,

Dutch in America, pp. 105–24, and Jon Gjerde, "Chain Migrations from the West Coast of Norway," in Rudolph J. Vecoli and Suzanne M. Sinke, eds., *A Century of European Migrations, 1830–1940* (Urbana: University of Illinois Press, 1991), pp. 173–74.

13. Ostergren, *A Community Transplanted*, p. 206.

14. Fred Bateman, "Labor Inputs and Productivity in American Dairy Agriculture, 1850–1910," *Journal of Economic History* 29 (June 1969): 212.

15. For an extended discussion of this issue, see Nancy Grey Osterud, *Bonds of Community: The Lives of Farm Women in Nineteenth-Century New York* (Ithaca: Cornell University Press, 1991).

16. See Barbara J. Steinson, "Memories of Hoosier Homemakers: A Review Essay," *Indiana Magazine of History* 86 (June 1990): 197–222 and Katherine Jellison, *Entitled to Power: Farm Women and Technology, 1913–1963* (Chapel Hill: University of North Carolina Press, 1993), chap. 1.

17. See Joan M. Jensen, *Loosening the Bonds: Mid-Atlantic Farm Women, 1750–1850* (New Haven: Yale University Press, 1986) and Sally McMurry, *Families and Farmhouses in Nineteenth-Century America: Vernacular Design and Social Change* (New York: Oxford University Press, 1988), chaps. 4, 7.

18. Rosemary O. Joyce, *A Woman's Place: The Life History of a Rural Ohio Grandmother* (Columbus: Ohio State University Press, 1982), p. 193.

19. See Maris A. Vinovskis, "Historical Perspectives on Rural Development and Human Fertility in Nineteenth Century America," in Wayne A. Schutjer and C. Shannon Stokes, eds., *Rural Development and Human Fertility* (New York: Macmillan, 1984), pp. 79–89; Richard A. Easterlin, "Population Change and Farm Settlement in the Northern United States," *Journal of Economic History* 36 (March 1976): 45–83; Jeremy Atack and Fred Bateman, *To Their Own Soil: Agriculture in the Antebellum North* (Ames: Iowa State University Press, 1988), pp. 50–70; Don R. Leet, "The Determinants of the Fertility Transition in Antebellum Ohio," *Journal of Economic History* 36 (June 1976): 359–78; Jenny Bourne Wahl, "Trading Quantity for Quality," and Richard H. Steckel, "The Fertility Transition in the United States," in Claudia Goldin and Hugh Rockoff, eds., *Strategic Factors in Nineteenth Century American Economic History: A Volume to Honor Robert W. Fogel* (Chicago: University of Chicago Press, 1992).

20. Conzen, "Peasant Pioneers," p. 279.

21. Michael Williams, *Americans and Their Forests: A Historical Geography* (New York: Oxford University Press, 1989), pp. 363–67.

22. Williams, *Americans and Their Forests*, pp. 114–15.

23. Williams, *Americans and Their Forests*, p. 117.

24. Bogue, *From Prairie to Cornbelt*, p. 81.

25. Henry C. Taylor, *Tarpleywick: A Century of Iowa Farming* (Ames: Iowa State University Press, 1970), p. 40.

26. Ostergren, *A Community Transplanted*, p. 195; also Jan Combs, "The Health of Central Wisconsin Residents in 1880: A New View of Midwestern Rural Life," *Wisconsin Magazine of History* 68 (Summer 1985): 290.

27. Atack and Bateman, *To Their Own Soil*, pp. 148–52.

28. Margaret Beattie Bogue, "Liberty Hyde Bailey, Jr., and the Bailey Family Farm," *Agricultural History* 63 (Winter 1989): 36.

29. Donald L. Winters, *Farmers without Farms: Agricultural Tenancy in Nineteenth Century Iowa* (Westport: Greenwood Press, 1978), pp. 44–45.

30. Brian Q. Cannon, "Immigrants in American Agriculture," *Agricultural History* 65 (Winter 1991): 30–35.

31. Jette Mackintosh, "Ethnic Patterns in Danish Immigrant Agriculture: A Study of Audubon and Shelby Counties, Iowa," *Agricultural History* 64 (Fall 1990): 62–67.

32. Taylor, *Tarpleywick*, p. 88.

33. Atack and Bateman, *To Their Own Soil*, p. 131; Winters, *Farmers without Farms*, pp. 24–25.

34. Leon E. Truesdell, *Farm Population of the U.S.*, *Census Monographs VI* (Washington: Government Printing Office, 1926), pp. 65–60.

35. Truesdell, *Farm Population*, p. 55.

36. See David E. Schob, *Hired Hands and Plowboys: Farm Labor in the Midwest, 1815–60* (Urbana: University of Illinois Press, 1975).

37. Jane Marie Pederson, "The Country Visitor: Patterns of Hospitality in Rural Wisconsin, 1880–1925," *Agricultural History* 58 (July 1984): 359.

38. Steinson, "Memories of Hoosier Homemakers," pp. 201–202.

39. Wheeler, "Land and Community," p. 113.

40. Pederson, "The Country Visitor," p. 351.

41. James Sanford Rikoon, "The White Plains, Indiana, Threshing Ring, 1920–1943," *Indiana Magazine of History* 80 (September 1984): 228–36.

42. Pederson, "The Country Visitor," p. 358.

43. Robert Leslie Jones, *History of Agriculture in Ohio* (Kent: Kent State University Press, 1983), pp. 263–78.

44. Peter H. Argersinger and Jo Ann E. Argersinger, "The Machine Breakers: Farmworkers and Social Change in the Rural Midwest in the 1870s," *Agricultural History* 58 (July 1984): 403.

45. Argersinger and Argersinger, "The Machine Breakers," p. 409.

46. Jones, *History of Agriculture*, pp. 315–16.

47. See Thomas J. Schlereth, *Victorian America: Transformations in Everyday Life, 1876–1915* (New York: Harper Collins, 1991), chaps. 3–4.

48. See Wayne E. Fuller, *The Old Country School: The Story of Rural Education in the Middle West* (Chicago: University of Chicago Press, 1982); Merle Curti, *The Making of an American Community: A Case Study of Democracy in a Frontier County* (Stanford: Stanford University Press, 1959), pp. 382–405; Howard E. Good, *Black Swamp Farm* (Columbus: Ohio State University Press, 1967), pp. 206–13.

49. Fuller, *The Old Country School*, pp. 119–26.

50. See Anne Mayhew, "A Reappraisal of the Causes of Farm Protest in the United States, 1870–1900," *Journal of Economic History* 32 (June 1972): 464–75.

51. George N. Miller, "Origins of the Iowa Granger Law," *Mississippi Valley Historical Review* 40 (March 1954): 657–80.

52. See D. Sven Nordin, *Rich Harvest: A History of the Grange, 1867–1900* (Jackson: University Press of Mississippi, 1974), chaps. 3–6; Donald B. Marti, "Sisters of the Grange: Rural Feminism in the Late Nineteenth Century," *Agricultural History* 58 (July 1984): 247–61; R. Douglas Hurt, "The Ohio Grange, 1870–1900," *Northwest Ohio Quarterly* 53 (Winter 1981): 19–32.

53. See William F. Holmes, "Populism: In Search of Context," *Agricultural History* 64 (Fall 1990): 37–39.

54. Roy V. Scott, *Agrarian Movement in Illinois* (Urbana: University of Illinois Press, 1962), pp. 37–64; R. Douglas Hurt, "The Farmers' Alliance and People's Party in Ohio," *Old Northwest* 10 (Winter 1984–1985): 440–43.

55. Scott, *Agrarian Movement in Illinois*, p. 37.

56. Roger E. Wyman, "Agrarian or Working Class Radicalism? The Electoral Basis of Populism in Wisconsin," *Political Science Quarterly* 89 (Winter 1974–1975): 825–47; Scott, *Agrarian Movement* pp. 130–35; Hurt, "Farmers' Alliance," pp. 446–59; Paul Kleppner, *The Cross of Culture: A Social Analysis of Midwestern Politics, 1850–1900* (New York: Free Press, 1970), pp. 182–90.

2. Industrial Workers, 1880–1900

1. John E. Bodnar, *The Transplanted: A History of Immigrants in Urban America* (Bloomington: Indiana University Press, 1985), pp. 71–83.

2. David Ward, *Cities and Immigrants* (New York: Oxford University Press, 1971), pp. 66–81.

3. Daniel E. Weinberg, "Ethnic Identity in Industrial Cleveland: The Hungarians, 1900–1920," *Ohio History* 86 (Summer 1977): 175. Also Josef J. Barton, *Peasants and Strangers: Italians, Rumanians, and Slovaks in an American City* (Cambridge: Harvard University Press, 1975), p. 57, and the essays by Yda Saueressig-Schreuder and David F. Vanderstel in Robert Swierenga, ed., *The Dutch in America: Immigration, Settlement, and Cultural Change* (New Brunswick: Rutgers University Press, 1985), pp. 105–24, 125–55.

4. Olivier Zunz, *The Changing Face of Inequality: Urbanization, Industrial Development, and Immigrants in Detroit, 1880–1920* (Chicago: University of Chicago Press, 1982), p. 39; Also see Hartmut Keil, "Immigrant Neighborhoods and American Society," in Hartmut Keil, ed., *German Workers' Culture in the United States, 1850 to 1920* (Washington: Smithsonian Institution Press, 1988), pp. 30–31.

5. See Anita R. Olson, "The Community Created: Chicago Swedes, 1680–1920," in Philip J. Anderson and Dag Blanck, *Swedish-American Life in Chicago: Cultural Life and Urban Aspects of an Immigrant People, 1850–1930* (Urbana: University of Illinois Press, 1992), pp. 50–55; Bodnar, *The Transplanted*, pp. 57–71.

6. Robert L. Burkofer, "From Voluntary Association to Welfare State: The Illinois Immigrants' Protective League, 1908, 1926," *Journal of American History* 58 (December 1971): 646.

7. See Joseph P. Ferrie, "'We Are Yankees Now': The Economic Mobility of Two Thousand Antebellum Immigrants to the United States," *Journal of Economic History* (June 1993): 388–90.

8. For midwestern examples see Stephan Thernstrom, *The Other Bostonians: Poverty and Progress in the American Metropolis, 1880–1970* (Cambridge: Harvard University Press, 1973), pp. 224–53; Dean R. Esslinger, *Immigrants and the City: Ethnicity and Mobility in a Nineteenth Century Midwestern Community* (Port Washington: Kennikat Press, 1975).

9. Joan Underhill Hannon, "City Size and Ethnic Discrimination: Michigan Agricultural Implements and Iron Working Industries, 1890," *Journal of Economic History* 42 (December 1982): 825–46.

10. Zunz, *Changing Face of Inequality*, pp. 38–39.

11. Humbert S. Nelli, "The Italian Padrone System in the United States," *Labor History* 5 (Spring 1964): 153–67.

12. See Sanford M. Jacoby and Sunil Sharma, "Employment Duration and Industrial Labor Force Mobility in the United States, 1880–1990," *Journal of Economic History* 52 (March 1992): 161–80.

13. See Robert Whaples and David Buffum, "Fraternalism, Paternalism, the Family and the Market: Insurance a Century Ago," *Social Science History* 15 (Spring 1991): 100–101; and Alexander Keyssar, *Out of Work: The First Century of Unemployment in Massachusetts* (Cambridge: Cambridge University Press, 1986), chaps. 3–4.

14. Zunz, *The Changing Face of Inequality,* pp. 227–28.

15. W. J. Rorabaugh, "Beer, Lemonade, and Prosperity in the Gilded Age," in Kathryn Grover, ed., *Dining in America, 1850–1900* (Amherst: University of Massachusetts Press, 1987), p. 25.

16. Humbert S. Nelli, *Italians in Chicago, 1880–1930: A Study in Ethnic Mobility* (New York: Oxford University Press, 1970), pp. 74–75. Also see Walter Licht, *Getting Work: Philadelphia, 1840–1950* (Cambridge: Harvard University Press, 1992), chap. 6.

17. Harvey A. Levenstein, *Revolution at the Table: The Transformation of the American Diet* (New York: Oxford University Press, 1988), pp. 102–108.

18. Levenstein, *Revolution at the Table,* p. 25.

19. See Tamara K. Hareven and John Modell, "The Malleable Household: Boarding and Lodging in American Families," *Journal of Marriage and the Family* 35 (August 1973): 467–79.

20. Robert C. Ostergren, *A Community Transplanted: The Trans-Atlantic Experience of a Swedish Immigrant Settlement in the Upper Middle West, 1835–1915* (Madison: University of Wisconsin Press, 1988), pp. 190, 195.

21. Eric D. Weitz, "Class Formation and Labor Protest in the Mining Communities of Southern Illinois and the Ruhr, 1890–1925," *Labor History* 47 (Winter 1985–86): 88–89; Dorothy Schwieder, Joseph Hraba, and Elmer Schwieder, *Buxton: Work and Racial Equality in a Coal Mining Community* (Ames: Iowa State University Press, 1987), p. 73; Dorothy Schwieder, *Black Diamonds: Life and Work in Iowa's Coal Mining Communities, 1895–1925* (Ames: Iowa State University Press, 1983), pp. 72, 98–99.

22. Richard Jensen, *The Winning of the Midwest: Social and Political Conflict, 1888–1896* (Chicago: University of Chicago Press, 1971), p. 262.

23. See Schwieder, *Black Diamonds,* pp. 38–56.

24. Randall E. Rohe, "The Evolution of the Great Lakes Logging Camps, 1830–1930," *Journal of Forest History* 30 (January 1986): 19.

25. Jeremy W. Kilar, "Great Lakes Lumber Towns and Frontier Violence: A Comparative Study," *Journal of Forest History* 31 (April 1987): 71–72.

26. Michael Eliseuson, *Tower Soudan: The State Park Down Under* (Minneapolis: Minnesota Parks Association, 1976), p. 30. Also see Arnold R. Alanen, "Companies as Caretakers: Paternalism, Welfare Capitalism, and Immigrants in the Lake Superior Mining Region," in Rudolph J. Vecoli and Suzanne M. Sinke, eds., *A Century of European Migrations, 1830–1930* (Urbana: University of Illinois Press, 1991), pp. 378–82.

27. Herbert G. Gutman, "Reconstruction in Ohio: Negroes in the Hocking Valley Coal Mines in 1873 and 1874," *Labor History* 3 (Fall 1962): 256–60; Also Raymond Boryczka and Lorin Lee Cary, *No Strength without Union: An Illustrated History of Ohio's Workers 1803–1980* (Columbus: Ohio Historical Society, 1982), pp. 65–67.

28. Ronald L. Lewis, *Black Coal Miners in America: Race, Class, and Community Conflict, 1780–1980* (Lexington: University of Kentucky Press, 1987), pp. 81–84; Jeremy W. Kilar, "Black Pioneers in the Michigan Lumber Industry," *Journal of Forest History* 24 (July 1980): 142–49.

29. Jensen, *Winning of the Midwest,* p. 240.

30. Arthur W. Thurner, *Rebels on the Range: The Michigan Copper Miners: Strike of 1913–14* (Lake Linden: John H. Forster Press, 1984), pp. 38–40; Larry Lankton, *Cradle to Grave: Life, Work, and Death at the Lake Superior Copper Mines* (New York: Oxford University Press, 1991), pp. 106, 221.

31. Thurner, *Rebels on the Range*, p. 36.

32. Charles K. Hyde, "Undercover and Underground: Labor Spies and Mine Management in the Early Twentieth Century," *Business History Review* 60 (Spring 1986): 6.

33. Michael Williams, *Americans and Their Forests: A Historical Geography* (New York: Cambridge University Press, 1989), p. 219.

34. Rohe, "Great Lakes Logging Camp," p. 28.

35. David A. Walker, *Iron Frontier: The Discovery and Early Development of Minnesota's Three Ranges* (Minneapolis: Minnesota Historical Society Press, 1979), pp. 134–35.

36. David R. Meyer, "Midwestern Industrialization and the American Manufacturing Belt in the Nineteenth Century," *Journal of Economic History* 49 (December 1989): 921–37.

37. Bruce Laurie and Mark Schmitz, "Manufacture and Productivity: The Making of an Industrial Base, Philadelphia, 1850–1880," in Theodore Hershberg, ed., *Philadelphia: Work, Space, Family, and Group Experience in the Nineteenth Century* (New York: Oxford University Press, 1981), p. 59.

38. Robert V. Robinson and Carl M. Briggs, "The Rise of Factories in Indianapolis, 1850–1880," *American Journal of Sociology* (November 1991): 622–56.

39. Hartmut Keil, "German Working Class Immigration and the Social Democratic Tradition in Germany," in Keil, *German Workers' Culture*, pp. 1–23; Keil, "The German Immigrant Working Class of Chicago, 1875–1890," in Dirk Hoerder, ed., *American Labor and Immigration History, 1877–1920s: Recent European Research* (Urbana: University of Illinois Press, 1983), pp. 160–62; Richard J. Oestreicher, *Solidarity and Fragmentation: Working People and Class Consciousness in Detroit, 1875–1900* (Urbana: University of Illinois Press, 1986); Steven J. Ross, *Workers on the Edge: Work, Leisure, and Politics in Industrializing Cincinnati, 1788–1890* (New York: Columbia University Press, 1985); Kathleen Neils Conzen, *Immigrant Milwaukee, 1836–1860: Accommodation and Community in a Frontier City* (Cambridge: Harvard University Press, 1976).

40. Ross, *Workers on the Edge*, p. 80.

41. Zunz, *Changing Face of Inequality*, p. 18.

42. See Edward P. Duggan, "Machines, Markets, and Labor: The Carriage and Wagon Industry in Late Nineteenth Century Cincinnati," *Business History Review* 51 (Autumn 1977): 308–25.

43. Duggan, "Machines, Markets, and Labor," p. 317.

44. Michael Nuwer, "From Batch to Flow: Production Technology and Work-Force Skills in the Steel Industry, 1880–1920," *Technology and Culture* 29 (October 1988), pp. 808–38; Alfred D. Chandler, Jr., *The Visible Hand: The Managerial Revolution in American Business* (Cambridge: Harvard University Press, 1977), pp. 259–69.

45. Margaret Walsh, "From Pork Merchant to Meat Packer: The Midwestern Meat Industry in the Mid-Nineteenth Century," *Agricultural History* 56 (January 1982): 127–37.

46. James R. Barrett, *Work and Community in the Jungle: Chicago's Packinghouse Workers, 1894–1922* (Urbana: University of Illinois Press, 1987), pp. 38–46.

47. Richard Schneirov, *Pride and Solidarity: A History of the Plumbers and Pipefitters of Columbus, Ohio, 1889–1989* (Ithaca: ILR Press, 1992), p. 40.

48. David M. Gordon, Richard Edwards, and Michael Reich, *Segmented Work, Divided Workers: The Historical Transformation of Labor in the United States* (Cambridge: Cambridge University Press, 1982), pp. 100–64.

49. See Nick Salvatore, *Eugene V. Debs, Citizen and Socialist* (Urbana: University of Illinois Press, 1982), chaps. 2–3.

50. See David Montgomery, *The Fall of the House of Labor* (Cambridge: Cambridge University Press, 1987) for many examples.

51. Keil, "German Immigrant Working Class of Chicago," pp. 159–60.

52. Robert Ozanne, *A Century of Labor-Management Relations at McCormick and International Harvester* (Madison: University of Wisconsin Press, 1967), pp. 5–6.

53. Louise Carroll Wade, *Chicago's Pride: The Stockyards, Packingtown, and Environs in the Nineteenth Century* (Urbana: University of Illinois Press, 1987), pp. 123–26; Wayne G. Broehl, Jr., *John Deere's Company: A History of Deere & Company and Its Times* (New York: Doubleday, 1984), pp. 237–38; Arnold R. Alanen, "Early Labor Strife on Minnesota's Mining Frontier, 1882–1906," *Minnesota History* 52 (Fall 1991): 246–63.

54. Oestreicher, *Solidarity and Fragmentation*, p. 162.

55. Keil, "German Immigrant Working Class," p. 163.

56. Oestreicher, *Solidarity and Fragmentation*, pp. 92–94.

57. Ralph Scharnau, "Workers and Politics: The Knights of Labor in Dubuque, Iowa, 1885–1890," *Annals of Iowa* 48 (Winter/Spring 1987): 356–60.

58. Susan Levine, "Labor's True Woman: Domesticity and Equal Rights in the Knights of Labor," *Journal of American History* 70 (September 1983): 325–29; Alice Kessler-Harris, *Out of Work: A History of Wage-Earning Women in the United States* (New York: Oxford University Press, 1982), p. 86.

59. Paul Avrich, *The Haymarket Tragedy* (Princeton: Princeton University Press, 1984), chap. 12.

60. Doris B. McLaughlin, *Michigan Labor: A Brief History from 1818 to the Present* (Ann Arbor: Institute of Labor and Industrial Relations, 1970), pp. 32–49; Jeremy W. Kilar, "Community and Authority Response to the Saginaw Valley Lumber Strike of 1885," *Journal of Forest History* 20(April 1976): 73–77.

61. George B. Cotkin, "Strikebreakers, Evictions, and Violence: Industrial Conflict in the Hocking Valley, 1884–1885," *Ohio History* 87 (Spring 1978): 140–50; Andrew Birdle, "Governor George Hoadley's Use of the Ohio National Guard in the Hocking Valley Coal Strike of 1884," *Ohio History* 91 (1982): 37–57.

62. Avrich, *Haymarket Tragedy*, p. 208; Ozanne, *A Century of Labor Management Relations*, pp. 22–23.

63. James M. Morris, "No Haymarket for Cincinnati," *Ohio History* 83 (Winter 1974): 17–32.

64. Robert W. Ozanne, *The Labor Movement in Wisconsin: A History* (Madison: State Historical Society of Wisconsin, 1984), pp. 9–11; Bayrd Still, *Milwaukee: The History of a City* (Madison: State Historical Society of Wisconsin, 1948), pp. 291–92; Thomas W. Gavett, *Development of the Labor Movement in Milwaukee* (Madison: University of Wisconsin Press, 1965), p. 64.

65. Leon Fink, *Workingmen's Democracy: The Knights of Labor and American Politics* (Urbana: University of Illinois Press, 1982), pp. 28–29.

66. Ross, *Workers on the Edge*, pp. 294–312; Fink, *Workingmen's Democracy*, pp. 196–202.

67. Scharnau, "Workers and Politics," pp. 374–76.

68. Elizabeth and Kenneth Fones-Wolf, "The War at Mingo Junction: The Autonomous Workman and the Decline of the Knights of Labor," *Ohio History* 92 (Annual, 1983): 49.

69. Richard Schneirov and Thomas J. Suhrbur, *Union Brotherhood, Union Town: The History of the Carpenters' Union of Chicago, 1863–1987* (Carbondale: Southern Illinois University Press, 1988), pp. 27–48.

70. Jensen, *Winning of the Midwest*, p. 212.

71. Jensen, *Winning of the Midwest*, p. 259.

72. Kleppner, *Cross of Culture*, pp. 240–47; Almont Lindsey, *The Pullman Strike: The Story of a Unique Experiment and a Great Labor Upheaval* (Chicago: University of Chicago Press, 1942); Stanley Buder, *Pullman: An Experiment in Industrial Order and Community Planning, 1880–1930* (New York: Oxford University Press, 1967), chaps. 12–15; Shelton Stromquist, *A Generation of Boomers: The Pattern of Railroad Labor Conflict in Nineteenth-Century America* (Urbana: University of Illinois Press, 1987), pp. 79–94.

73. Price V. Fishback, *Soft Coal, Hard Choices: The Economic Welfare of the Bituminous Coal Miners, 1890–1930* (New York: Oxford University Press, 1992), p. 90.

74. See Sanford M. Jacoby, "American Exceptionalism Revisited: The Importance of Management," in Jacoby, ed., *Masters to Managers: Historical and Comparative Perspectives on American Employers* (New York: Columbia University Press, 1991), pp. 173–200.

3. White-Collar Workers, 1880–1900

1. W. J. Rorabaugh, "Beer, Lemonade, and Prosperity in the Gilded Age," in Kathryn Grover, ed., *Dining in America, 1850–1900* (Amherst: University of Massachusetts Press, 1987), p. 26.

2. John F. Kasson, "Rituals of Dining: Table Manners in Victorian America," in Grover, ed., *Dining in America*, p. 123.

3. Merle Curti, *The Making of an American Community: A Case Study of Democracy in a Frontier County* (Stanford: Stanford University Press, 1959), p. 224.

4. See Lewis Atherton, *Main Street on the Middle Border* (Bloomington: Indiana University Press, 1954), pp. 229–33.

5. Samuel Haber, *The Quest for Authority and Honor in the American Professions, 1750–1900* (Chicago: University of Chicago Press, 1991), pp. 188–89.

6. Joyce Maynard Ghent and Frederic Cople Jaher, "The Chicago Business Elite: 1830–1930: A Collective Biography," *Business History Review* 50 (Autumn 1976): 296–99.

7. Olivier Zunz, *The Changing Face of Inequality: Urbanization, Industrial Development, and Immigrants in Detroit, 1880–1920* (Chicago: University of Chicago Press, 1982), p. 205.

8. John N. Ingham, "Rags to Riches Revisited: The Effects of City Size and Related Factors on the Recruitment of Business Leaders," *Journal of American History* 63 (December 1976): 627, 630.

9. See Ingham, "Rags to Riches Revisited," 628–30.

10. Steven A. Sass, *The Pragmatic Imagination: A History of the Wharton School, 1881–1981* (Philadelphia: University of Pennsylvania Press, 1982), p. 5.

11. See Stuart Morris, "Stalled Professionalism: The Recruitment of Railway Officials in the United States, 1885–1940," *Business History Review* 47 (Autumn 1973): 317–34.

12. David Tyack and Elisabeth Hansot, *Learning Together: A History of Coeducation in American Schools* (New Haven: Yale University Press, 1990), p. 136.

13. Susan B. Carter and Mark Prus, "The Labor Market and the American High School Girl, 1890–1928," *Journal of Economic History* 42 (March 1982): 163–80. For a useful case study, see Edward M. Miggins, "The Search for the One Best System: Cleveland Public Schools and Educational Reform, 1836–1920," in David D. Van Tassel and John J. Grabowski, eds., *Cleveland: A Tradition of Reform* (Kent: Kent State University Press, 1986), pp. 146–54.

14. See Walter Licht, *Getting Work: Philadelphia 1840–1950* (Cambridge: Harvard University Press, 1992), chap. 3; Ileen A. DeVault, *Sons and Daughters of Labor: Class and Clerical Work in Turn-of-the-Century Pittsburgh* (Ithaca: Cornell University Press, 1990).

15. See Stuart M. Blumin, *The Emergence of the Middle Class: Social Experience in the American City, 1760–1900* (Cambridge: Cambridge University Press, 1989).

16. JoAnne Yates, *Control through Communication: The Rise of System in American Management* (Baltimore: Johns Hopkins University Press, 1989), chap. 2.

17. Lisa M. Fine, *The Souls of the Skyscraper: Female Clerical Workers in Chicago, 1870–1930* (Philadelphia: Temple University Press, 1990), p. 22.

18. Tyack and Hansot, *Learning Together*, pp. 185–87.

19. Fine, *Souls of the Skyscraper*, p. 123.

20. Based on Fine, *Souls of the Skyscraper*, p. 43, and Joshua L. Rosenbloom, "Occupational Differences in Labor Market Integration: The U.S. in 1890," *Journal of Economic History* 51 (June 1991): 430. For living conditions of independent women in Chicago, see Joanne J. Meyerowitz, *Women Adrift: Independent Wage Earners in Chicago, 1880–1930* (Chicago: University of Chicago Press, 1988).

21. Fine, *Souls of the Skyscraper*, p. 87.

22. See Susan Porter Benson, *Counter Cultures: Saleswomen, Managers, and Customers in American Department Stores, 1890–1940* (Urbana: University of Illinois Press, 1986), pp. 23–26 and chaps. 4–6.

23. Robert W. Twyman, *History of Marshall Field & Co., 1852–1906* (Philadelphia: University of Pennsylvania Press, 1954), pp. 68–72.

24. Faye E. Dudden, *Serving Women: Household Service in Nineteenth Century America* (Middletown: Wesleyan University Press, 1983), chap. 1.

25. David M. Katzman, *Seven Days a Week: Women and Domestic Service in Industrializing America* (New York: Oxford University Press, 1978), p. 45.

26. Harvey A. Levenstein, *Revolution at the Table: The Transformation of the American Diet* (New York: Oxford University Press, 1988), p. 63.

27. Katzman, *Seven Days a Week*, p. 61.

28. Joy K. Lintelman, "'On My Own': Single, Swedish, and Female in Turn-of-the-Century Chicago," in Philip J. Anderson and Dag Blanck, eds., *Swedish-American Life in Chicago: Cultural and Urban Aspects of an Immigrant People, 1850–1930* (Urbana: University of Illinois Press, 1992), p. 91.

29. Alice Kessler-Harris, *Out to Work: A History of Wage-Earning Women in the United States* (New York: Oxford University Press, 1982), pp. 103–104.

30. Dudden, *Serving Women*, pp. 209–11.

4. Revolutions in Production and Work, 1900–1930

1. David B. Danborn, "The Agricultural Experiment Station and Professionalization: Scientists' Goals for Agriculture," *Agricultural History* 60 (Spring 1986): 247.

2. Edward H. Beardsley, *Harry L. Russell and Agricultural Science in Wisconsin* (Madison: University of Wisconsin Press, 1969), p. 65; Wilson Smith, "'Cow College' Mythology and Social History: A View of Some Centennial Literature," *Agricultural History* 44 (July 1970): 301; Alan I. Marcus, "The Ivory Silo: Farmer-Agricultural College Tensions in the 1870s and 1880s," *Agricultural History* 60 (Spring 1986): 22–36.

3. Harry C. McDean, "Professionalism in the Rural Social Sciences," *Agricultural History* 58 (July 1984): 375–77.

4. Roy V. Scott, *The Reluctant Farmer: The Rise of Agricultural Extension to 1914* (Urbana: University of Illinois Press, 1970), p. 93.

5. Scott, *Reluctant Farmer*, p. 106.

6. Scott, *Reluctant Farmer*, p. 194.

7. Scott, *Reluctant Farmer*, p. 286.

8. David B. Danborn, *The Resisted Revolution: Urban America and the Industrialization of Agriculture, 1890–1930* (Ames: Iowa State University Press, 1979), chap. 2; Danborn, "Rural Education Reform and the Country Life Movement," *Agricultural History* 53 (April 1979): 462–63.

9. Danborn, *Resisted Revolution*, pp. 77–78; Wayne E. Fuller, *The Old Country School: The Story of Rural Education in the Middle West* (Chicago: University of Chicago Press, 1982), chap. 11.

10. Brian William Beltman, "Rural Renaissance in an Urban Age: The Country Life Movement in Wisconsin, 1895–1918" (Ph.D. diss., University of Wisconsin, 1974), pp. 154–55.

11. Richard J. Jensen and Mark Friedberger, "Education and Social Structure: An Historical Study of Iowa, 1870–1930," National Institute of Education Project (Chicago: Newberry Library, 1976), pp. 2, 10.

12. David B. Danborn, "Rural Education Reform and the Country Life Movement, 1900–1920," *Agricultural History* 53 (April 1979): 470–71.

13. Beltman, "Rural Renaissance," p. 121.

14. See Eric L. Lampard, *The Rise of the Dairy Industry in Wisconsin* (Madison: State Historical Society of Wisconsin, 1958), chaps. 6–7.

15. Beardsley, *Harry L. Russell*, p. 89.

16. W. Elliot Brownlee, Jr., "Income Taxation and the Political Economy of Wisconsin, 1890–1930," *Wisconsin Magazine of History* 59 (Summer 1976): 299–324.

17. Dorothy Schwieder, "The Iowa State College Cooperative Extension Service through Two World Wars," *Agricultural History* 64 (Spring 1990): 223. Also see Leland L. Sage, "Rural Iowa in the 1920s and 1930s," *Annals of Iowa* 47 (Fall 1983): 96–97, and Katherine Jellison, *Entitled to Power: Farm Women and Technology, 1913–1963* (Chapel Hill: University of North Carolina Press, 1993), pp. 21–24.

18. See Robert L. Morlan, *Political Prairie Fire: The Nonpartisan League, 1915–1922* (Minneapolis: University of Minnesota Press, 1955); Richard M. Valelly, *Radicalism in the States: The Minnesota Farmer-Labor Party and the American Political Economy* (Chicago, 1989), chap. 3; Millard L. Gieske, *Minnesota Farmer-Laborism: The Third Party Alternative* (Minneapolis: University of Minnesota Press, 1979), chaps. 4–5.

19. U.S. Department of Agriculture, *Agricultural Statistics, 1937* (Washington: Government Printing Office, 1937), p. 390. Also see Lee J. Alston, "Farm Foreclosures in the United States during the Interwar Period," *Journal of Economic History* 43 (December 1983): 887–94.

20. See Gilbert Fite, *George N. Peek and the Fight for Farm Parity* (Norman: University of Oklahoma Press, 1954); Donald L. Winters, *Henry Cantwell Wallace as Secretary of Agriculture, 1921–1924* (Urbana: University of Illinois Press, 1970).

21. Robert E. Ankli, "Horses vs. Tractors on the Corn Belt," *Agricultural History* 54 (January 1980): 135–37; Robert C. Williams, *Fordson, Farmall, and Poppin' Johnny: A History of the Farm Tractor and Its Impact on America* (Urbana: University of Illinois Press, 1987).

22. Ankli, "Horses vs. Tractors," p. 146.

23. Ankli, "Horses vs. Tractors"; Allan G. Bogue, "Changes in Mechanical and Plant Technology: The Corn Belt, 1910–1940," *Journal of Economic History* 43 (March 1983): 2–3.

24. Daniel Nelson, *Managers and Workers: Origins of the New Factory System in the United States, 1880–1920* (Madison: University of Wisconsin Press, 1975), pp. 7–9.

25. Arthur G. Woolf, "Electricity, Productivity, and Labor Saving: American Manufacturing, 1900–1929," *Explorations in Economic History* 21 (1984): 183–84.

26. See Philip Scranton, "Diversity in Diversity: Flexible Production and American Industrialization, 1880–1930," *Business History Review* 65 (Spring 1991): 27–90.

27. JoAnne Yates, *Control through Communications: The Rise of System in American Management* (Baltimore: Johns Hopkins University Press, 1989), pp. 133–58; also Nelson, *Managers and Workers*, pp. 48–54.

28. Daniel Nelson, "The New Factory System and the Unions: The NCR Dispute of 1901," *Labor History* 15 (Winter 1974): 89–97; Judith Sealander, *Grand Plans: Business Progressivism and Social Change in Ohio's Miami Valley, 1890–1929* (Lexington: University of Kentucky Press, 1988), pp. 18–42; Sanford M. Jacoby, *Employing Bureaucracy: Managers, Unions, and the Transformation of Work in American Industry, 1900–1945* (New York: Columbia University Press, 1985).

29. Robert Ozanne, *A Century of Labor-Management Relations at McCormick and International Harvester* (Madison: University of Wisconsin Press, 1967), chap. 4; Nelson, *Managers and Workers*, pp. 101–21.

30. David J. Goldberg, "Richard A. Feiss, Mary Barnett Gilson, and Scientific Management at Joseph & Feiss, 1909–1925," in Daniel Nelson, ed., *A Mental Revolution* (Columbus: Ohio State University Press, 1992), p. 43.

31. Goldberg, "Richard A. Feiss," p. 45.

32. Goldberg, "Richard A. Feiss," pp. 50–53.

33. Robert Paul Thomas, "The Automobile Industry and Its Tycoon," *Explorations in Entrepreneurial History* 6 (1979): 147.

34. David A. Hounshell, *From the American System to Mass Production, 1880–1932: The Development of Manufacturing Technology in the United States* (Baltimore: Johns Hopkins University Press, 1984), pp. 217–62; Daniel M. G. Raff, "Wage Determination Theory and the Five-Dollar Day at Ford," *Journal of Economic History* 48 (June 1988): 387–99.

35. William J. Abernathy, *The Productivity Dilemma: Roadblock to Innovation in the Automobile Industry* (Baltimore: Johns Hopkins University Press, 1978), p. 25.

36. See Wayne A. Lewchuk, "Men and Monotony: Fraternalism as a Managerial Strategy at the Ford Motor Company," *Journal of Economic History* 53 (December 1993): 824–57.

37. Allan Nevins, *Ford: The Times, The Man, The Company* (New York: Scribner, 1954), pp. 542–44; Larry Lankton, *Cradle to Grave: Life, Work, and Death at the Lake Superior Copper Mines* (New York: Oxford University Press, 1991), p. 241.

38. August Meier and Elliott Rudwick, *Black Detroit and the Rise of the UAW* (New York: Oxford University Press, 1979), pp. 8–16; Zaragosa Vargas, *Proletarians of the North: A History of Mexican Industrial Workers in Detroit and the Midwest, 1917–1933* (Berkeley: University of California Press, 1993), pp. 47–51.

39. The 1935 data is based on Ford Motor Company, Rouge Plant, "Number of Men on Each Occupation," August 7, 1935, Ford Archives. For an earlier effort, see Charles Reitell, "Machinery and Its Effect Upon the Workers in the Auto Industry," *Annals of the American Academy of Political and Social Science* 116 (November 1924): 39–40.

40. Stephen Meyer II, *The Five Dollar Day: Labor, Management and Social Control in the Ford Motor Company, 1908–1921* (Albany: SUNY Press, 1981), pp. 50–51.

41. Allan Nevins, *Ford: Expansion and Challenge 1915–1933* (New York: Scribner, 1957), pp. 255–56; Abernathy, *Productivity Dilemma*, pp. 20–21.

42. Gilbert F. Richards, *Budd on the Move: Innovation for a Nation on Wheels* (New York: Newcomen Society, 1975), pp. 10–11; Abernathy, *Productivity Dilemma*, pp. 18–19, 24–26, 183–84.

43. Federal Trade Commission, *Report on Motor Vehicle Industry* (Pursuant to Joint Resolution No. 87, 75th Congress, 3rd session) (Washington: Government Printing Office, 1939), p. 546.

44. Lawrence H. Seltzer, *A Financial History of the American Automobile Industry* (Boston: Houghton-Mifflin, 1928), pp. 96, 160; E. D. Kennedy, *The Automobile Industry: The Coming of Age of Capitalism's Favorite Child* (Clifton: A. M. Kelley, 1972), pp. 89, 156; Charles K. Hyde, "'Dodge Main' and the Detroit Automobile Industry, 1910–1980," *Detroit in Perspective* 6 (Spring 1983): 10.

45. See Walter P. Chrysler, *Life of an American Workman* (New York: Dodd Mead, 1950), pp. 133–37.

46. Hyde, "Dodge Main," p. 8.

47. Daniel Raff, "The Puzzling Profusion of Compensation Schemes in the 1920s Automobile Industry," unpublished paper, 1988.

48. E. S. Cowdrick, "Methods of Wage Payment," (1927) General Motors Report, Bethlehem Steel Company Papers, Accession 1699 (Hagley Library, Wilmington).

49. Norman G. Shidle, "How Industry Is Approaching the Wage Payment Problem," *Automotive Industries* (September 24, 1925): 498–99.

50. Sidney Fine, *Sit-Down: The General Motors Strike of 1936–37* (Ann Arbor: University of Michigan Press, 1969), pp. 23–25; Jacoby, *Employing Bureaucracy*, pp. 137, 234–37.

51. John Dean Gaffey, *The Productivity of Labor in the Rubber Tire Manufacturing Industry* (New York: Columbia University Press, 1940), p. 90.

52. Boris Stern, "Labor Productivity in the Automobile Tire Industry," U.S. Bureau of Labor Statistics *Bulletin* 585 (July 1933): 61.

53. Mary J. Drucker, *The Rubber Industry in Ohio* (Columbus: Works Progress Administration, 1937); "Summary of Enrollment," National Labor Relations Board Papers, National Archives RG 25, Box 2116, File 1832.

54. Quoted in Daniel Nelson, "Mass Production and the U.S. Tire Industry," *Journal of Economic History* 47 (June 1987): 336.

55. Nelson, "Mass Production," p. 337.

56. Nelson, "Mass Production," p. 338.

57. See Donald Finlay Davis, *Conspicuous Production: Automobiles and Elites in Detroit, 1899–1933* (Philadelphia: Temple University Press, 1988).

58. Goldberg, "Richard A. Feiss," p. 47.

59. See Alfred D. Chandler, Jr., *The Visible Hand: The Managerial Revolution in American Business* (Cambridge: Harvard University Press, 1977) and Olivier Zunz, *Making America Corporate, 1870–1920* (Chicago: University of Chicago Press, 1990).

60. Sharon Hartman Strom, *Beyond the Typewriter: Gender, Class, and the Origins of Modern American Office Work, 1900–1930* (Urbana: University of Illinois Press, 1992), pp. 198–201.

61. See Margery W. Davies, *Woman's Place Is at the Typewriter: Office Work and Office Workers, 1870–1930* (Philadelphia: Temple University Press, 1982), pp. 97–128; Sharon Hartman Strom, "Light Manufacturing: The Feminization of American Office Work, 1900–1930," *Industrial and Labor Relations Review* 43 (October 1989): 64–69; Elyce J. Rotella, "The Transformation of the American Office: Changes in Employment and Technology," *Journal of Economic History* 41 (March 1981): 51–58.

62. Susan Benson Porter, *Counter Cultures: Saleswomen, Managers, and Customers in American Department Stores, 1890–1940* (Urbana: University of Illinois Press, 1986), pp. 143–59.

63. C. Bertrand Thompson, "Scientific Management in Retailing," in C. B. Thompson, ed., *Scientific Management* (Cambridge: Harvard University Press, 1914), pp. 546–47.

64. Elyce J. Rotella, *From Home to Office: U.S. Women at Work* (Ann Arbor: University of Michigan Press, 1981), p. 34.

65. Strom, *Beyond the Typewriter*, p. 201.

66. Strom, *Beyond the Typewriter*, p. 197.

67. Winifred D. Wandersee, *Women's Work and Family Values, 1920–1940* (Cambridge: Harvard University Press, 1981), p. 100.

68. Wandersee, *Women's Work*, pp. 80–81.

69. Zunz, *Making America Corporate*, p. 69.

70. Strom, *Beyond the Typewriter*, pp. 280–92.

71. Dorothy Sue Cobble, *Dishing It Out: Waitresses and Their Unions in the Twentieth Century* (Urbana: University of Illinois Press, 1991), chaps. 2, 3.

72. David E. Nye, *Electrifying America: Social Meanings of a New Technology, 1880–1940* (Cambridge: MIT Press, 1940), chap. 6.

73. David M. Katzman, *Seven Days a Week: Women and Domestic Service in Industrializing America* (New York: Oxford University Press, 1978), p. 130.

74. Ruth Schwartz Cowan, *More Work for Mother: The Ironies of Household Technology from the Open Hearth to the Microwave* (New York: Basic Books, 1983), chap. 6; Harvey A. Levenstein, *Revolution at the Table: The Transformation of the American Diet* (New York: Oxford University Press, 1988), p. 162.

75. Robert S. Lynd and Helen Merrell Lynd, *Middletown: A Study in American Culture* (New York: Harcourt, Brace & World, 1929), pp. 408–409.

76. Daniel E. Sutherland, "Modernizing Domestic Service" in Jessica H. Foy and Thomas J. Schlereth, eds., *American Home Life, 1880–1930: A Social History of Spaces and Services* (Knoxville: University of Tennessee Press, 1992), pp. 252–55.

5. Urban Workers in a Revolutionary Era, 1900–1930

1. Catherine Esther Gregg, "Ethnic Membership in Community Organizations of an Ohio Steel Town: A Study of the Rate of Social Assimilation" (Ph.D. diss., Columbia University, 1954), p. 54.

2. See Lisabeth Cohen, *Making a New Deal: Industrial Workers in Chicago, 1919–1939* (New York: Cambridge University Press, 1990), p. 30; Olivier Zunz, *The Changing Face of Inequality: Urbanization, Industrial Development, and Immigrants in Detroit, 1880–1920* (Chicago: Chicago University Press, 1982), pp. 349–50; Humbert S. Nelli, *Italians in Chicago, 1880–1930: A Study in Ethnic Mobility* (New York: Oxford University Press, 1970), chap. 3; John J. Bukowczyk, *And My Children Did Not Know Me: A History of Polish Americans* (Bloomington: Indiana University Press, 1987), chap. 2; Dominic A. Pacyga, *Polish Immigrants and Industrial Chicago: Workers on the South Side, 1880–1922* (Columbus: Ohio State University Press, 1991), chaps. 1–3.

3. James R. Barrett, *Work and Community in the Jungle: Chicago's Packinghouse Workers, 1894–1922* (Urbana: University of Illinois Press, 1987), p. 39; Donald Pienkos, "Politics, Religion, and Change in Polish Milwaukee, 1900–1930," *Wisconsin Magazine of History* 61 (Spring 1978): 181.

4. Nelli, *Italians in Chicago*, chap. 3.

5. Zunz, *Changing Face of Inequality*, pp. 340–41.

6. Zunz, *Changing Face of Inequality*, pp. 320–33, 350–51.

7. See, for example, Lloyd P. Gartner, *History of the Jews of Cleveland* (Cleveland: Western Reserve Historical Society, 1978), chap. 4, and Marc Lee Raphael, *Jews and Judaism in a Midwestern Community: Columbus, Ohio, 1840–1975* (Columbus: Ohio Historical Society, 1979), chaps. 6–7.

8. David A. Gerber, *Black Ohio and the Color Line, 1860–1915* (Urbana: University of Illinois Press, 1976), pp. 301–306; Nancy Bertaux, "Structural Economic Change and Occupational Decline among Black Workers in Nineteenth-Century Cincinnati," in Henry Louis Taylor, Jr., ed., *Race and the City: Work, Community, and Protest in Cincinnati, 1820–1970* (Urbana: University of Illinois Press, 1993), pp. 143–44.

9. Pacyga, *Polish Immigrants*, p. 155.

10. Edward R. Kantowicz, "Polish Chicago: Survival through Solidarity," in Melvin G. Holli and Peter d'A. Jones, eds., *Ethnic Chicago* (Grand Rapids: William B. Eerdmans, 1984), p. 218.

11. See Nick Salvatore, *Eugene V. Debs, Citizen and Socialist* (Urbana: University of Illinois Press, 1982); David Montgomery, *The Fall of the House of Labor: The Workplace, the State, and American Labor Activism, 1865–1925* (Cambridge: Cambridge University Press, 1987).

12. See Gwendolyn Mink, *Old Labor and New Immigrants in American Political Development: Union, Party, and State, 1875–1920* (Ithaca: Cornell University Press, 1986).

13. Gerald Friedman, "Dividing Labor," in Claudia Goldin and Hugh Rockoff, eds., *Strategic Factors in Nineteenth Century American Economic History: A Volume to Honor Robert W. Fogel* (Chicago: Chicago University Press, 1992), pp. 447–64.

14. Friedman, "Dividing Labor," pp. 461–62.

15. Richard Schneirov and Thomas J. Suhrbur, *Union Brotherhood, Union Town: The History of the Carpenters' Union of Chicago, 1863–1987* (Carbondale: Southern Illinois University Press, 1988), pp. 76–93.

16. Steven L. Piott, "The Chicago Teamsters; Strike of 1902: A Community Confronts the Beef Trust," *Labor History* 26 (Spring 1985): 250–67.

17. Friedman, "Dividing Chicago," pp. 462–63.

18. Robert Ozanne, *A Century of Labor-Management Relations at McCormick and International Harvester* (Madison: University of Wisconsin Press, 1967), pp. 46–59.

19. David Brody, *The Butcher Workmen: A Study of Unionization* (Cambridge: Harvard University Press, 1964), pp. 34–61.

20. Milton Derber, *Labor in Illinois: The Affluent Years, 1945–1980* (Urbana: University of Illinois Press, 1989), p. 40; Steve Fraser, *Labor Will Rule: Sidney Hillman and the Rise of American Labor* (New York: Free Press, 1991), chap. 3.

21. Pienkos, "Politics, Religion, and Change in Polish Milwaukee," pp. 179–81.

22. Thomas W. Gavett, *Development of the Labor Movement in Milwaukee* (Madison: University of Wisconsin Press, 1965), pp. 81, 114.

23. Gavett, *Development of the Labor Movement*, pp. 96, 98. Also see Robert W. Ozanne, *The Labor Movement in Wisconsin: A History* (Madison: State Historical Society of Wisconsin, 1984), pp. 31–43; Bayrd Still, *Milwaukee: The History of a City* (Madison: State Historical Society of Wisconsin, 1948), pp. 303–17; Sally M. Miller, *Victor Berger and the Promise of Constructive Socialism, 1910–1920* (Westport: Greenwood Press, 1973).

24. See Miller, *Victor Berger*, and Miller, "Casting a Wide Net: The Milwaukee Movement to 1920," in Donald T. Critchlow, ed., *Socialism in the Heartland: The Midwestern Experience, 1900–1925* (Notre Dame: University of Notre Dame Press, 1986), pp. 30–34.

25. See the accounts by Gavett, Ozanne, and Still cited above. Also see Gerd Korman, *Industrialization, Immigrants and Americanizers: The View from Milwaukee* (Madison: State Historical Society of Wisconsin, 1967).

26. Pienkos, "Politics, Religion, and Change in Polish Milwaukee," pp. 194–95.

27. Richard J. Oestreicher, *Solidarity and Fragmentation: Working People and Class Consciousness in Detroit, 1875–1900* (Urbana: University of Illinois Press, 1986), chap. 7.

28. See Melvin G. Holli, *Reform in Detroit: Hazen G. Pingree and Urban Politics* (New York: Oxford University Press, 1969).

29. Thomas Klug, "Employer's Strategies in the Detroit Labor Market" in Nelson Lichtenstein and Stephen Meyer, eds., *On the Line: Essays in the History of Auto Work* (Urbana: University of Illinois Press, 1989), pp. 42–72.

30. Christopher H. Johnson, *Maurice Sugar: Law, Labor, and the Left in Detroit, 1912–1950* (Detroit: Wayne State University Press, 1988), chaps. 3–4.

31. James F. Richardson, "Political Reform in Cleveland," in David D. Van Tassel and John J. Grabowski, eds., *Cleveland: A Tradition of Reform* (Kent: Kent State University Press, 1986), pp. 159–61; Arthur DeMatteo, "The Downfall of a Progressive: Mayor Tom L. Johnson and the Cleveland Streetcar Strike of 1908," *Ohio History* 104 (Winter-Spring 1995): 24–41.

32. Morgan J. Barclay, "Reform in Toledo: The Political Career of Samuel M. Jones," *Northwest Ohio Quarterly* 50 (Summer 1978): 79–89; George W. Knepper, *Ohio and Its People* (Kent: Kent State University Press, 1988), pp. 328–29.

33. Ozanne, *Labor Movement in Wisconsin*, p. 30.

34. Daniel Nelson, *American Rubber Workers and Organized Labor, 1900–1941* (Princeton: Princeton University Press, 1988), pp. 23–43.

35. John T. Walker, "Socialism in Dayton, Ohio, 1912–1925: Its Membership, Organization, and Demise," *Labor History* 26 (Summer 1985): 383, 389.

36. Richard W. Judd, "Restoring Consensus in Flint, Michigan: The Socialist Party in Municipal Politics, 1910–1912," in Critchlow, *Socialism in the Heartland*, p. 94.

37. Errol Wayne Stevens, "Main Street Socialism: The Socialist Party of America in Marion, Indiana, 1900–1921," in Critchlow, *Socialism in the Heartland*, pp. 359–60.

38. Lysle E. Meyer, "Radical Responses to Capitalism in Ohio before 1913," *Ohio History* 79 (Summer-Autumn 1970): 204; William H. Cumberland, "The Red Flag Comes to Iowa," *Annals of Iowa* 39 (Fall 1968): 453; William H. Cumberland, "The Davenport Socialists of 1920," *Annals of Iowa* 47 (Summer 1984): 451–74; James J. Lorence, "'Dynamite for the Brain': The Growth and Decline of Socialism in Central and Lakeshore Wisconsin, 1910–1920," *Wisconsin Magazine of History* 66 (Summer 1983): 251–73.

39. John E. Haynes, "The *New Times*, a Frustrated Voice of Socialism, 1910–1919," *Minnesota History* 52 (Spring 1991): 184.

40. Price V. Fishback, *Soft Coal, Hard Choices: The Economic Welfare of Bituminous Coal Miners, 1890–1930* (New York: Oxford University Press, 1992), p. 24.

41. John H. M. Laslett, "Swan Song or New Social Movement? Socialism and Illinois District 12, United Mine Workers of America, 1919–1926," in Critchlow, *Socialism in the Heartland*, p. 172.

42. Ronald L. Lewis, *Black Coal Miners in America: Race, Class, and Community Conflict, 1780–1980* (Lexington: University of Kentucky Press, 1987), pp. 83–84, 96–97.

43. Fishback, *Soft Coal, Hard Choices*, p. 29.

44. Auvo Kostiainen, "For or against Americanization? The Case of the Finnish Immigrant Radicals," in Dirk Hoerder, ed., *American Labor and Immigration History, 1877–1920s: Recent European Research* (Urbana: University of Illinois Press, 1983), p. 261; Larry Lankton, *Cradle to Grave: Life, Work, and Death at the Lake Superior Copper Mines* (New York: Oxford University Press, 1991), pp. 212–13. Also see Michael G. Karni, "Finnish Immigrant Leftists in America: The Golden Years, 1900–1918," in Dirk Hoerder, ed., *"Struggle a Hard Battle": Essays on Working Class Immigrants* (DeKalb: Northern Illinois University Press, 1986), pp. 199–228.

45. Arnold R. Alanen, "Early Labor Strife on Minnesota's Mining Frontiers, 1882–1906," *Minnesota History* 52 (Fall 1991): 257.

46. Charles K. Hyde, "Undercover and Underground: Labor Spies and Mine Management in the Early Twentieth Century," *Business History Review* 60 (Spring 1986): 12–13.

47. Neil Betten, "Strike on the Mesabi—1907," *Minnesota History* 40 (Fall 1967): 343–47; Alanen, "Early Labor Strife," p. 262.

48. Arthur W. Thurner, *Rebels on the Range: The Michigan Copper Miners' Strike of 1913–1914* (Lake Linden: John H. Forster Press, 1984), chap. 9; Lankton, *Cradle to Grave*, pp. 129–40.

49. Daniel Nelson, *Managers and Workers: Origins of the New Factory System, 1880–1920* (Madison: University of Wisconsin Press, 1975), pp. 143–47. For the southern labor market, see Gavin Wright, *Old South, New South: Revolutions in the Southern Economy since the Civil War* (New York: Norton, 1986).

50. See Jack Temple Kirby, "The Southern Exodus, 1910–1960: A Primer for Historians," *Journal of Southern History* 49 (November 1983): 594.

51. James R. Grossman, *Land of Hope: Chicago, Black Southerners, and the Great Migration* (Chicago: University of Chicago Press, 1989), pp. 74–85; also see the essays in Joe William Trotter, Jr., ed., *The Great Migration in Historical Perspective: New Dimensions of Race, Class, and Gender* (Bloomington: Indiana University Press, 1991).

52. Zunz, *Changing Face of Inequality*, p. 288; Lee Williams, "Newcomers to the City: A Study of Black Population Growth in Toledo, Ohio, 1910–1930," *Ohio History* 89 (Winter 1980): 5–24.

53. William M. Tuttle, Jr., "Labor Conflict and Racial Violence: The Black Worker in Chicago," *Labor History* 10 (Summer 1969): 421.

54. Cohen, *Making a New Deal*, p. 152.

55. Elliott M. Rudwick, *Race Riot in East St. Louis, July 2, 1917* (Carbondale: Southern Illinois University Press, 1963), pp. 142, 218.

56. Tuttle, "Labor Conflict and Racial Violence," p. 415.

57. Dianne M. Pinderhughes, *Race and Ethnicity in Chicago Politics: A Reexamination of Pluralist Theory* (Urbana: University of Illinois Press, 1987), p. 29.

58. Donald G. Sofchalk, "Organized Labor and the Iron Ore Mines of Northern Minnesota," *Labor History* (Spring 1971): 225.

59. Neil Betten, "Riot, Revolution, Repression in the Iron Range Strike of 1916," *Minnesota History* 41 (Summer 1968): 82–94.

60. Sofchalk, "Organized Labor and the Iron Ore Miners," p. 231.

61. See David Brody, *Steelworkers in America: The Nonunion Era* (Cambridge: Harvard University Press, 1960), pp. 231–62; Brody, *Labor in Crisis: The Steel Strike of 1919* (Philadelphia: Lippincott, 1965). For turmoil in the auto industry, see Raymond Boryczka and Lorin Lee Cary, *No Strength without Union: An Illustrated History of Ohio Workers, 1803–1980* (Columbus: Ohio Historical Society, 1982), pp. 161–63.

62. Brody, *The Butcher Workmen*, pp. 97–105; Pacyga, *Polish Immigrants and Industrial Chicago*, pp. 239–54.

63. Daniel Nelson, "The Company Union Movement, 1900–1937: A Reexamination," *Business History Review* 56 (1982): 335–57.

64. Gavett, *Development of the Labor Movement*, pp. 128–31.

65. Stanley Shapiro, "'Hand and Brain': The Farmer-Labor Party of 1920," *Labor History* 26 (Summer 1985): 411.

66. Mary Watters, *Illinois in the Second World War, Volume II: The Production Front* (Springfield: Illinois State Historical Library, 1951), p. 204.

67. Richard Straw, "An Act of Faith: Southeastern Ohio Miners in the Coal Strike of 1927," *Labor History* 21 (Spring 1980): 221–38; Melvyn Dubofsky and Warren Van Tine, *John L. Lewis: A Biography* (Urbana: University of Illinois Press, 1986), chaps. 6–7.

68. Barbara Warne Newell, *Chicago and the Labor Movement: Metropolitan Unionism in the 1930s* (Urbana: University of Illinois Press, 1961), pp. 70–71; Schneirov and Suhrbar, *Union Brotherhood, Union Town*, pp. 104–12; Erik Olssen, "The Making of a Political Machine: The Railroad Unions Enter Politics," *Labor History* 19 (Summer 1978): 373–96.

69. Gavett, *Development of the Labor Movement*, pp. 137–50; Darryl Holter, "Labor Spies and Union-Busting in Wisconsin, 1890–1940," *Wisconsin Magazine of History* 68 (Summer 1985): 243–65.

70. Gavett, *Development of the Labor Movement*, pp. 146–51.

71. Thomas J. Jablonsky, *Pride in the Jungle: Community and Everyday Life in Back of the Yards Chicago* (Baltimore: Johns Hopkins University Press, 1993), p. 52.

72. Jablonsky, *Pride in the Jungle*, p. 94.

73. Levenstein, *Revolution at the Table*, pp. 175–76.

74. William W. Giffin, "The Political Realignment of Black Voters in Indianapolis, 1924," *Indiana Magazine of History* 79 (June 1983): 133–66.

75. William Wayne Giffin, "The Negro in Ohio, 1914–1949" (Ph.D. diss., Ohio State University, 1968), pp. 148–57; Joe William Trotter, *Black Milwaukee: The Making of an Industrial Proletariat, 1915–45* (Urbana: University of Illinois Press, 1988), p. 45; Kenneth Kusmer, *A Ghetto Takes Shape: Black Cleveland, 1870–1900* (Urbana: University of Illinois Press, 1976), p. 160.

76. James H. Madison, *Indiana through Tradition and Change: A History of the Hoosier State and Its People, 1920–1945* (Indianapolis: Indiana Historical Society, 1982), pp. 208, 211–13, 230–31.

77. Ronald Edsforth, *Class Conflict and Cultural Consensus: The Making of a Mass Consumer Society in Flint, Michigan* (New Brunswick: Rutgers University Press, 1987), pp. 94–95; Robert S. LaForte and Richard Himmel, "Middletown Looks at the Lynds: A Contemporary Critique by the Reverend Dr. Hillyer H. Stratton of Muncie, Indiana, 1937," *Indiana Magazine of History* 49 (September 1983): 248–64; Daniel Horowitz, *The Morality of Spending: Attitudes toward the Consumer Society in America, 1875–1940* (Baltimore: Johns Hopkins University Press, 1985), pp. 134–53. Also see Lisa M. Fine, "'Our Big Factory Family': Masculinity and Paternalism at the Reo Motor Car Company of Lansing, Michigan," *Labor History* 34 (Spring-Summer 1993): 280–88.

78. See Daniel Nelson, "Scientific Management and the Workplace," in Sanford M. Jacoby, ed., *Masters to Managers: Historical and Comparative Perspectives on American Employers* (New York: Columbia University Press, 1991), pp. 74–89.

79. David Fairris, "From Exit to Voice in Shopfloor Governance: The Case of Company Unions," Unpublished paper, 1993.

80. Daniel Nelson, *American Rubber Workers & Organized Labor, 1900–1941* (Princeton: Princeton University Press, 1988), p. 104.

81. Ozanne, *A Century of Labor Relations*, pp. 124–33.

82. Kathleen M. Blee, *Women of the Klan: Racism and Gender in the 1920s* (Berkeley: University of California Press, 1991), pp. 104–11; Carl V. Hallberg, "'For God, Country, and Home': The Ku Klux Klan in Pekin, 1923–1925," *Journal of the Illinois Historical Society* 77 (Summer 1984): 82–93.

83. Leonard J. Moore, *Citizen Klansmen: The Ku Klux Klan in Indiana, 1921–1928* (Chapel Hill: University of North Carolina Press, 1991), p. 7.

84. Paul M. Angle, *Bloody Williamson: A Chapter in American Lawlessness* (New York: Alfred A. Knopf, 1952), p. 205.

85. William D. Jenkins, *Steel Valley Klan: The Ku Klux Klan in Ohio's Mahoning Valley* (Kent: Kent State University Press, 1990); Ronald L. Lewis, *Black Coal Miners in America: Race, Class, and Community Conflict, 1780–1980* (Lexington: University of Kentucky Press, 1987), pp. 104–105; William W. Giffin, "The Political Realignment of Black Voters in Indianapolis, 1927," *Indiana Magazine of History* 79 (June 1983): 133–66; Robert A. Goldberg, "The Ku Klux Klan in Madison, 1922–1927," *Wisconsin Magazine of History* 58 (Autumn 1974): 31–44.

86. Jenkins, *Steel Valley Klan*, p. 151.

87. Angle, *Bloody Williamson*, pp. 135–269.

88. Nelson, *American Rubber Workers*, p. 101.

89. Blee, *Women of the Klan*, p. 149; Dwight W. Hoover, "To Be a Jew in Middletown: A Muncie Oral History Project," *Indiana Magazine of History* 81 (June 1985): 131–58.

6. A New Deal for Midwestern Workers, 1930–1939

1. David E. Nye, *Electrifying America: Social Meanings of a New Technology, 1880–1910* (Cambridge: MIT University Press, 1990), chap. 7. Also see Dorothy Schwieder, "Rural Iowa in the 1920s," *Annals of Iowa* 47 (Fall 1983): 104–11.

2. John L. Shover, *Cornbelt Rebellion: The Farmers' Holiday Association* (Urbana: University of Illinois Press, 1965), p. 39.

3. H. Roger Grant and L. Edward Purcell, *Years of Struggle: The Farm Diary of Elmer G. Powers, 1931–1936* (Ames: Iowa State University Press, 1976), p. 41.

4. Shover, *Cornbelt Rebellion*, p. 16. Also see Lee J. Alston, "Farm Foreclosures in the United States During the Interwar Period," *Journal of Economic History* 43 (December 1983): 887–88.

5. Shover, *Cornbelt Rebellion*, pp. 86–88; Lee J. Alston, "Farm Foreclosure Moratorium Legislation: A Lesson from the Past," *American Economic Review* 74 (June 1984): 445–46; Rodney D. Karr, "Farm Rebels in Plymouth County, Iowa, 1932–1933," *Annals of Iowa* 47 (Winter 1985): 638–43. On the Plymouth County violence, also see the exchange between Joseph Frazier Wall and George Mills in the Fall 1983 *Annals of Iowa*, pp. 124–31.

6. Walter W. Wilcox, *The Farmer in the Second World War* (Ames: Iowa State College Press, 1947), pp. 10–11.

7. William F. Thompson, *The History of Wisconsin, Vol. VI: Continuity and Change, 1940–1965* (Madison: State Historical Society of Wisconsin, 1988), p. 177.

8. Sally Clarke, "'Innovation' in U.S. Agriculture: A Role for New Deal Regulation," *Business and Economic History* 21 (1992): 49–50.

9. Barbara J. Steinson, "Memories of Hoosier Homemakers: A Review Essay," *Indiana Magazine of History* 86 (June 1990): 204–206; Robert T. Beall, "Rural Electrification," in U.S. Department of Agriculture, *Farmers in a Changing World, Yearbook of Agriculture, 1940* (Washington: Government Printing Office, 1940), pp. 802–806; Deborah Fink, *Open Country Iowa: Rural Women, Tradition and Change* (Albany: State University of New York Press, 1986), p. 47.

10. Wilcox, *Farmer in the Second World War*, p. 13.

11. Mary Watters, *Illinois in the Second World War, Vol. II: The Production Front* (Springfield: Illinois State Historical Library, 1952), p. 401.

12. Watters, *Illinois in the Second World War*, p. 404.

13. John Joseph Wallis, "Employment in the Great Depression: New Data and Hypotheses," *Explorations in Economic History* 26 (1989): 53.

14. Richard J. Jensen, "The Causes and Cures of Unemployment in the Great Depression," *Journal of Interdisciplinary History* 19 (Spring 1989): 553–83.

15. See Robert M. Collins, *The Business Response to Keynes, 1929–1964* (New York: Columbia University Press, 1981), chaps. 3–4.

16. Lisabeth Cohen, *Making a New Deal: Industrial Workers in Chicago, 1919–1939* (New York: Cambridge University Press, 1990), p. 241; Paul M. Angle, *Bloody Williamson: A Chapter in American Lawlessness* (New York: Alfred A. Knopf, 1952), p. 269; Larry D. O'Brien, "The Ohio National Guard in the Coal Strike of 1932," *Ohio History* 84 (Summer 1975): 127–44; Larry Lankton, *Cradle to Grave: Life, Work and Death at the Lake Superior Copper Mines* (New York: Oxford University Press, 1991), pp. 252–53.

17. William Wayne Giffin, "The Negro in Ohio, 1914–1939" (Ph.D. diss., Ohio

State University, 1968), pp. 308–309; Joe William Trotter, *Black Milwaukee: The Making of an Industrial Proletariat, 1915–1945* (Urbana: University of Illinois Press, 1988), p. 151.

18. Cohen, *Making a New Deal*, p. 241.

19. Harvey A. Levenstein, *Paradox of Plenty: A Social History of Eating in Modern America* (New York: Oxford University Press, 1993), pp. 25, 265; John Modell, *Into One's Own: From Youth to Adulthood in the United States, 1920–1975* (Berkeley: University of California Press, 1989), pp. 124–27; Elizabeth Faue, *Community of Suffering & Struggle: Women, Men, and the Labor Movement in Minneapolis, 1915–1945* (Chapel Hill: University of North Carolina Press, 1991), p. 43.

20. Levenstein, *Paradox of Plenty*, p. 25.

21. Modell, *Into One's Own*, p. 130; Cohen, *Making a New Deal*, pp. 226–31; Winifred D. Wandersee, *Women's Work and Family Values, 1920–1940* (Cambridge: Harvard University Press, 1981), p. 38.

22. Jurgen Kocka, *White Collar Workers in America 1890–1940: A Social-Political History in International Perspective* (London: Sage Publishing, 1986), chap. 4; Richard Schneirov and Thomas J. Suhrbur, *Union Brotherhood, Union Town: The History of the Carpenters' Union of Chicago, 1863–1987* (Carbondale: Southern Illinois University Press, 1988), p. 116; William Graebner, *A History of Retirement: The Meaning and Function of an American Institution, 1885–1978* (New Haven: Yale University Press, 1980), chap. 7.

23. Zaragosa Vargas, *Proletarians of the North: A History of Mexican Industrial Workers in Detroit and the Midwest, 1917–1933* (Berkeley: University of California Press, 1993), pp. 176–89; Francisco Arturo Rosales and Daniel T. Simon, "Mexican Immigrant Experience in the Urban Midwest: East Chicago, Indiana, 1919–1945," *Indiana Magazine of History* 77 (December 1981): 347–49.

24. Irving Bernstein, *The Lean Years: A History of the American Worker, 1920–1933* (Boston: Houghton Mifflin, 1960), pp. 296–97, 300–301.

25. Iwan Morgan, "Fort Wayne and the Great Depression: The Early Years, 1929–1933," *Indiana Magazine of History* 80 (June 1984): 130, 136.

26. Morgan, "Fort Wayne and the Great Depression," p. 142. Also see John A. Garraty, *Unemployment in History: Economic Thought and Public Policy* (New York: Harper & Row, 1978), pp. 178–86.

27. Bernstein, *Lean Years*, p. 428; Faue, *Community of Suffering and Struggle*, pp. 64–65; St. Clair Drake and Horace R. Layton, *Black Metropolis: A Study of Negro Life in a Northern City, Vol. I* (New York: Harcourt Brace, 1945), pp. 86–87; Daniel Leab, "'United We Eat': The Creation and Organization of the Unemployed Councils in 1930," *Labor History* 8 (1967): 300–15.

28. Alex Baskin, "The Ford Hunger March—1932," *Labor History* 13 (Summer 1972): 331–60.

29. Roy Rosenzweig, "Radicals and the Jobless: The Musteites and the Unemployed Leagues, 1932–1936," *Labor History* 16 (Winter 1975): 60–61.

30. Roy Rosenzweig, "Socialism in Our Time: The Socialist Party and the Unemployed, 1929–1936," *Labor History* 20 (Fall 1979): 491–92.

31. Frank P. Vazzano, "Harry Hopkins and Martin Davey: Federal Relief and Ohio Politics during the Depression," *Ohio History* 96 (Summer-Autumn 1987): 125.

32. See Richard J. Jensen, "The Causes and Cures of Unemployment," 553–83.

33. Dianne M. Pinderhughes, *Race and Ethnicity in Chicago Politics: A Reexamination of Pluralist Theory* (Urbana: University of Illinois Press, 1987), pp. 72–79; Steven P. Erie, *Rainbow's End: Irish Americans and the Dilemmas of Urban Machine*

Politics, 1840–1985 (Berkeley: University of California Press, 1988), pp. 132–37; Cohen, *Making a New Deal*, pp. 256–57.

34. James H. Madison, *Indiana through Tradition and Change: A History of the Hoosier State and Its People, 1920–1945* (Indianapolis: Indiana Historical Society, 1982), pp. 116–24; Philip G. Payne, "The AFL and the CIO in Ironton [Ohio], 1935–1938," Unpublished essay, 1991.

35. See James H. Gross, *The Making of the National Labor Relations Board: A Study in Economics, Politics, and the Law* (Albany: State University of New York Press, 1974); Irving Bernstein, *Turbulent Years: A History of the American Worker, 1933–1941* (Boston: Houghton Mifflin, 1970), chaps. 5, 7, 13.

36. Daniel Nelson, *American Rubber Workers & Organized Labor, 1900–1941* (Princeton: Princeton University Press, 1988), p. 117.

37. Gary L. Bailey, "The Terre Haute, Indiana, General Strike, 1935," *Indiana Magazine of History* 80 (September 1984): 198.

38. Nelson, *American Rubber Workers & Organized Labor*, p. 122.

39. Daniel Nelson, "How the UAW Grew," *Labor History* 35 (Winter 1994): 10; Steve Babson, *Building the Union: Skilled Workers and Anglo-Gaelic Immigrants in the Rise of the UAW* (New Brunswick: Rutgers University Press, 1991), chap. 4.

40. John Bodnar, "Power and Memory in Oral History: Workers and Managers at Studebaker," *Journal of American History* 75 (March 1989): 1201–21.

41. Daniel Nelson, "Managers and Non-Union Workers in the Rubber Industry: Union Avoidance Strategies in the 1930s," *Industrial and Labor Relations Review* 43 (October 1989): 43.

42. Walter H. Uphoff, *Kohler on Strike: Thirty Years of Conflict* (Boston: Beacon Press, 1966), pp. 28–95.

43. Roger Keeran, *The Communist Party and the Auto Workers Unions* (Bloomington: Indiana University Press, 1980), pp. 38–95; Ronald Edsforth, *Class Conflict and Cultural Consensus: The Making of a Mass Consumer Society in Flint, Michigan* (New Brunswick: Rutgers University Press, 1987), pp. 128–35.

44. Wyndham Mortimer, *Organize! My Life as a Union Man* (Boston: Beacon Press, 1971), pp. 54–59.

45. Larry D. Englemann, "'We Were the Poor People'—The Hormel Strike of 1933," *Labor History* 15 (Fall 1974): 483–510; Bernstein, *Turbulent Years*, chaps. 2–4.

46. Sidney Fine, *The Automobile Under the Blue Eagle: Labor Management and the Automobile Manufacturing Code* (Ann Arbor: University of Michigan Press, 1963), pp. 163–71.

47. Bernstein, *Turbulent Years*, chap. 6.

48. Bernard Sternsher, "Scioto Marsh Onion Workers Strike, Hardin County, Ohio, 1934," *Northwest Ohio Quarterly* 58 (Spring-Summer 1986): 39–92.

49. Nelson, *American Rubber Workers & Organized Labor*, pp. 136–42.

50. Nelson, *American Rubber Workers & Organized Labor*, pp. 185–203.

51. Alfred Winslow Jones, *Life, Liberty and Property: A Story of Conflict and a Measurement of Conflicting Rights* (Philadelphia: Lippincott, 1941), chap. 10.

52. Nelson, *American Rubber Workers & Organized Labor*, pp. 256–57; Lester H. Brune, "Union Holiday—Closed Till Further Notice: The 1936 General Strike at Pekin, Illinois," *Journal of the Illinois Historical Society* 75 (Spring 1982): 29–38; Roger Horowitz, "'It Wasn't a Time to Compromise': The Unionization of Sioux City's Packinghouses, 1937–1942," *Annals of Iowa* 50 (Fall 1989-Winter 1990): 256–65.

53. Nelson, *American Rubber Workers & Organized Labor*, pp. 204–13; Sidney Fine, *Sit-Down: The General Motors Strike of 1936–37* (Ann Arbor: University of Michigan Press, 1969), chap. 5.

54. Fine, *Sit-Down*, chap. 8.

55. Sidney Fine, *Frank Murphy: The New Deal Years* (Chicago: University of Chicago Press, 1979), pp. 326–52; Carlos A. Schwantes, "'We've Got 'Em on the Run, Brothers': The 1937 Non-Automotive Sit-Downs in Detroit," *Michigan History* 56 (1972): 179–99.

56. Bernstein, *Turbulent Years*, chap. 10; Barbara Warne Newell, *Chicago and the Labor Movement: Metropolitan Unionism in the 1930s* (Urbana: University of Illinois Press, 1961), pp. 128–33.

57. James L. Baughman, "Classes and Company Towns: Legends of the 1937 Little Steel Strike," *Ohio History* 87 (Spring 1978): 175–92.

58. William Kornblum, *Blue Collar Community* (Chicago: University of Chicago Press, 1974), pp. 104–106; Donald G. Sofchalk, "The Chicago Memorial Day Incident: An Episode of Mass Action," *Labor History* 6 (Winter 1965): 9–19.

59. Baughman, "Classes and Company Towns," p. 176; John F. Shiner, "The 1937 Steel Labor Dispute and the Ohio National Guard," *Ohio History* 84 (Autumn 1975): 182–95.

60. Gene Smiley, "Recent Unemployment Rate Estimates for the 1920s and 1930s," *Journal of Economic History* 43 (June 1983): 488.

61. Nelson, "How the UAW Grew," 7; Nelson, *American Rubber Workers*, p. 265.

62. Cohen, *Making a New Deal*, pp. 340–41.

63. See Walter Licht and Hal Seth Barron, "Labor's Men: A Collective Biography of Union Officialdom During the New Deal Years," *Labor History* 19 (Fall 1978): 532–45.

64. Newell, *Chicago and the Labor Movement*, pp. 182–85; Thomas W. Gavett, *Development of the Labor Movement in Milwaukee* (Madison: University of Wisconsin Press, 1965), pp. 161–66; Nelson, *American Rubber Workers & Organized Labor*, pp. 229–31, 293–94; Warren Van Tine, "The CIO Split from the AFL in Columbus," Unpublished essay, 1991.

65. Gavett, *Development of the Labor Movement*, p. 179; John Earl Haynes, *Dubious Alliance: The Making of Minnesota's DFL Party* (Minneapolis: University of Minnesota Press, 1984), pp. 4, 42–43.

66. Gavett, *Development of the Labor Movement*, pp. 179–81; Stephen Meyer, *"Stalin over Wisconsin": The Making and Unmaking of Militant Unionism, 1900–1950* (New Brunswick: Rutgers University Press, 1992), pp. 83–101; Darryl Holter, "Sources of CIO Success: The New Deal Years in Milwaukee," *Labor History* 29 (Spring 1988): 222–23.

67. Bailey, "Terre Haute General Strike," 216–22; Shiner, "1937 Steel Labor Dispute," 182–95.

68. Hugh T. Lovin, "The Automobile Workers Unions and the Fight for Labor Politics in the 1930s," *Indiana Magazine of History* 77 (June 1981): 123–39; Lovin, "The Ohio 'Farmer-Labor' Movement in the 1930s," *Ohio History* 87 (Autumn 1978): 419–37.

69. Nelson, *American Rubber Workers & Organized Labor*, pp. 223–33.

7. Change and Continuity, 1939–1953

1. Alan S. Milward, *War, Economy, and Society, 1939–1945* (Berkeley: University of California Press, 1977), pp. 64–69.

2. Murray Benedict, *Farm Policies of the United States, 1790–1950: A Study of Their Origins and Development* (New York: 20th Century Foundation, 1953), p. 402; Milward, *War, Economy, and Society*, pp. 274–75.

3. Walter W. Wilcox, *The Farmer in the Second World War* (Ames: Iowa State College Press, 1947), p. 104.

4. Quoted in William F. Thompson, *History of Wisconsin, Vol. VI: Continuity and Change, 1945–1965* (Madison: State Historical Society of Wisconsin, 1988), p. 87.

5. Mary Watters, *Illinois in the Second World War, Vol. II: The Production Front* (Springfield: Illinois State Historical Library, 1952), pp. 415–21; Thompson, *History of Wisconsin*, pp. 91–93.

6. Wilcox, *Farmer in Second World War*, pp. 88–89.

7. Watters, *Illinois in the Second World War, Vol. II*, pp. 154–55.

8. *Monthly Labor Review* 54 (January 1942): 34–48.

9. U.S. Department of Commerce, Bureau of the Census, "Population," Series CA–3, no. 10, table 6 (Washington: Government Printing Office, 1944).

10. *Monthly Labor Review* 59 (September 1944): 485.

11. Lowell Juilliard Carr and James Edson Stermer, *Willow Run* (New York: Harper, 1952), pp. 356–57.

12. *Monthly Labor Review* 52 (June 1941): 1397–1401.

13. Bureau of Census, "Population," 1944; John Modell, *Into One's Own: From Youth to Adulthood in the United States, 1920–1975* (Berkeley: University of California Press, 1989), pp. 166–67; *Monthly Labor Review* 61 (November 1945): 843; Richard M. Ugland, "Viewpoints and Morale of Urban High School Students During World War II—Indianapolis as a Case Study," *Indiana Magazine of History* 77 (June 1981): 164–65.

14. Elizabeth Faue, *Community of Suffering and Struggle: Women, Men, and the Labor Movement in Minneapolis, 1915–1945* (Chapel Hill: University of North Carolina Press, 1991), pp. 172–73.

15. Thompson, *History of Wisconsin, Vol. VI*, p. 99.

16. *Monthly Labor Review* 61 (December 1945): 1088.

17. See Susan M. Hartmann, *The Home Front and Beyond: American Women in the 1940s* (Boston: Twayne Publishing, 1982), chap. 4.

18. Watters, *Illinois in the Second World War, Vol. I: Operation Home Front*, p. 247.

19. Modell, *Into One's Own*, p. 171.

20. D'Ann Campbell, *Women at War with America: Private Lives in a Patriotic Era* (Cambridge: Harvard University Press, 1984), p. 96.

21. Bureau of the Census, "Population," 1944.

22. Mary M. Schweitzer, "World War II and Female Labor Force Participation Rates," *Journal of Economic History* 40 (March 1980): 92–93. For day care in Michigan and Illinois, see Alan Clive, "Women Workers in World War II: Michigan as a Test Case," *Labor History* 20 (Winter 1979): 59–65, and Watters, *Illinois in the Second World War, Vol. I*, pp. 346–55.

23. Robert Ozanne, *A Century of Labor-Management Relations at McCormick and International Harvester* (Madison: University of Wisconsin Press, 1967), p. 188.

24. Herbert R. Northrup, *The Negro in the Automobile Industry* (Philadelphia: University of Pennsylvania Press, 1968), p. 9.

25. Watters, *Illinois in the Second World War, Vol. II*, p. 272.

26. *Monthly Labor Review* 55 (August 1942): 232.

27. Malcolm H. Ross, *All Manner of Men* (New York: Greenwood, 1969), pp. 49–66.

28. Joe William Trotter, *Black Milwaukee: The Making of an Industrial Proletariat, 1915–45* (Urbana: University of Illinois Press), pp. 165–71; Merl E. Reed, *Seedtime for the Modern Civil Rights Movement: The President's Committee on Fair Employment Practice, 1941–1946* (Baton Rouge: Louisiana State University Press, 1991), pp. 217–22; Andrew Kersten, "Fighting for Fair Employment: The FEPC in Cincinnati, Ohio, 1943–1945," unpublished manuscript, April 1994.

29. Watters, *Illinois in the Second World War, Vol. II*, pp. 264–66.

30. August Meier and Elliott Rudwick, *Black Detroit and the Rise of the UAW* (New York: Oxford University Press, 1979), pp. 130–35.

31. See Dominic J. Capeci, *Race Relations in Wartime Detroit: The Sojourner Truth Housing Controversy of 1942* (Philadelphia: Temple University Press, 1977).

32. Harvard Sitcoff, "Racial Militancy and Interracial Violence in the Second World War," *Journal of American History* 58 (December 1971): 673.

33. Robert Shogan and Tom Craig, *The Detroit Race Riot: A Study in Violence* (Philadelphia: Chilton Books, 1964), p. 89; Harvard Sitcoff, "The Detroit Race Riot of 1943," *Michigan History* 53 (Fall 1969): 183–206; Alan Clive, *State of War: Michigan in World War II* (Ann Arbor: University of Michigan Press, 1979), chap. 4.

34. Meier and Rudwick, *Black Detroit*, pp. 193–94; Alfred McClung Lee and Norman D. Humphrey, *Race Riot, Detroit 1943* (New York: Octagon Books, 1968), pp. 74–78.

35. Dominic J. Capeci, Jr., and Martha Wilkerson, *Layered Violence: The Detroit Rioters of 1943* (Jackson: University Press of Mississippi, 1991), p. 90.

36. Sidney Fine, *Violence in the Model City: The Cavanagh Administration, Race Relations, and the Detroit Riot of 1967* (Ann Arbor: University of Michigan Press, 1989), p. 2.

37. Leo Troy, *Distribution of Union Membership among the States, 1939 and 1953: Occasional Paper 56* (New York: National Bureau of Economic Research, 1957), pp. 6–9.

38. Daniel Nelson, "How the UAW Grew," *Labor History* 35 (Winter 1994): 16.

39. Barry Knitzberg, "An Unfinished Chapter in White-Collar Unionism: The Formative Years of the Chicago Newspaper Guild, Local 171, American Newspaper Guild, AFL-CIO," *Labor History* 14 (Summer 1973): 397–413.

40. Thomas L. Pahl, "G-String Conspiracy, Political Reprisal, or Armed Revolt? The Minneapolis Trotskyite Trial," *Labor History* 8 (Winter 1967): 30–52; John Earl Haynes, *Dubious Alliance: The Making of Minnesota's DFL Party* (Minneapolis: University of Minnesota Press, 1984), pp. 81–82. For UAW politics see Martin Halpern, "The 1939 UAW Convention: Turning Point for Communist Power in the Auto Union?" *Labor History* 33 (Spring 1992): 190–216. For the impact of the Minneapolis Teamsters, see Erling N. Sannes, "'Make Sioux City a Good Place to Live': Organizing Teamsters in Sioux City, 1933–1938," *Annals of Iowa* 50 (Fall 1989-Winter 1990): 214–40.

41. Stephen Meyer, *"Stalin over Wisconsin": The Making and Unmaking of Militant Unionism, 1900–1950* (New Brunswick: Rutgers University Press, 1992), pp. 92–103.

42. Robert W. Ozanne, *The Labor Movement in Wisconsin: A History* (Madison: State Historical Society of Wisconsin, 1984), p. 107.

43. See Steve Fraser, *Labor Will Rule: Sidney Hillman and the Rise of American Labor* (New York: Free Press, 1991), chap. 16; and Melvyn Dubofsky, *The State and Labor in Modern America* (Chapel Hill: University of North Carolina Press, 1994), chaps. 6–7.

44. Ozanne, *A Century of Labor-Management Relations*, pp. 196–209; Watters, *Illinois in the Second World War, Vol. II*, pp. 343–45; Wayne G. Broehl, Jr., *John Deere's Company: A History of Deere & Company and Its Times* (New York: Doubleday, 1984), pp. 554–57; *Monthly Labor Review* 57 (January 1944): 77–79.

45. Nelson, "How the UAW Grew," 16–17.

46. Bert Cochran, *Labor and Communism: The Conflict That Shaped American Unions* (Princeton: Princeton University Press, 1977), p. 257.

47. See Martin Halpern, *UAW Politics in the Cold War Era* (Albany: State University of New York Press, 1988).

48. Meier and Rudwick, *Black Detroit and the Rise of the UAW*, chap. 2.

49. Meier and Rudwick, *Black Detroit and the Rise of the UAW*, chap. 5.

50. Nancy F. Gabin, *Feminism in the Labor Movement: Women and the United Auto Workers, 1935–1975* (Ithaca: Cornell University Press, 1990), p. 59.

51. Gabin, *Feminism in the Labor Movement*, pp. 79–91.

52. *Monthly Labor Review* 59 (September 1944): 473. Also see Shelton Stromquist, *Solidarity & Survival: An Oral History of Iowa Labor in the Twentieth Century* (Iowa City: University of Iowa Press, 1993), pp. 127–28.

53. Nelson Lichtenstein, *Labor's War at Home* (New York: Cambridge University Press, 1982), pp. 134–35.

54. U.S. Senate, *Hearings before a Special Committee Investigating the National Defense Program*, Part 28, 79th Cong., 1st sess. (Washington, 1945), pp. 13795–96.

55. *Hearings*, pp. 13621–25.

56. *Hearings*, pp. 13621–25.

57. Carr and Stermer, *Willow Run*; Allan Nevins and Frank Ernest Hill, *Ford, Decline and Rebirth, 1933–1962* (New York: Scribner, 1962), pp. 209–17; Keith Sward, *The Legend of Henry Ford* (New York: Holt, Rinehart & Winston, 1948), pp. 429–50.

58. Steve Jefferys, *Management and Managed: Fifty Years of Crisis at Chrysler* (New York: Cambridge University Press, 1986), pp. 94–96.

59. Milton Derber, *Labor in Illinois: The Affluent Years, 1945–80* (Urbana: University of Illinois Press, 1989), p. 296.

60. Wilson J. Warren, "The Heyday of the CIO in Iowa: Ottumwa's Meatpacking Workers, 1937–1954," *Annals of Iowa* 51 (Spring 1992): 376–85; Roger Horowitz, "Organizing the Makers of Meat: Shop Floor Bargaining and Industrial Unionism in Meat Packing, 1930–1990" (unpublished manuscript, 1994), pp. 412–25; David Brody, *The Butcher Workmen: A Study of Unionization* (Cambridge: Harvard University Press, 1964), pp. 233–35; Stromquist, *Solidarity and Survival*, pp. 177–86.

61. Ozanne, *A Century of Labor-Management Relations*, pp. 213–14.

62. Derber, *Labor in Illinois*, pp. 274–78; Broehl, *John Deere's Company*, pp. 576–80.

63. Ozanne, *Labor Movement in Wisconsin*, p. 97.

64. Meyer, *"Stalin over Wisconsin,"* pp. 157–209; Roger Keeran, *The Communist Party and the Auto Workers Union* (Bloomington: Indiana University Press, 1980), pp. 267–78.

65. Theodore V. Purcell, *Blue Collar Man: Pattern of Dual Allegiance in Industry* (Cambridge: Harvard University Press, 1960), pp. 138–40.

66. See John Barnard, *Walter J. Reuther and the Rise of the Auto Workers* (Boston: Little, Brown, 1983); Frank Marquart, *An Auto Worker's Journal: The UAW from Crusade to One-Party Union* (University Park: Pennsylvania State University Press, 1975); Jack Stieber, *Governing the UAW* (New York: John Wiley & Sons, 1962); Stephen Amberg, *The Union Inspiration in American Politics: The Autoworkers and the Making of a Liberal Industrial Order* (forthcoming), chap. 4.

67. John Bartlow Martin, *Adlai Stevenson of Illinois: The Life of Adlai Stevenson* (New York: Doubleday, 1976), p. 300.

68. Derber, *Labor in Illinois*, pp. 86–89, 94–97.

69. Ralph C. James and Estelle Dinerstein James, *Hoffa and the Teamsters* (Princeton: D. Van Nostrand, 1965), p. 75.

70. Arthur A. Sloane, *Hoffa* (Cambridge: MIT Press, 1991), p. 33.

71. Jack Stieber, *The Steel Industry Wage Structure: A Study of the Joint Union-Management Job Evaluation Program in the Basic Steel Industry* (Cambridge: Harvard University Press, 1959), pp. 7–27, 62–63.

72. James W. Kuhn, *Bargaining in Grievance Settlement: The Power of Industrial Work Groups* (New York: Columbia University Press, 1961), pp. 149–70.

73. Derber, *Labor in Illinois*, pp. 109–11.

74. Kuhn, *Bargaining in Grievance Settlement*, p. 119.

75. Elizabeth Fons-Wolf, "Industrial Recreation, the Second World War, and the Revival of Welfare Capitalism, 1934–1960," *Business History Review* 60 (Summer 1986): 250–55.

76. Sumner H. Slichter, James J. Healy, and E. Robert Livernash, *The Impact of Collective Bargaining on Management* (Washington: Brookings Institution, 1960), pp. 374–75; Beth Stevens, "Labor Unions, Employee Benefits, and the Privatization of the American Welfare State," *Journal of Policy History* 2 (1990): 233–60; Alan Derickson, "Health Security for All? Social Unionism and Universal Health Insurance, 1935–1958," *Journal of American History* 80 (March 1994): 1347–51.

77. Slichter, Healy, and Livernash, *Impact of Collective Bargaining*, pp. 376–77.

78. Robert M. MacDonald, *Collective Bargaining in the Automobile Industry: A Study of Wage Structure and Competitive Relations* (New Haven: Yale University Press, 1963), p. 34.

79. See J. David Greenstone, *Labor in American Politics* (New York: Alfred A. Knopf, 1969).

80. Derber, *Labor in Illinois*, chap. 5.

81. Stephen B. Sarasohn and Vera H. Sarasohn, *Political Party Patterns in Michigan* (Detroit: Wayne State University Press, 1957), pp. 36–39.

82. Doris B. McLaughlin, *Michigan Labor: A Brief History from 1818 to the Present* (Ann Arbor: Institute of Labor and Industrial Relations, 1970), p. 130; Fay Calkins, *The CIO and the Democratic Party* (Chicago: University of Chicago Press, 1952), pp. 115–37.

83. See John Earl Haynes, "Farm Coops and the Election of Hubert Humphrey to the Senate," *Agricultural History* 57 (April 1983): 201–11; Carl Solberg, *Hubert Humphrey: A Biography* (New York: W. W. Norton, 1984).

84. David M. Oshinsky, "Wisconsin Labor and the Campaign of 1952," *Wisconsin Magazine of History* 56 (Winter 1972–73): 109–18.

85. See Carl Dean Snyder, *White Collar Workers and the UAW* (Urbana: University of Illinois Press, 1973).

86. Boris Emmet and John E. Jenck, *Catalogues and Counters: A History of Sears, Roebuck and Company* (Chicago: University of Chicago Press, 1950), p. 585.

87. Claudia Goldin, *Understanding the Gender Gap: An Economic History of American Women* (New York: Oxford University Press, 1990), pp. 176–77.

8. End of an Era, 1953–1983

1. See Arthur Kornhauser, Harold L. Sheppard, Albert J. Mayer, *When Labor Votes: A Study of Auto Workers* (New York: University Books, 1966).

2. Melvyn Dubofsky and Warren Van Tine, *John L. Lewis: A Biography* (Urbana: University of Illinois Press, 1986), chap. 20; Curtis Seltzer, *Fire in the Hole: Miners and Managers in the American Coal Industry* (Lexington: University Press of Kentucky, 1985), chaps. 6–7.

3. Albert Churella, "Lima Locomotive Works and the Dieselization Revolution, 1930–1950: Corporate Response to Technological Change," unpublished essay, 1992, p. 8.

4. Richard Schneirov and Thomas J. Suhrbur, *Union Brotherhood, Union Town: The History of the Carpenters' Union of Chicago, 1863–1987* (Carbondale: Southern Illinois University Press, 1988), p. 144. Also Schneirov, *Pride and Solidarity: A History of the Plumbers and Pipefitters of Columbus, Ohio, 1889–1989* (Ithaca: ILR Press, 1992), pp. 90–92.

5. Deborah Fink, *Open Country, Iowa: Rural Women, Tradition, and Change* (Albany: State University of New York Press, 1986), chap. 6.

6. Marty Strange, *Family Farming: A New Economic Vision* (Lincoln: University of Nebraska Press, 1988), pp. 84–100.

7. Sally Clarke, "Innovation in U.S. Agriculture: A Role for New Deal Regulation," *Business and Economic History* 21 (1992): 51.

8. R. Douglas Hurt, "Ohio Agriculture since World War II," *Ohio History* 97 (Winter-Spring 1988): 53–55. Compare this situation with that of central Illinois Amish farmers who clung to more traditional practices. John Hostetler, *Amish Society*, 4th ed. (Baltimore: Johns Hopkins University Press, 1993), pp. 121–22.

9. Gilbert C. Fite, *American Farmers: The New Minority* (Bloomington: Indiana University Press, 1981), pp. 188–93.

10. Fite, *American Farmers*, p. 193.

11. William F. Thompson, *The History of Wisconsin, Vol. VI: Change and Continuity, 1940–1965* (Madison: State Historical Society of Wisconsin, 1988), p. 115.

12. Virginia S. Fink, "The Impact of Changing Technologies on the Roles of Farm and Ranch Wives in Southeastern Ohio," in Wava G. Haney and June B. Knowles, eds., *Women and Farming: Changing Roles, Changing Structures* (Boulder: Westview Press, 1988), pp. 234–35.

13. Quoted in Thompson, *History of Wisconsin*, p. 156.

14. Fite, *American Farmers*, pp. 158–64.

15. See U.S. Census, *Population*, 1950, table 30 and 1960, table 61 for each of the midwestern states.

16. Claudia Goldin, *Understanding the Gender Gap: An Economic History of*

American Women (New York: Oxford University Press, 1990), pp. 138–49; and Goldin, "The Evolution of Married Women's Labour Force Participation in America: The Role of World War II," in Erik Aerts, Paul M. M. Klep, Jurgen Kocka, and Marina Thorberg, eds., *Women in the Labor Force: Comparative Studies on Labor Market and Organization of Work Since the Eighteenth Century* (Leuven: Leuven University Press, 1990), pp. 32–47.

17. Joan Vanek, "Time Spent in Housework," *Scientific American* 231 (November 1974): 116–20. Also see Ruth Schwartz Cowan, *More Work for Mother: The Ironies of Household Technology from the Open Hearth to the Microwave* (New York: Basic Books, 1983), pp. 199–206.

18. Wesley A. Wildman, "Teachers and Collective Negotiations," in Albert A. Blum et al., *White Collar Workers* (New York: Random House, 1971), pp. 134–42.

19. William W. Philliber, *Appalachian Immigrants in Urban America: Cultural Conflict or Ethnic Group Formation?* (New York: Praeger Publishers, 1981), p. 26; Martin B. Sussman and R. Clyde White, *Hough, Cleveland, Ohio: A Study of Social Life and Change* (Cleveland: Press of Western Reserve University, 1959).

20. Jon C. Teaford, *Cities of the Heartland: The Rise and Fall of the Industrial Midwest* (Bloomington: Indiana University Press, 1993), pp. 230–31.

21. Richard J. Arnould, "Changing Patterns of Concentration in American Meat Packing, 1880–1963," *Business History Review* 45 (Spring 1971): 27.

22. See Frederick H. Harbison and Robert Dubin, *Patterns of Union-Management Relations* (Chicago: Science Research Associates, 1947); Robert M. MacDonald, *Collective Bargaining in the Automobile Industry: A Study of Wage Structure and Competitive Relations* (New Haven: Yale University Press, 1963).

23. Stephen Amberg, "The Triumph of Industrial Orthodoxy: The Collapse of Studebaker-Packard," in Nelson Lichtenstein and Stephen Meyer, eds., *On the Line: Essays in the History of Auto Work* (Urbana: University of Illinois Press, 1989), pp. 190–218.

24. Paul A. Tiffany, *The Decline of American Steel: How Management, Labor, and Government Went Wrong* (New York: Oxford University Press, 1988), p. 131.

25. Robert W. Crandall, *Manufacturing on the Move* (Washington: Brookings Institution, 1993), pp. 18–19; Tiffany, *Decline of American Steel*, pp. 160–65. Also David Brody, *Workers in Industrial America: Essays on the Twentieth Century Struggle* (New York: Oxford University Press, 1980), pp. 195–98.

26. Howell John Harris, *The Right to Manage: Industrial Relations Policies of American Business in the 1940s* (Madison: University of Wisconsin Press, 1982), chaps. 4–5.

27. Walter H. Uphoff, *Kohler on Strike: Thirty Years of Conflict* (Boston: Beacon Press, 1966), pp. 111–358.

28. See Richard A. Lester, *As Unions Mature: An Analysis of the Evolution of American Unionism* (Princeton: Princeton University Press, 1958).

29. Milton Derber, *Labor in Illinois: The Affluent Years, 1945–80* (Urbana: University of Illinois Press, 1989), pp. 118–19, 122–23; Barbara Marsh, *A Corporate Tragedy: The Agony of International Harvester Company* (New York: Doubleday, 1985), p. 91.

30. See William Serrin, *The Company and the Union: The "Civilized Relationship" of the General Motors Corporation and the United Automobile Workers* (New York: Vintage Press, 1974).

31. James W. Kuhn, *Bargaining in Grievance Settlement: The Power of Industrial Work Groups* (New York: Columbia University Press, 1961), pp. 170–77.

32. David Fairris, "Appearance and Reality in Postwar Shopfloor Relations," *Review of Radical Political Economics* 22 (1990): 17–43.

33. See Joel Seidman, Jack London, Bernard Karsh, and Daisey L. Tagliacozzo, *The Worker Views His Union* (Chicago: University of Chicago Press, 1958).

34. Sumner L. Slichter, James J. Healy, and E. Robert Livernash, *The Impact of Collective Bargaining on Management* (Washington: Brookings Institution, 1960), p. 545. For examples, see Shelton Stromquist, *Solidarity & Survival: An Oral History of Iowa Labor in the Twentieth Century* (Iowa City: University of Iowa Press, 1993), pp. 192–99.

35. Eli Chimoy, *Automobile Workers and the American Dream* (Urbana: University of Illinois Press, 1992), chaps. 6–7.

36. See Edward D. Berkowitz, "How to Think about the Welfare State," *Labor History* 32 (Fall 1991): 489–502.

37. Seidman, *Worker Views His Union*, pp. 230–31, 239.

38. Doris B. McLaughlin, *Michigan Labor: A Brief History from 1818 to the Present* (Ann Arbor: Institute of Labor and Industrial Relations, 1970), pp. 134–53.

39. Gilbert J. Gall, *The Politics of Right to Work: The Labor Federations as Special Interests, 1943–1979* (Westport: Greenwood Press, 1988), pp. 94–121; Glenn W. Miller and Stephen B. Ware, "Organized Labor in the Political Process: A Case Study of the Right-to-Work Campaign in Ohio," *Labor History* 4 (Winter 1963): 51–67; Richard O. Davies, *Defender of the Old Guard: John Bricker and American Politics* (Columbus: Ohio State University Press, 1993), pp. 195–202.

40. J. David Greenstone, *Labor in American Politics* (New York: Alfred A. Knopf, 1969), pp. 82–84; Derber, *Labor in Illinois*, chap. 5.

41. Seidman, *Worker Views His Union*, p. 229.

42. Greenstone, *Labor in American Politics*, pp. 120–22.

43. John Fraser Hart, "Field Patterns in Indiana," *The Geographical Review* 58 (1968): 464, 470.

44. Rene Perez Rosenbaum, "Unionization of Tomato Field Workers in Northwest Ohio, 1967–1969," *Labor History* 35 (Summer 1994): 329–44. Migrant pickle workers in Wisconsin organized successfully in 1967 but lost their jobs when the processors introduced mechanical pickers. See Rosenbaum, "Success in Organizing, Failure in Collective Bargaining: The Case of Pickle Workers in Wisconsin, 1967–68," working paper no. 11, Julian Samora Research Institute, Michigan State University, August 1991.

45. UAW, President's Office, UAW Papers, Wayne State University, Box 24.

46. Dave Hage and Paul Klauda, *No Retreat, No Surrender: Labor's War at Hormel* (New York: William Morrow, 1989), pp. 96–97; Sue Sorisek, "The Man Who Wouldn't Lie Down," *Ohio Magazine* (August 1992): 29–32, 128–30.

47. See Thomas Kochan, Harry C. Katz, and Robert McKersie, *The Transformation of American Industrial Relations* (New York: Basic Books, 1986), pp. 62–64.

48. Barry T. Hirsch, *Labor Unions and the Economic Performance of Firms* (Kalamazoo: W. E. Upjohn Institute, 1991).

49. Kochan, Katz, and McKersie, *Transformation*, pp. 55–78; D. Quinn Mills, "Management Performance," in Jack Stieber, Robert B. McKersie, and D. Quinn Mills, eds., *U.S. Industrial Relations 1950–1980: A Critical Assessment* (Madison: Industrial Relations Research Associates, 1981), pp. 99–128.

50. Herbert R. Northrup, *The Negro in the Rubber Industry* (Philadelphia: University of Pennsylvania Press, 1969), p. 113.

51. Northrup, *Negro in Rubber Industry*, p. 13.

52. Charles Jeszeck, "Structural Change in GB: The U.S. Tire Industry," *Industrial Relations* 25 (Fall 1986): 239.

53. Charles Jeszeck, "Decline of Tire Manufacturing in Akron," in Charles Craypo and Bruce Nissen, eds., *Grand Designs: The Impact of Corporate Strategies on Workers, Unions, and Communities* (Ithaca: ILR Press, 1993), pp. 18–44.

54. Harry C. Katz, *Shifting Gears: Changing Labor Relations in the U.S. Automobile Industry* (Cambridge: MIT Press, 1985), pp. 42–43.

55. Herbert R. Northrup, *The Negro in the Automobile Industry* (Philadelphia: University of Pennsylvania Press, 1968), pp. 59–60.

56. Emma Rothschild, *Paradise Lost: The Decline of the Auto-Industrial Age* (New York: Random House, 1973), p. 102; Stanley Aronowitz, *False Promises: The Shaping of American Working Class Consciousness* (New York: McGraw Hill, 1973), pp. 22–50.

57. Eileen Appelbaum and Rosemary Batt, *The New American Workplace: Transforming Work Systems in the United States* (Ithaca: ILR Press, 1994), p. 59.

58. Harry C. Katz and Charles F. Sabel, "Industrial Relations and Industrial Adjustment in the Car Industry," *Industrial Relations* 24 (Fall 1985): 302–303; Katz, *Shifting Gears*, pp. 74–79.

59. John A. Orr, "The Rise and Fall of Steel's Human Relations Committee," *Labor History* 14 (Winter 1973): 69–83.

60. Derber, *Labor in Illinois*, pp. 101–102.

61. Derber, *Labor in Illinois*, pp. 101–105.

62. Carol O. Smith and Stephen B. Sarasohn, "Hate Propaganda in Detroit," *Public Opinion Quarterly* 10 (Spring 1946): 28–32; Greenstone, *Labor in American Politics*, chap. 4; Sidney Fine, *Violence in the Model City: The Cavanagh Administration, Race Relations, and the Detroit Riot of 1967* (Ann Arbor: University of Michigan Press, 1989), chap. 1–2.

63. Steven P. Erie, *Rainbow's End: Irish Americans and the Dilemmas of Urban Machine Politics, 1840–1985* (Berkeley: University of California Press, 1988), pp. 162–69; Arnold Hirsch, "The Black Struggle for Integrated Housing in Chicago," in Melvin G. Holli and Peter d'A. Jones, eds., *Ethnic Chicago* (Grand Rapids: William B. Eerdmans, 1984), pp. 383–405.

64. William Kornblum, *Blue Collar Community* (Chicago: University of Chicago Press, 1974), p. 26.

65. Northrup, *Negro in Auto Industry*, p. 56.

66. Theodore V. Purcell, *Blue Collar Man: Patterns of Dual Allegiance in Industry* (Cambridge: Harvard University Press, 1960), pp. 127–28. Roger Horowitz, "Organizing the Makers of Meat: Shop Floor Bargaining and Industrial Unionism in Meatpacking, 1930–1990" (unpublished manuscript), pp. 495–502.

67. Fine, *Violence in the Model City*, chap. 16; Dominic J. Capeci, Jr., and Martha Wilkerson, *Layered Violence: The Detroit Rioters of 1943* (Jackson: University Press of Mississippi, 1991), pp. 166–69.

68. Schneirov, *Pride and Solidarity*, p. 105.

69. See Phyllis A. Wallace and James W. Driscold, "Social Issues in Collective Bargaining," in Stieber et al., *U.S. Industrial Relations*, pp. 199–254.

70. Derber, *Labor in Illinois*, pp. 73–81; Robert Ozanne, *A Century of Labor-Management Relations at McCormick and International Harvester* (Madison: University of Wisconsin Press, 1967), pp. 164–65. Also Richard Rowan and Lester Rubin, *Opening the Skilled Construction Trades to Blacks: A Study of the Washington and Indianapolis Plans for Minority Employment* (Philadelphia: Wharton School, 1972), pp. 123–35.

71. Richard C. Haney, "Wallace in Wisconsin: The Presidential Primary of 1964," *Wisconsin Magazine of History* 61 (Summer 1976): 259–78.

72. Alan Draper, "Labor and the 1966 Elections," *Labor History* 30 (Winter 1989): 85–86.

73. Lloyd Rodwin, "Deindustrialization and Regional Transformation," in Lloyd Rodwin and Hidehiko Sazanami, eds., *Deindustrialization and Regional Economic Transformation: The Experience of the United States* (Boston: Unwin Hyman, 1989), pp. 12–15.

74. James Bovard, *The Farm Fiasco* (San Francisco: ICS Press), pp. 130–50.

75. *The Economist,* Nov. 28, 1991, pp. 21–23.

76. Mickey Lauria and Peter Fisher, *Plant Closings in Iowa: Causes, Consequences, and Legislative Options* (Iowa City: Institution of Urban and Regional Research, 1983), p. 41; Horowitz, "Organizing the Makers of Meat," pp. 580–92; Jimmy M. Skaggs, *Prime Cut: Livestock Raising and Meatpacking in the United States, 1607–1983* (College Station: Texas A & M Press, 1986), pp. 204–207.

77. John Portz, *The Politics of Plant Closings* (Lawrence: University Press of Kansas, 1990), pp. 57–82.

78. Hage and Klauda, *No Retreat, No Surrender,* pp. 50–51; Hardy Green, *On Strike at Hormel* (Philadelphia: Temple University Press, 1990), pp. 43–44.

79. See Marsh, *A Corporate Tragedy,* p. 80.

80. Kenneth Warren, *The American Steel Industry, 1850–1970: A Geographical Interpretation* (Oxford: Clarendon Press, 1973), p. 300.

81. Staughton Lynd, *The Fight against Shutdowns: Youngstown's Steel Mill Closings* (San Pedro: Singlejack Books, 1982) and Thomas G. Fuechtman, *Steeples and Stacks: Religion and Steel Crisis in Youngstown* (New York: Cambridge University Press, 1989). For similar events and struggles in Chicago, see David Bensman and Roberta Lynch, *Rusted Dreams: Hard Times in a Steel Community* (New York: McGraw-Hill, 1987), pp. 39–70, 136–46.

82. Terry F. Buss and F. Stevens Redburn, *Shutdown at Youngstown: Public Policy for Mass Unemployment* (Albany: State University of New York Press, 1983), p. 83.

83. Michael Moritz and Barrett Seaman, *Going for Broke: The Chrysler Story* (Garden City: Doubleday & Co., 1981), p. 279.

84. Andrew Battista, "Labor and Coalition Politics: The Progressive Alliance," *Labor History* 32 (Summer 1991): 413–15.

85. *New York Times,* January 20, 1981; Bensman and Lynch, *Rusted Dreams,* p. 92; UAW, President's Report, 1983 (Detroit: UAW, 1983), pp. 153–54.

86. *Wall Street Journal,* September 14, 1992.

87. Gregory Pappas, *The Magic City: Unemployment in a Working-Class Community* (Ithaca: Cornell University Press, 1989), chap. 9.

88. Allison Zippay, *From Middle Income to Poor: Downward Mobility among Displaced Steelworkers* (New York: Praeger, 1991), pp. 9–13.

89. Michael A. Curme, Barry T. Hirsch, and David A. Macpherson, "Union Membership and Contract Coverage in the United States, 1983–1988," *Industrial and Labor Relations Review* 44 (October 1991): 22–26.

90. On General Motors, see Paul R. Lawrence and Davis Dyer, *Renewing American Industry* (New York: Free Press, 1983), chap. 2 and *Wall Street Journal,* December 1, 1992, December 15, 1992.

91. Derber, *Labor in Illinois,* pp. 186–87.

9. Afterword

1. Mary R. McCarthy, Priscilla Salant, and William E. Saupe, "Off-Farm Labor Allocation by Married Farm Women: Research Review and New Evidence from Wisconsin," in Wava G. Haney and Jane B. Knowles, eds., *Changing Roles, Changing Structures* (Boulder: Westview Press, 1988), pp. 139–40. For "contrary" farming, see Gene Logsdon, *The Contrary Farmer* (Post Mills, Vermont: Chelsea Green Publishing Company, 1993).

2. Robert W. Crandall, *Manufacturing on the Move* (Washington: Brookings Institution, 1993), pp. 7–8, 39–41.

3. See *Wall Street Journal*, December 3, 1994.

4. See Richard Preston, *American Steel: Hot Metal Men and the Resurrection of the Rust Belt* (New York: Prentice Hall, 1991).

5. *Wall Street Journal*, March 9, 1992.

6. David Gelsanliter, *Jump Start: Japan Comes to the Heartland* (New York: Farrar, Straus and Giroux, 1990), p. 28.

7. Gelsanliter, *Jump Start*, pp. 100–105.

8. Crandall, *Manufacturing on the Move*, p. 71.

9. See Richard B. Freeman and Joel Rogers, "Who Speaks for Us? Employee Representation in a Nonunion Labor Market," and Henry S. Farber and Alan B. Krueger, "Union Membership in the United States: The Decline Continues," in Bruce E. Kaufman and Morris M. Kleiner, eds., *Employee Representation: Alternatives and Future Directions* (Madison: Industrial Relations Research Association, 1993), pp. 13–80, 105–34.

10. Dave Hage and Paul Klauda, *No Retreat, No Surrender: Labor's War at Hormel* (New York: William Morrow, 1989).

11. Hage and Klauda, *No Retreat, No Surrender*, p. 201; Hardy Green *On Strike at Hormel* (Philadelphia: Temple University Press, 1990); Peter Rachleff, *Hard-Pressed in the Heartland: The Hormel Strike and the Future of the Labor Movement* (Boston: South End Press, 1993), chap. 4.

12. *Wall Street Journal*, January 18, 1994.

13. See *Wall Street Journal*, June 9, 1994, for examples.

14. *Wall Street Journal*, June 13, 1994.

Index

A. B. Dick Company: introduces mimeograph, 53

Abernathy, William J., 217n35, 218nn41, 42

African American workers: Ford employees, 77; lose craft jobs, 91; occupations in Detroit, 90–91; join meatpacking union, 93; strikebreakers in mines, 99; to North in World War I, 101; limited economic opportunity, 101; strikebreakers in Chicago, 101–102; riot in Chicago, 104; experience in 1920s, 107; high unemployment, 120; impact of relief, 124; employed in World War II, 145–49; migration to Detroit, 147; attracted to UAW, 152; favor CIO in meatpacking, 157; migration pattern, 174; support Sadlowski, 184–85; job opportunities, 185–86; Chrysler crisis, 190; declining opportunities, 198

Agricultural Adjustment Act: adopted, 118; creates cartels, 125

agricultural extension: development, 64–68; spread, 68

agricultural innovation: organizational changes, 64–68

Agricultural Marketing Act: splits farm activists, 116

agricultural service state: LaFollette creates, 68; Farmer-Labor Party promotes, 69

Akron: auto parts center, 76; tire plant technology, 80; 1913 strike, 97–98; Klan role, 110; unions grow, 126; CIO candidates, 137; women workers recruited, 144; July 1943 strike, 153; decline as manufacturing center, 182–83

Alanen, Arnold R., 211n53, 213n53, 222nn45, 47

alfalfa hay: Holden promotes, 65

Alger, Russell: opposes strike, 42

Allen County Unemployment Association: emphasizes barter, 122

alliances, farmers': in Midwest, 21–22

Allis-Chalmers: Communists control local union, 136; company defeats union, 156; decline in 1970s, 189

Alston, Lee J., 217n19, 225n5

Amalgamated Association of Iron and Steel Workers: defeats Knights of Labor, 44; Lewis transforms, 132–33

Amalgamated Clothing Workers: Feiss fights, 75

Amalgamated Meat Cutters: enlists Chicago workers, 93–94; organizes during World War I, 104; at Swift, 156–57; race relations, 185

Amberg, Stephen, 232n66, 234n23

The American Farmer (1902): portrays farmers as workers, 3

American Federation of Labor: founded in Columbus, 44; active in Akron strike, 97; contributes to East St. Louis riot, 101; role in Mesabi strike, 103; expands in cities, 103; Milwaukee unions support, 105; competition with CIO, 126; organizes manufacturing workers, 127; leaders compared to CIO, 135; conflict with CIO, 136–37; opposes CIO candidates, 137; resists integration, 146; opposes CIO, 149; defeats Ohio right-to-work, 178. *See also* Congress of Industrial Organizations

American Federation of State, County, and Municipal Employees (AFSCME): growth in Midwest, 193

American Legion: expels Mexican workers, 121

American Newspaper Guild: fights AFL and Hearst, 149

American Plan: open shop campaign, 105

American Railway Union: loses Pullman strike, 45

Amlie, Thomas: promotes farmer-labor party, 137

Anderson, Indiana: GM plants, 108

Angle, Paul M.: studied Ku Klux Klan, 109; 224nn84, 87, 225n16

Ankli, Robert E., 217n21

Annual Improvement Factor: 1948 GM contract, 158

Appelbaum, Eileen, 236n57

apprenticeship: in offices, 50; declines in 1930s, 121

DANIEL NELSON is Professor of History at the University of Akron. He is the author of *American Rubber Workers and Organized Labor, 1900–1941* and *Managers and Workers: Origins of the New Factory System in the United States, 1880–1920*.